THE COMPLETE
BOOK OF THE
CAR

ISBN 1 85868 337 8

Project Editor: Simon Kirrane
Art Editor: Paul Messam
Design: Simon Balley
Production: Garry Lewis

Printed in Dubai

GENERAL EDITOR:
Alan Anderson One time senior
editor of *Which Car?* magazine Alan
Anderson now works on a broad cross-
section of UK-based magazines.

CONTRIBUTORS:
Tony Bosworth Motoring expert,
Tony Bosworth has been a regular on
national radio and contributed to many
national newspapers.

Martin Vincent Martin has designed
and marketed his own range of kit car
specials and was editor of *Which Kit*?

Chris Rees An established classic car
expert Chris Rees was a staff writer
for *Your Classic* magazine before
going freelance.

David Sutherland Is a journalist at
What Car?, contributor to all the major
UK motoring titles and is editor of *The
Golf* magazine.

THE COMPLETE
BOOK OF THE
CAR

The definitive illustrated guide
to the world's favourite automobiles

GENERAL EDITOR:
ALAN ANDERSON

CARLTON

Contents

The car is many things to many people and has had a massive impact on people's lives, and indeed, civilisation throughout the 20th Century.

Next to accommodation cars tend to account for the largest slice of the household budget and those who don't worship their car invariably depend upon it both for transport and, in many cases, for employment. We live in a car society and this will remain to be the case for many years to come. Yet despite cars and drivers being taxed at greater and greater rates and falling under increasing legislative control the love affair with the car is just as passionate as it has always been. This book is dedicated to car lovers everywhere and celebrates more than 100 years of life with man's most important invention since the wheel. It does not pretend to be the most comprehensive publication on the history of the motor car, nor the most technologically biased but rather an insight into the car's evolution since its introduction in 1885, from crude horseless carriages to computer-aided 200mph sportscars.

Alan Anderson
General Editor

The
HISTORY
of the
CAR

There have been many great inventions during the Twentieth Century – the telephone, air travel, television and the atomic bomb – are just four with universal impact. But one stands out from the crowd as having had more influence on more people in more places – the car. The thing that takes us to work and to play, that is pictured on every other billboard or magazine, something that possession of which has become a rite of passage from adolescence to adulthood.

It is ironic then that this great invention, a machine that created the suburbs of the world's great cities, that virtually drew up the blueprints for every major American settlement now claims more lives each year than war and pestilence, and is seen by some as doing irreparable damage to the planet.

But perhaps it is this great irony that has captured people's imagination. To most the ownership of this great machine is worth the risks involved. As a representation of Western development, the car has no equal. It is loved, loathed, needed and feared. Created by humans, it makes us what we are. This celebration of the car is needed.

The significance of the motor car to the recent history of civilisation is beyond question. The car's precise date of introduction, however, will be debated for decades to come. That's because, ever since the invention of the wheel around 4000 BC, humans have tried to design a self-propelled machine to replace the horse.

Karl Benz and Gottlieb Daimler may have been credited with producing the first vehicles powered by the internal combustion engine in 1885, but

Henry Ford with his legendary Model T, the vehicle that pioneered mass-production techniques

the origins of the car go back as far as the Old Testament. This foretold of machines propelling themselves on land and in the air. The great 13th-century scientist and philosopher Roger Bacon predicted the advent of machine-powered vehicles on land and water, while Leonardo de Vinci's diagrams of a self-propelled carriage are a matter of record. Clockwork and wind-assisted vehicles all played their part in the pre-history of the car but the greatest influence came from the Steam Age. In the early 1760s Frenchman Captain Nicolas Joseph Cugnot built a powerful steam-driven tractor to tow artillery hardware. Only partly successful, it was left to a group of British,

American and European inventors to pursue the development further. Of these, Richard Trevithick's London Carriage was both the most practical and effective.

The steam era saw, not only the advent of a succession of road coaches, but also the more recent railway locomotive. The former was handicapped by public resistance and government legislation, while those involved in the horse trade saw these new contraptions as a danger to their livelihood. This led not only to heavy taxation through toll roads but also the implementation of the Red Flag Act. This ruled that all forms of 'road locomotives' should have a man with a red flag walking ahead of them. This ridiculous law

was not repealed until many years later.

THE POWER STRUGGLE

It was the development of the internal combustion engine from the mid-1800s onwards which spurred inventors on to develop 'horseless carriages'. Nikolaus Otto is generally regarded as being the father of today's petrol engine but its origins date back much further. The initial idea can be traced to the 1670s, from when there survive the first descriptions of a piston sliding within a cylinder, powered by gun powder – in effect, a development of the cannon. This was put into practice by a number

FIRST · CAR

of engineers, one of whom was the Swiss, Francois Issac de Rivaz, who even used electricity to supply the ignition.

Arguments still rage today among automotive historians concerning the identity of the individual who created the first 'true' internal combustion engine. Etienne Lenior won the race to patent his design first in 1859, but the Italians Barsanti and Matteucci had working designs on display several years earlier. Lenior's patent was more in line with the modern engine as we know it however, and was a spur to future innovators like Nickolaus Otto, Gottlieb Daimler and Karl Benz. Otto's four-stroke engine (the four 'strokes' of the cycle being: Induction, Compression, Ignition, Exhaust) was a refinement of Lenior's idea, and provided the motive power for the motor car in more ways than one.

Otto had a tough time realising his vision. Having learned of Lenior's gas engine, and being further inspired by seeing the Barsanti and Matteucci idea on a trip to England, he developed a similar unit designed to run on liquid fuel. However, as the history of the automobile constantly shows, some of the greatest innovators had poor business minds. Otto needed future car enthusiast Eugen Langen to both help secure a patent and also see the venture through bleak times when technical problems halted sales for a while.

It is unfair to credit any one person with the creation of the car. Gottlieb Daimler, who worked with Otto until their differing views caused a fall-out, developed his own engines. These were not solely for car use, but he did build the first four-wheel horseless carriage. Karl

Benz, who lived less than 100 miles away, designed his advanced tricycle which proved to be the first truly purpose-built machine. Amazingly, not only did the pair never meet, but were even unaware of each other's efforts as they worked on parallel designs.

By 1886 the motor car was definitely ready to roll.

THE DRIVE TO GAIN ACCEPTANCE

Germany received the credit for fathering the automobile but it was France which gave it the warmest welcome. Both Daimler and Benz came under strong criticism in their home country for their inventions, but the French, who already had a healthy road network to cater for their enthusiasm for bicycles, staged one of the most significant events designed to popularise the motor car, in 1889.

The Paris World Exhibition attracted 400,000 visitors, who poured through the doors to see the first car. Daimler and Benz enjoyed

success at the event, while Peugeot gained the right to build cars with Daimler engines. Despite opposition from some quarters, there was no turning back.

Across the Atlantic, the first automobile ran in 1891, built by John Lambert of Ohio. Four years later the Duryea brothers established the first car-manufacturing plant. The birth of the car in the US was a difficult one. George Baldwin Selwyn, a lawyer specialising in patents, had decided to monopolise the automobile by drawing up a definitive patent for the car. Any future fuel-powered designs would be an infringement upon it. His case was strengthened by ALAM – the Association of Licensed Automobile Manufacturers – and it took the courage of a certain Henry Ford, no less, to contest this judgement and win the case.

The absurd Red Flag Act in the UK stifled enthusiasm for the car until 1896 when it was finally scrapped. A speed limit of 12 mph was imposed in its place. To

Karl Benz: builder of the first true car

celebrate the occasion, which effectively marked the birth of the British car industry, a drive from the capital to Brighton was instigated. This annual London to Brighton run is still enjoyed today.

By the end of the century, and while still the preserve of the elite, the Automobile Club of Great Britain and Ireland staged a famous 1000-mile trial around the country. Some 65 cars took part to show the population – many of whom had

Steam power met with considerable resistance. This shot from 1869 shows the dreaded red flag in action

never seen a car before – the future way to travel. The motor car had truly arrived.

FAST AND FURIOUS

Like so many great inventions in the past, further development was easier once the initial blueprint was established. The action was fast and furious in the first years of the new century. Because many of the car manufacturers were being run by engineers and not businessmen, they had the authority, and the

---

Wartime, and the motor car became a vital weapon

---

audacity, to build exactly what they wanted.

We may think that our fuel-injected, 16-valve, electronically-chipped and heavily-appointed cars of the 1990s represent the pinnacle of automotive design, but this is not the case. In fact, apart from the electronics, most of the concepts found in a typical modern car are little more than an advancement of an idea originally devised decades ago. Only the lack of suitable materials available to engineers at that time stifled inspired thought.

Another factor, of course, was the price. As the car's popularity spread, so to did the demand for cheap, simple transport for the

masses, epitomised by the Ford Model T By the mid-1920s nearly 700,000 cars were in daily use on British roads and more than ten million could be found in the USA. Things weren't rosy for all vehicle manufacturers, however, with many small outfits floundering early-on. As the car became big business across the world only the strongest survived.

This was never more evident than in the aftermath of an economic slump in Europe in the early 1920s, followed several years later across the Atlantic during the Great Depression.

To help the British car industry survive in these tough times, the government set up a special

horsepower tax which penalised foreign imports. The idea was to tax cars on their power output. This basically sound idea was seriously hampered because the levy imposed (based on calculations performed by the Royal Automobile Club) was derived from a formula which would have baffled even Albert Einstein. Instead of it being related to engine size, it was bizarrely connected to the size of an engine's pistons. Thus, 'small-bore/long-stroke' engines – the most inefficient design of all – achieved the lowest taxation. As a result, engine development in the UK was crippled for years. The tax was finally replaced in 1947 by a flat-

rate charge better known today as the road fund licence. Incidentally this coincided with the launch of the Standard Vanguard, with a 'short-stroke' engine aimed directly at export markets.

The 1930s saw a significant shift towards the affordable car, both in the US and in the UK. Ford's Y Popular became the company's first truly British car. It cost just £100 – easily within the realms of the ordinary worker, as contemporary advertisements at the time showed. With more than 1.5 million cars on the UK's streets by this time, the car was fast being viewed as not simply a luxury, but more a necessity. Expectations rose too. Safety glass, proper windscreen wipers and better interiors were now standard even in the cheapest car.

The advent of World War II saw progress in aero-engine design which decades later would have an effect on the car. Multi-valve engines were used by Rolls-Royce for extra power and superior high-octane fuels were introduced for added performance. One American fighter used an engine which made use of an embryonic variable valve-timing system – an innovation which is increasingly being seen on car engines 50 years later.

The immediate postwar years were bleak on the automotive front, however. In Britain, car manufacturers were ordered by the Government to export, so half of all production was destined for overseas. There was a real shortage of cars, fuel and even tyres, and used-car prices soared to meet the increasing demand. To stop any speculating and selling-on for an instant profit, new car buyers were forced to sign a pledge that stated that they would not sell the car for a minimum of two years.

While the countries of Europe tightened their collective belts with the continued imposition of rationing, the US car industry returned to its pre-war ways by offering unprecedented levels of refinement to potential car buyers.

The London to Brighton run, established to celebrate the ending of the red flag act

Fully automatic transmission, cruise control and powered brakes, seats and windows were all common fittings.

In the UK new car designs were scarce, with most postwar models being carry-overs from the 1930s. It was left to the humble, yet technically advanced Morris Minor and the stunning Jaguar XK120 to woo enthusiasts at the 1948 Motor Show in London.

That same year saw a remarkable car launched in America – the Tucker '48'. Preston Tucker was a flamboyant small-time car manufacturer who wanted to make it big with what was described at the time as the first completely new car for half a century. With features like a special passenger safety cage and standard

seat belts, the Tucker was decades ahead of its rivals, but it flopped due to the company having little business acumen. Tucker made big claims and promises to raise the $12 million he required, and although later charged with fraud, his only real crime was over-enthusiasm.

Preston Tucker thought the big car-makers were out to get him but his failure was due principally to being out of his depth and expecting too much too soon. Had the '48' been a success, the progress of auto technology may have moved on much more rapidly.

The 1950s was a time when the car industry tried to shake off its postwar blues. Although these were still austere times, it turned out to be a golden age in motoring. American bosses of both Ford and

Vauxhall became more involved in the designs of their UK satellites, while the sheer size of product output by parent companies in the US saw the demise of many superb, but small, European car-makers.

From a technical viewpoint, the 1950s was a decade of advancement thanks to the universal quest to improve the motor car. Engineers and pioneers were given licence to express and exploit their ideas with a freedom which has only recently returned. Rover experimented with gas turbine power, the rotary engine was designed and advanced automatic transmissions using continually-variable gear ratios were produced.

Not surprisingly, the 1950s also brought us two of the most significant designs in automotive history – the Citroën DS and the evergreen Mini.

The DS was a technological delight, with its complex hydraulic system powering the brakes and suspension, which in turn imbued the car with levels of performance hitherto unseen on a family car.

The Mini was the result of a world fuel crisis which highlighted the need for a practical economy vehicle, rather than the three-wheel 'bubble' city cars that had became a popular sight in Europe after the Suez War of 1956.

With the space race just beginning between the super-powers and the Cold War showing little sign of thawing, the pace of technological progress was frightening. Anything and everything looked possible.

It didn't last long. By the mid-1960s realism was starting to creep in. Of all the major car developments of the previous decade only three – the Mini, tubeless tyres and disc brakes – gained popularity. The rest disappeared almost as quickly as they came. Even the Mini, which is now approaching 40 years of age, didn't make a profit in its first decade of production.

NADER'S LEGACY

It wasn't only company 'bean counters' who now decided on the way car designs would be heading. In America an ambitious young lawyer by the name of Ralph Nader would also have a profound effect on the motor car in terms of the way it would be viewed by consumers. His classic 1966 book, *Unsafe at Any Speed*, attacked the motor car, and in particular General Motors for producing what he considered to be a dangerous car in the shape of the Chevrolet Corvair. Accompanied by a blaze of publicity, Nader took on GM in a crusade for safety.

The Corvair was essentially an American Volkswagen Beetle in terms of its rear-engine layout and its compact size. However, it was a much sleeker and faster design, due both to its styling and larger engine. It also used a chassis design alien to most US drivers, which resulted in the oversteering Corvair catching out so many motorists that it became known as accident-prone. Nader believed that this was largely due to poor design and development on General Motor's behalf, and GM dropped the car due, partly, to poor sales.

The outcome shocked the car industry, bringing safety and consumer issues to a head. The legacy of Nader was that car-makers wouldn't dare do anything other than play safe again.

The revolution of the 1950s gave way to automotive 'nannyism'. Today, with environmental issues starting to gain momentum, the car is once again coming under serious assault for the second time in its short life, as ever-tightening rules on exhaust emissions and noise levels take hold.

The 1960s also saw the first stages in the meteoric growth of the Japanese car industry. Voices of concern from certain quarters of the industry went unheeded and,

Ralph Nader, safety crusader

having already dominated motorcycle manufacturing, Japan again caught the rest of the world napping.

The Citröen DS was one of the most revolutionary car designs ever produced, and still admired as such

In the UK, car manufacturing had already started its decline – the ailing Rootes Group comprising Hillman, Humber, Sunbeam and Singer (all historic names) was bought out by Chrysler in the mid 1960s, just a few years after the innovative, but unreliable, Imp had been launched. BMC, which started the first of its sequence of 'shotgun marriages' in 1952 with the merger of Austin and Morris, gobbled up Rover and Jaguar, before becoming British Leyland Motor Corporation in 1968.

It was the start of one of the greatest automotive embarrassments in history, littered with blunders where badge engineering ruled. This is the strategy of calling an identical car by another name, trying to sell it on its badge rather than its qualities and it helped kill off most of the once-great British car industry.

Not surprisingly, the 1970s are generally remembered for bringing some bleak times to the global motor industry. Ironically, the decade had started with UK car sales peaking at an all time high in 1972, but two wars in the Middle East, oil shortages and the spread of economic recession across the globe soon led to an all-encompassing mood of conservatism and consolidation.

It was a time for pure survival above everything else, which in turn cultivated just the right environment for the Japanese automobile industry to prosper.

With nothing to lose, it exploited the vast deficiencies which existed in the automotive products of America and Europe, both in terms of design and customer satisfaction. The rest is history.

In total contrast British Leyland (BL) lurched from bad to worse. Nationalised in 1975, industrial strife, appalling build-quality and the gradual blackening of great names such as Jaguar, Rover and Triumph, drove BL to the edge of the abyss. It was only a partnership with Honda that pulled it back from the brink and gave the company some respectability.

Vauxhall was another company in big trouble and it took the wholesale scrapping of Luton-based products in favour of re-badged, but better built, Opels from Germany to reverse the company's fortunes. Citroën, the most radical-thinking of all French car manufacturers, faced a similar problem. Despite its vehicles being technically brilliant, Citroën wasn't making enough money to ensure survival and was duly bought by Peugeot in 1974.

American companies were also in trouble, with the Chrysler 'empire' crumbling on a global scale. Even the legendary Cadillac suffered huge losses.

Fortunately the new decade brought happier times. Car demand gradually started to creep up, ranges were rationalised and engineers were at last left alone by company accountants. However, the sheer cost of developing totally new designs meant that an increasing number of car-makers enlisted arch rivals as partners in the production of new models common to both interests, thus reducing levels of duplication in component manufacturing.

This, in some instances, led to dedicated plants being built. Some car manufacturers – notably the Japanese – established factories abroad. Soon, companies from other countries were setting up manufacturing bases around the world. The age of the global car company coincided with the fading of the postwar stigma attached to buying foreign products. A 'British' Ford is now possibly built in Germany or Spain, while French Peugeots are produced at the old Rootes/Chrysler sites in the English Midlands.

To save on costs, the need for true 'world' cars suitable for all markets was now apparent. As the

1990s dawned, a new threat was mounted on the 'establishment' by Korean firms with odd names like Daewoo and Hyundai. Unlike the Japanese invasion of 30 years before, however, this one is being taken far more seriously by the established manufacturers.

The BMC/BLMC/Austin-Rover group finally became Rover and was then sold to BMW in 1994. From being a once-dominant car-maker that annually grabbed well over one-third of all UK sales, it has now become a small and select low-volume manufacturer. Its limited range dovetails with BMW's. Rather ironically, the German giant had started life building Austins under licence some six decades before.

The 1990s have also seen electric cars pushed back in the frame in order to cut pollution and provide the answer to dwindling oil supplies. The first electric-and-petrol-powered car was produced as long ago as 1906, but it has taken 90 years for car-makers to begin seriously offering acceptable alternatives to the Otto engine.

Despite a crop of new designs from major companies like General Motors, Ford, Mercedes-Benz and Peugeot, electric cars are still being resisted by public and industry alike. Plans to introduce a law in California stating that two per cent of all newly-registered vehicles must be electrically-powered has had to be postponed.

Now, more than ever, the car

needs to get in step with changing times and attitudes to its use. A century has passed since Benz and Daimler showed off their inventions to a hostile public and still the car faces severe criticisms over its place in society. Moves to tax, curb and resist its role as a provider of independent transport and mass employment are gathering momentum. Industry historians may be feeling a certain hint of *deja vu*. As mentioned earlier, little is really new in the history of the motor car.

As a new century dawns thoughts have again turned to the electric car concept in a bid to reduce pollution

Classic
CARS

Some cars have a certain cachet which sets them apart from their peers and sees them accumulate fanatical followings and steadily rising price tags. These classic cars appeal to the driver who is tired of modern, colourless, computer designed clones and hankers for something with a little more style, a little more class and a lot more character.

The classic car industry has developed over the past two decades and there is now a dedicated industry which deals with classic car restoration, upkeep and appreciation.

When dealing with classic cars 'appreciation' is a term one often comes across, not only because people enjoy their pride and joy but also because some of these cars can literally be worth their weight in gold.

Here a selection of world classics that are celebrated for their good looks, charm and huge followings. It is doubtful that any of these cars will be strangers to you but even more doubtful that you aren't smitten by them.

FERRARI
250GTO

The seven letters of the name 'Ferrari' produce a quickening of the pulse for any car enthusiast. If you're a dedicated Ferrari fan however, just the three letters GTO are all it takes to get the adrenaline pumping. To the devoted, everything else is just a little ordinary by comparison; even the F40s, Berlinetta Boxers and 275GTBs. The GTO is THE Ferrari – and perhaps THE car of all time.

Why is the GTO so special? There are several compelling reasons. Firstly, the GTO helped Ferrari win three World Championships in a row from 1962 to 1964. Yet it was a real rarity, a racer that could be driven on the road. On top of that, only 39 were ever made. That makes the 250GTO ultra-desirable whichever way you care to look at it.

To understand the GTO, car enthusiasts have to realise why it was conceived. Racing during the 1950s had become very much faster and consequently more dangerous. The death of 82 people at Le Mans in 1955 was the catalyst which split top-flight racing into categories. One of these was the new grand tourer class, which required that cars should have closed coupe bodies which resembled to a large degree those of the manufacturer's road cars. A minimum of 100 examples of each of these race cars had to be built.

By the beginning of the 1960s, Enzo Ferrari's cars were dominant in racing, so he took the new class very seriously. He certainly faced some stiff competition from the Aston Martin DB4 Zagato and the new Jaguar E-Type. Ferrari's competitor was the 250GT, the first volume-produced Ferrari. It used the same basic chassis as that of the 166, first seen in 1947, which provided excellent handling. However, the 250GT was not strong on all-out speed.

Enzo thought that he could beat the opposition with a more powerful engine but Chief engineer Carlo Chiti argued that the car's blunt aerodynamics were at fault. He went to great pains to have a wind tunnel installed at Ferrari's HQ in Modena. The result was that the engine remained much the same as before: a glorious 3.0-litre V12 unit designed by Gioacchino Colombo. The size of each individual cylinder was 250cc, hence the '250' name. In specification, it mirrored the Testa Rossa pure racing car, including dry sump lubrication and six twin-choke Weber carburettors.

Ferrari developed a new five-speed, all-synchromesh gearbox but the chassis remained much as before but with a short wheelbase. The reasoning was that Ferrari faced enough problems getting the car through the 100-car homologation rule without having

The fabulous GTO is arguably the greatest Ferrari ever made. Only 39 were built, ensuring its exclusivity

to argue about the chassis as well. Standard 250GT suspension used coil springs at the front and a rigid axle with leaf springs at the back. Development engineer Giotto Bizzarrini wanted to up-rate the rear to coil springs as well but Enzo did not agree.

The new car arrived in February 1962 and was christened 250GTO, the magical letters standing for Gran Turismo Omologato. Each car was virtually hand-built, mostly for very wealthy private individuals who fancied their chances at a racing career. All GTOs were given odd chassis numbers (at a time when racing cars were traditionally allocated even numbers), which has given rise to some confusion over the exact number of GTOs built. However, most historians now agree on 39, a figure which fell way below the supposed 'minimum' of 100. Each one was slightly different and some, like Bizzarrini's triplet of restyled 'bread van' GTOs, were very different.

The styling was gorgeous, the work of Ferrari's own engineers. It made use of the Kamm tail principle, which yielded enhanced aerodynamics for cars with sloping tails. Overall, the GTO was 6.6in longer and 3.5in lower than the short wheelbase 250GT Berlinetta. Construction was very lightweight, with all-aluminium bodies created in the tiny Modena workshop of Sergio Scaglietti. The body styling would later change on the 1964 Series II to incorporate a notchback.

As a race car, the 250GTO was highly successful. From its first outings it proved its superiority over the opposition in endurance events and the World Championship. Phil Hill came second in the 1962 Sebring, the GTO's debut event. In the hands of

This highly successful sportscar could also be used on the road to stylish effect

drivers like Mike Parkes and the late, great Rodriguez brothers, it made Ferrari dominant on the track. In Class III of the 1962 championship, Ferrari GTOs won a crushing victory with maximum points – despite the Italian giant not having an official works team.

Its only competition came from the lightweight Jaguar E-Type (from 1963) and the AC Cobra (from 1964).

A single 4.0-litre GTO was developed and raced by Parkes and Mairesse at the 1962 Nurburgring 1000km. It finished second but came off at Mulsanne at Le Mans later in the year. Ferrari

scored a spectacular success at the 1962 Paris 1000km, occupying the first six places, four of which were GTOs. Many other drivers raced GTOs, including such illustrious names as Graham Hill, Innes Ireland and Roger Penske.

Not only was the GTO a racing success, it could also used be on the road. As expected, handling and raw performance were exemplary. Car enthusiasts might not, however, have expected it to be a tractable and usable machine, especially in town – but it was.

The downside (from the point of view of someone wanting to use it as a road car) was difficult braking, uncomfortable accommodation, draughts and the sheer level of noise.

The 250GTO was the last of a long line of great front-engined racing Ferraris. By 1963, the mid-engined 250LM had arrived and would show the way ahead: its

potential for ultimate handling balance tended to place it ahead of the GTO. The new car would effectively have rendered the GTO obsolete immediately, but racing officials refused to sanction it because too few had been made to satisfy homologation.

There were also several 'pseudo' GTOs, such as the 'bread vans' built by Piero Drogo and Giotto Bizzarrini, and Count Volpi's converted 250GT, which did battle with genuine GTOs on the track. They had little success.

Today the really fanatical Ferrari collector simply must have a GTO in his or her garage. However, that person will certainly need to be extraordinarily rich: the going price for a 250GTO is around the £2.5 million mark. For that a car enthusiast could buy seven brand new Ferrari F50s. In Britain, several music business personalities have bought GTOs, though the cars are

very seldom seen in public because of their stratospheric value.

One side-effect of this situation has been the widespread replication of the GTO. Quite a few standard 250GT Ferraris have been butchered over the years to make replicas. Some have even been passed off as originals, a process encouraged by the confusion over chassis numbers. More recently (in 1984), the GTO name was revived for another very special homologation car, the mid-engined 288GTO – but that, as they say, is another story.

FACTS & FIGURES

- **Engine:** 2953cc, V12 cylinders, 295-300 bhp
- **Max Speed:** 155mph *(250kmh)*
- **Years produced:** 1962-6
- **Numbers built:** 39

MERCEDES-BENZ
300SL

Since Karl Benz's first bold experiment with internal combustion in 1885, Mercedes-Benz has maintained an eminence in the motoring world. The name is synonymous with quality, power and a fine sporting tradition.

Perhaps the last great sporting era for Mercedes-Benz began with the 300SL... and the 300SL began with the gigantic Mercedes-Benz 300 saloon, launched in 1951. This top-class range of cars used a six-

The perfect W194, later known as the 300SL, was made with racing in mind

cylinder, 3.0-litre, overhead-cam engine with an alloy head and twin carburettors, plus such advanced features as an all-synchromesh gearbox, hypoid drive (the first German car to have this) and independent rear suspension.

It was a natural choice for Mercedes-Benz engineers to base a new sporting model on. Engineer Rudolf Uhlenhaut realised that, if he used the basic mechanicals in a space frame chassis of the type being used by Aston Martin, Jaguar and Cisitalia, he could have a competitive racing car. And so the W194 project began.

The chassis took the form of two large cross-members joined

by a lattice of smaller steel tubes. To achieve the necessary stiffness, the tubes had to run beside the cockpit and it was this factor which gave rise to the gullwing doors of the 300SL. A stressed aluminium body was designed by Karl Wilfert around the space frame. It was a coupe because this body type was believed to give the best aerodynamics.

Surprisingly, the new racing coupe was given drum brakes, not discs. The 3.0-litre engine had to be inclined at 50 degrees to fit within the complex lattice of tubes, a new cylinder head was designed and dry sumping was used. There were also three carburettors, an uprated

camshaft and a new exhaust, the net result was an output of 171 bhp which was very impressive for its day.

Mercedes-Benz's larger-than-life racing director, Hans Neubauer, didn't like the prototype and insisted that more power, better brakes and a five-speed gearbox should be fitted. Thus Mercedes-Benz re-entered sports-car racing. With Rudi Caracciola, Karl Kling and Hermann Lang at the wheel, the team attacked the 1952 Mille Miglia. Kling came in second behind Giovanni Bracco's Ferrari V12. However, at the next race, the Swiss Grand Prix, the 300SL scored a memorable 1-2-3

victory. This was followed by a convincing 1-2 at Le Mans.

For the 1952 Nurburgring race, Mercedes-Benz chopped the top off three 300SL coupes to create racing roadsters. Not surprisingly, the all-conquering Mercedes team stormed to victory with another 1-2-3 result and Lang led the trio home. The only other race run by the 300SL was the gruelling Carrera Panamericana in Mexico. This yielded yet another victory for Kling and Mercedes, with Lang in second place. Mercedes-Benz would not race in 1953, officially because 'they had learnt all they needed to know'.

After this crushingly successful competition record, the road-going version was eagerly awaited. It might never have happened had not the American Mercedes-Benz importer, Max Hoffman, placed an advance order for 1,000 cars.

Some modifications were made: the body was substantially re-designed by Paul Bracq to become more aerodynamic and steel became the main material of construction (except for a run of 29 all-aluminium cars). The 3.0-litre engine's power and torque rose significantly and it was given Bosch fuel-injection – a pioneering step.

The suspension was modified to cure oversteer caused by the swing-axle rear, recirculating ball steering replaced the old worm-and-nut system and proper heating was installed (though ventilation would always be a problem with the Gullwing).

The new 300SL made its debut at the 1954 New York International Motor Show. It caused a considerable stir with its amazing gullwing doors, dramatic lines and advanced specification. There was no shortage of flapping cheque books at the show, despite the

The drop-head roadster followed the classic Gullwing coupe and although rarer is not so valuable

exorbitant price being charged.

With some 215 bhp on tap, and up to 240 bhp with the right modifications, the new Mercedes could do an amazing 145-160 mph depending on rear axle ratio, and reach 60 mph from rest in a little over 8 seconds.

The 300SL was by no means perfect: entry and exit was decidedly awkward, the gullwing doors irksome to open, luggage space rather restricted and ventilation poor. Driving it required great skill, as it would snake when the driver floored the throttle and it still had a propensity for oversteering.

Although Mercedes-Benz never fielded official 300SL racers, it supported private owners. These often had great success, like Fitch and Gendebien's class win in the Mille Miglia, Tak's victory in the Tulip Rally and Engel's European Touring Car Championship.

There was also a spin-off of the 300SL, the 300SLR, which was conceived to compete in Grand Prix racing. Stirling Moss drove the 300SLR in its debut race at the 1955 Mille Miglia, winning after a punishing ten-hour drive. At Le Mans, Levegh's 300SLR plunged into the crowd with devastating results, leading to the team withdrawing from the event. Mercedes-Benz won the 1955 World Sports Car Championship.

A Roadster version had always been planned but, when it arrived in 1957, it replaced the Coupe rather than supplementing it. The claustrophobic and impractical Gullwing was frankly unsuited to American tastes and climate and, after all, Californians did buy most of the 1,371 Coupes made.

The Roadster debuted at the 1957 Geneva Salon. It had a proper folding hood which disappeared into boot and the novelty of winding windows. The gullwings were replaced by conventionally-opening doors. Suspension modifications improved handling, the headlamps were restyled and the engine now developed between 225 bhp and 250 bhp. A removable hard top was offered from 1958 and four-wheel disc brakes were standardised in 1961. By the time 300SL Roadster production ceased in 1963, Mercedes-Benz had built 1,858 of them. Some of the Roadster's reflected glory was apparent in the cheaper 190SL, made from 1954-63. This had only 105 bhp available however, and was more of a boulevard cruiser than a true sportscar.

There are few examples of a classic car which is worth more in closed coupe form than it is in convertible form. The Mercedes-Benz 300SL Gullwing is such a car. Its awe-inspiring presence guarantees a premium over the more effete Roadster. The magic which it cannot fail to weave on all who set eyes on it continues today and examples can fetch extraordinary sums.

FACTS & FIGURES

- **Engine:** 2996cc, 6 cylinders, 215-250 bhp
- **Max speed:** 140-160 mph (225-258 km/h)
- **Years produced:** 1954-63
- **Numbers built:** 3,229

AC
COBRA

Cobra... The very name conjures up images of awesome performance, evocatively-shaped haunches, a blistering soundtrack and a white-knuckle ride. It is, in short, a legend.

How can a car which was in production for a mere five years, and which sold only around 1,000 examples, achieve such legendary status? The story is all the more remarkable considering the Cobra grew out of a not particularly exceptional sportscar, made by a tiny English firm by the name of AC, and its combination of a frail-looking ladder chassis and a brutish V8 power plant that was hardly subtle.

One name provides the answer: that of a larger-than-life Texan racer and chicken farmer called Carroll Shelby. It was he who had the vision to mate the AC Ace sportscar chassis with an American Ford V8 engine and it was Shelby who actually screwed the cars together in his racing workshops in Santa Fe, California.

Shelby had heard that AC's engine supplier, Bristol, was stopping making the 2.0-litre engines used in the Ace sportscar. He got in touch with AC Cars of Thames Ditton, Surrey, in 1961 with a suggestion: How about using an American-made engine in

American tuning ace Carroll Shelby was the instigator of the classic AC Cobra. After discovering the old Bristol engine was being discontinued he suggested using a Ford V8. The result was one of the most brutish cars ever — a similar charge can be levelled at his Viper

the form of a 260 cu in (4260cc) V8 unit from a Ford Fairlane? The idea of putting an American V8 engine in a European sportscar was not new but no-one had dared to approach the heights to which the Cobra would ascend.

AC agreed to try the idea. Amazingly, the Ace's very simple twin-tube ladder chassis was retained virtually unchanged, although Girling in-board rear disc brakes and a reinforcing frame for the rear suspension were fitted.

At both ends, lower wishbones were combined with transverse leaf spring upper links and telescopic dampers.

Production of the Cobra got underway in 1962. The chassis and lightweight (22.5kg) aluminium body were hand-built by AC in Thames Ditton. Most of the road equipment was then fitted and shipped to California for final assembly by Shelby, using Ford engines, close ratio Borg-Warner four-speed gearboxes and strengthened drive shafts.

The Cobra first appeared on the Ford stand at the 1962 New York Auto Show, where it caused a sensation, an impact which was reinforced by a number of high-profile road test reports. *Sports Car Graphic* described the Cobra as "one of the most impressive production sportscars we've ever driven", adding that its acceleration

was "explosive". Their official road test recorded the astonishing times of 0-60 mph in 4.1 seconds and the standing 1/4 mile in 12.9 seconds. Those figures can put to shame most current supercars, let alone the sort of machinery which was available in 1962.

The secret of the Cobra's performance was not a massive power output – it had a 'mere' 260 bhp to begin with – but its light weight. The Cobra measured only 151in (384cm) long, so weight was kept down to 2020lb (916kg), producing a power-to-weight ratio of 288 bhp per ton – better than the contemporary Ferrari Testa Rossa.

In America, the model was generally known as the Shelby Cobra but European markets always had cars badged as the AC Cobra, and later just AC 289 Sports. The advertising presented it as the perfect match of British styling and craftsmanship with American power and reliability.

Right from the start, it was offered with competition options for owners who wanted to take their cars racing. Owners could buy roll hoops, racing seats, cut-down windscreen, extra vents and a whole host of engine options. Racers would soon be following in successful footsteps for the Cobra was the first British finisher in the 1963 Le Mans, scored many victories in American SCCA events

and met with success in numerous European races.

On the back of its racing pedigree, the Cobra sold well, especially in America. It was actually cheaper than the old Bristol-powered Ace had been, selling for around the same price as the poorer-performing Jaguar E-Type. Shelby was forced to move to bigger premises to cope with the growing demand.

In alliance with Shelby, Ford itself ironed out many of the Cobra's problems. A lot of work went into balancing the chassis. Rack-and-pinion steering replaced the archaic worm-and-roller system. Then Ford offered Shelby their bigger 289 cu in engine.

This was merely a stepping-stone to the ultimate Cobra: the 427 of 1965. Conceived as a giant-killing race-winner, it was essentially a Cobra fitted with a big block 427 cu in (6997cc) V8 from the Ford Galaxie 500. The 271 bhp Cobra 289 was already a performance legend, so the impact of the 425 bhp Cobra 427 was going to be shattering. And that was in standard tune – with the right tuning gear, there was potential for that to go up to 480 bhp and beyond.

Two examples were completed with Paxton superchargers and claimed to deliver no less than a frightening 800 bhp.

To cope with the extra power, the chassis was completely redesigned. The basic ladder frame layout remained but the tubes were far thicker and the suspension towers were now tubular affairs, not fabricated sheet metal.

At last, the old leaf spring

suspension gave way to coil spring dampers and double wishbones, refined by Ford Engineering to be fully adjustable. Larger brakes, beefed-up drive shafts and extra cooling completed the picture.

The 427 also looked more muscular. Only the bonnet and doors stayed the same – everything else had been pumped up to accommodate much fatter 8.15in (207mm) tyres.

The 427 did not have much of a competition life, because by 1965 it would have clashed with Ford's own GT40. Nevertheless, a Semi-Competition (S/C) model was offered to private buyers as "the fastest production car in the world", with a top speed of around 165 mph and a 0-60 mph time of 4.0 seconds. One 427 managed to accelerate to 100 mph and back to zero again in just 13.8 seconds.

Safety and environmental legislation killed the Cobra in 1968. AC tried to update the concept with the Frua-bodied AC 428 but this did not last long in the fuel crisis of the 1970s.

All types of Cobra are extremely rare and sought after today, with authenticated 427s commanding prices well in excess of £150,000. With so few originals ever made, it is hardly surprising that a vast industry has sprung up dedicated to making AC replicas.

As well as literally dozens of companies producing fibreglass copies the world over, an official AC Cobra Mk IV has been manufactured from 1983 by Autokraft, which is the only company legally entitled to use the AC name.

Carroll Shelby himself launched a controversial new Cobra in the 1990s, which he said was based on chassis left over from the 1960s. However, none of the replicas could ever hope to match the raw magic of an original 1960s Shelby-built Cobra, one of the greatest motoring legends of all time and certainly one of the most exhilarating.

The mightiest Cobra was the 427 produced in 1965. And it looks just as mean too — the perfect mix of style and power

FACTS & FIGURES

- **Engine:** 4260cc /4727cc/ 6984cc/6997cc, V8 cylinders, 260-480 bhp
- **Max speed:** 144-180 mph *(225-258 km/h)*
- **Years produced:** 1962-68
- **Numbers built:** 979

SPIDER

There can be no mistaking an Alfa Romeo Spider. The delicacy of its lines and its unique character could not have come from any other car-maker. Nor would any other manufacturer ever consider making essentially the same sports-car for no less than 27 years. Sports-cars are normally a genre reserved for the cutting edge of car design.

The truth is that Alfa Romeo never really needed to replace the Spider. It was always an intensely likable car and it gained a passionate following of devotees, especially in America. In the early 1980s, when sportscars were almost universally dropped from other car-makers' price lists, the Alfa Romeo Spider pretty much had the ground all to itself.

Few people could have realised the little Alfa sportscar would become such a classic when it was launched in 1966 as the Duetto (duet), a name selected from hundreds of entries in a nationwide competition. Alfa Romeo even gave away a new car to the lucky winner of the contest.

The Duetto used the advanced mechanicals from the Giulia saloon, including the 1570cc engine in its most powerful (109 bhp) twin-carb state-of-tune, plus a five-speed gearbox and all-round disc brakes. It was very advanced for 1966. With its unmistakable long, flat, rounded tail, the Duetto was judged by the motoring press to be an outstanding sportscar.

In Britain at least, it was rather too expensive to make much impact, as it cost almost as much as an E-Type Jaguar.

After just one year, the engine was changed for a new 1779cc engine with 118 bhp on tap and the old Duetto name was dropped in favour of the Alfa Romeo 1750 Spider Veloce. In 1968, a short-lived 1300 Spider Junior was also launched, although that model is little-known outside Italy.

Visually, the biggest change to the Spider came in 1970 when the car's delicately rounded rump was replaced with a harder and arguably prettier 'Kamm'-style cut-off tail. A year later the engine was increased in capacity once more, to 1962cc, and output leapt up to a punchy 132 bhp. The early 1970s was undoubtedly the Spider's heyday: it was quicker, prettier and purer than at any other time in its life.

Then it all fell apart. In Britain, it was decided that converting Spiders to right-hand drive was uneconomic and official imports ceased in 1977. If purchasers were keen enough, they could still buy a Spider through specialists Bell & Colvill, who would even convert it to right-hand drive if wished, but it was always a marginal product. Then US law decreed that rubber impact bumpers and catalysts had to be fitted. Soon after, in 1982, the Spider's glorious twin-carb engine was stultified by fuel injection, blunting its power down to a pale 115 bhp.

In this fashion, the Spider lasted right up until 1990, when Alfa Romeo boldly decided to give the Spider one last lease of life with a major re-style by Pininfarina. The central bodywork remained the same except for some plastic sill covers, but the front and rear ends were heavily revamped. Most significant were the wrap-around body-coloured plastic bumpers front and rear, and the re-shaped boot and rear wings. The engine was modernised with electronic fuel injection, variable valve-timing and a catalytic converter. Inside, the interior was considerably reworked. With this last breath of fresh air, the Spider lasted for two years; Alfa Romeo did not pull the plug on its most coveted model until 1993.

It's amazing that the Spider proved so long-lived. Pininfarina's styling was controversial even when the car was new and, by 1970 the influential American magazine, *Road & Track*, was already describing both the shape and the ergonomics as "outdated". It always had a bucketful of the usual Alfa quirks, such as the gear lever which sprouted from the dashboard and worked in a near-vertical plane.

Yet the Spider's appeal was remarkably durable. Spurred on by one of the most celebrated film appearances ever for a car, when Dustin Hoffman swept Katherine Ross off her feet in *The Graduate*, the American market became the Spider's mainstay during the bleak 1970s. Around 90 per cent of all Alfa Spiders were sold in the US during this time. From 1985, the base model Spider was even called the Graduate in America.

Typically Italian in style and in its uncompromising engineering approach, perhaps the Spider's

The Alfa Romeo badge has always stood for something special and this is typified by the Spider

best point was its silky sweet four-cylinder twin-cam engines. Like all sportscars, the Spider was a victim of advancing legislation, developing performance-blunting fuel injection and catalysts in response to American demands. It never lost its essential charm though. Indeed, in engineering terms it always remained firmly rooted in the 1960s.

Despite its admirable handling, refinement and ride being overtaken by other sportscars, the Spider remained convincing. Performance was lively and the sound from the exhaust was distinctively Alfa. There were wonderful design touches and the feel was of a very special car.

That means that it inevitably became a desirable classic. Despite the oft-repeated stories of rampaging rust and delicate engines, there is no shortage of enthusiasts who appreciate the Spider's finer qualities. There is no shortage of people who remember *The Graduate* either. The Spider is simply too stylish to avoid being a fashion statement as well as a great sportscar.

With the memory of its legendary Spider still fresh in the mind, Alfa Romeo presented, in

Alfa's amazing Spider lived for almost three decades and is one of the most desirable and affordable classics around. Its sheer character compensated for its aging design

1994, an all-new Spider. However, it shared only the name with its ancestor, as it was radically different in concept and design. Front-wheel drive is the biggest difference and the new car's modern styling sets the pace for rival sportscars. The new Spider promises a great future for Alfa Romeo's venerable sportscar tradition.

As the company's 1980s advertising slogan boasted: "The magic lives on... "

FACTS & FIGURES

- **Engine:** 1290cc /1570cc/ 1779cc/1962cc, 4 cylinders, 87-132 bhp
- **Max speed:** 106-124 mph *(170-200 km/h)*
- **Years produced:** 1966-93
- **Numbers built:** 105,226

VOLKSWAGEN
BEETLE

No other car in history has mobilised more people than the Volkswagen Beetle – and yet it almost never made it into production. When the Allied Forces evaluated the prototypes at the end of World War II, it was considered too crude, ugly and underdeveloped for production.

Designed before WW2 the Beetle was almost killed off before going on sale. Once production started the world couldn't get enough of them

Sir William Rootes even said that it "does not meet the fundamental requirements of a motor car". Necessity prevailed and the Volkswagen – or People's Car – was given life.

The Beetle's origins can be traced back to 1934, when Ferdinand Porsche began work on Adolf Hitler's dream of a Volksauto. This was to be a four-seater, air-cooled car to cost less than DM1000 (around £50/$250). However, the car couldn't be bought for cash, only through a saving stamps scheme. Two

prototypes were completed by October 1936 and, after further development, a factory was opened in 1938 to build the 'Kraft-durch-Freude Wagen' – the 'Strength Through Joy' car. Production never really began, since the war required that the factory was turned over to making the Kubelwagen – a military vehicle with the same mechanical basics.

After the war, Major Ivan Hirst was given the task of rebuilding the factory, which had been destroyed by Allied bombing. Among the ruins was found the remains of a

KdF Wagen. The military advised that this should be produced as a means of supplying local light transport. So a production line was set up – in appalling conditions at first – and supplies flowed to all of the occupying forces.

It was felt that the Volkswagen, as it was now called, stood a chance as a regular production car – it was cheap and simple, ideal for those austere post-war years. Exports to France and Russia began in 1946 and civilian orders were being fulfilled within two years. British control was handed over in

1949 and VW became a manufacturer in its own right.

The basis of the Volkswagen was a backbone chassis/platform with a rear-mounted, 1131cc, flat-four engine, which was air-cooled to cope with severe German winters. Unusually for the time, it had four-wheel independent suspension by torsion bars. The simple steel bodywork bolted on top and because of its shape, it was nicknamed the 'Beetle' by the Americans.

The early Volkswagens had split rear windows and very austere trim with no chromework. Export

The familiar Beetle shape is still being produced in Mexico to this day. The earliest split rear screen is most treasured

models were slightly more luxurious and technically more sophisticated. Early 'split window' Beetles are now treasured collectors' pieces.

No Beetle is more highly prized than the convertible. Volkswagen sanctioned only two official conversions. The first was a 2+2 version, manufactured by Hebmuller. The sills, bulkhead and rear were all strengthened, so it felt very rigid. The original windscreen was retained, though the side windows and engine lid were new, and the hood could be raised with one hand. Hebmuller never really recovered from a serious factory fire in the year of its launch (1949). It suffered financial problems and production ground to a halt after only 696 had been built.

The second convertible Beetle was a full four-seater, created by

Karmann of Osnabruck, which became the definitive item. Rigidity was addressed by adding members under the sills and around the doors, which pushed the weight up by 90lb (40kg). Externally it was identical to a Beetle below the waist (except for repositioned semaphore indicators) but there were new winding front and rear windows and an elegant fabric hood with glass rear window, which grew larger as the years passed. The hood stacked up high behind rear seats. Production of the Karmann Cabriolet ceased as late as 1980.

The first major change to the saloon occurred in 1953, when the rear window became oval-shaped and the engine increased in size to 1192cc, pushing power up from 25 bhp to 30 bhp. The Beetle got into its stride from now on, becoming the definitive 'people's car' of

Germany – and the world – notching up million after million sales, pouring out of factories across the globe.

By the time the rear window changed again to its more familiar rectangular shape in 1957, sales in America were soaring. They were up to 64,000 that year and eventually peaked in 1970 at over 582,000 units. The Beetle's success was partly spurred on by an inventive advertisement campaign which played on the contrast of the Beetle's unchanging appearance versus Detroit's chaotic annual revisions. The Beetle was also widely viewed as the most reliable car around.

Gradually things became a little more sophisticated, as the engines grew in size, the gearbox gained synchromesh, automatic transmission became optional and

Designed by Ferdinand Porsche: the Beetle laid the foundations for his legendary sportscars

the improved 1302 Beetle came on stream. Volkswagen, however, never lost sight of the attributes which endeared it to its owners: simplicity, value and reliability. Instead it created more up-market variants on the same basic floorpan, like Karmann-Ghia's lovely coupe, a 1500 saloon and the 411 range.

On 17 February 1972, the Beetle passed the magic milestone of 15,007,034 units produced, overtaking the record set by the Ford Model T. That made it the most popular car in history and its total is unlikely to be exceeded by any other single model. The Toyota Corolla's claim to have caught the Beetle is only believable if all the very different versions of the Japanese car are added together.

Even after German production ceased in January 1978, the Beetle continued to be made at factories in countries like Brazil and Mexico, where Beetles are still being churned out at the rate of almost 500 a day. The current total exceeds

The interiors were always stark, but were surprisingly comfortable and sturdy nonetheless

a staggering 21 million cars.

The popularity of the Beetle has never waned. It is still viewed with tremendous affection and owners are often loyal to the point of fanaticism. This is reflected in fairly high prices for Beetles sold as classics, especially the convertibles.

The Beetle also sired a whole

series of crazes. The first of these was the American fad for racing off-road. A wide variety of 'sand rails' were built in the late 1950s and early 1960s, and a sub-culture of performance tuning parts sprang up. This in turn led to the great dune buggy explosion, ignited when Bruce Meyers put a fibreglass body tub on a Beetle floorpan. Hundreds of firms sprang up overnight to supply an insatiable desire for 'Beach Buggy' machines.

More recently, there has been a craze for customising. Young

people attracted by the Beetle's timeless lines often spent large sums subtly evolving their cars.

For instance, 'Cal-Look' Beetles smoothed out the lines, lowered the suspension and added wild and gaudy paint schemes.

There is a strong case for naming the VW Beetle as 'Car of the Century' – indeed a panel of German motoring journalists has already done so. It has brought affordable and reliable motoring to countless millions, not just in its home market, but in the United States, Australia, South America, Africa and across the rest of the entire globe and it will continue to do so for some time to come.

FACTS & FIGURES

- **Engine:** 1131cc /1192cc/ 1285cc/1493cc/1584cc, 4 cylinders, 25-50 bhp
- **Max speed:** 60-84 mph *(97-135 km/h)*
- **Years produced:** 1945-date
- **Numbers built:** 21 million (...and rising)

JAGUAR
E-TYPE

Right from the very origins of William Lyons' marque, Jaguar has meant two things: luxurious sporting saloon cars with 'Grace, Space, Pace' – and pace-setting high performance sportscars. Arguably the greatest sportscar of them all was the Jaguar E-Type.

The E-Type name still has a magical ring to it. When it was first shown to the public at the 1961 Geneva Motor Show, it was nothing short of sensational. Here

When launched in 1961 the 150 mph E-Type offered unbelievable value – just like its 1990s successor the XK8

was a car which looked absolutely stunning, a car which would soon prove to be capable of 150 mph, and a car which cost just over £2,000 new. The only other car capable of these speeds, the Ferrari 250GT, cost more than £6,300.

Although it was a direct replacement for the ageing XK150, the E-Type's name played on the Le Mans winning heritage of its C-Type and D-Type racing forebears of the 1950s. In style, it certainly bore a striking resemblance to the sleek lines of the D-Type, as both cars were designed by the same man, Malcolm Sayer.

There were two models at the launch: an open-topped sports model and a fixed-head coupe.

Both were strict two-seaters, though the coupe was more practical thanks to its side-hinged rear hatch and long load platform for luggage.

Unlike the old XK series, the E-Type had no chassis: it was a complex unitary structure with an enormously long bonnet which hinged forward for access. Underneath that bonnet lay the latest incarnation of the fabulous six-cylinder XK engine, first seen in 1948. It had no less than 265 bhp on tap, at that time an extraordinary figure for a 3.8-litre 'six'. Jaguar supplied E-Types to motoring magazines for test, determined to reach the magic 150 mph – which the car did, thanks to

some rather special high-speed tyres. Almost all the rest of the mechanical specification was new. The four-speed gearbox was carried over but much of the rest was developed specially for the Jaguar: double-wishbone front suspension, power-assisted front disc brakes, and rear suspension mounted on a separate subframe.

Inside, there was less of the traditional leather-and-wood approach: for instance, owners now just got a moulded plastic dash with aluminium edgings and vinyl door trims.

The buying public went mad for the new E-Type. Demand was so high that used examples were fetching more than new ones. The

Left: *V12 models had power but were fatter and heavier*

mania was fuelled when racing drivers such as Roy Salvadori, John Coombs and Graham Hill took to the circuits with great success in the early days. The E-Type's best competition record had to wait until 1963, however, when a batch of Lightweight E-Types were made specifically for racing.

In 1964, the E-Type was given a 4.2-litre engine and a new gearbox. The engine provided much better torque (though no extra top-end performance), and the all-synchromesh gearbox was much quicker between changes than the slow original.

Two years later came a third E-Type body style – the 2+2. In order to fit an extra pair of children's seats in the rear, the E-Type shell had to be stretched by nine inches and the roof was raised by two inches to create extra head room. The result may not have been aesthetically pleasing but it certainly enhanced the appeal of Jaguar's sportscar range. Another option starting at this time was an automatic gearbox.

In 1968 a much revised Series 2 E-Type was launched at Earls Court. Most of the changes were to answer new American Federal regulations about lighting and bumper height. Hence, the Series 2 had a new bonnet incorporating uncowled headlamps, which were sited two inches higher, and there were larger, wrap-around bumpers fitted.

There were also new laws about emissions in America, so examples exported to the States began to get modified engines with restricted power outputs. Home-market cars still had 265 bhp but emissions-restricted ones had just 171 bhp. Today, purists regard the Series 2 as a diluted version of the original E-Type, but the period when it was sold (1968-70) represented the era of the E's greatest popularity.

The final development of the E-Type came in 1971, when a brand new V12 engine became standard across the board. This fabulous and sizeable engine was the result of £3 million of development and featured all-aluminium construction, overhead cams on each bank of cylinders and no less than four Stromberg carburettors. Power was up to 272 bhp but more significantly, torque rose to an amazing 304 lb ft. A 0-60 mph time of 6.4 seconds was quoted, although in outright performance it was probably no better than the very first and much lighter models.

The so-called Series 3 also looked very different: the nose incorporated a controversial 'cheese grater' grille, the wheels and arches were much wider and all models (roadster and fixed head coupe) now came on the long wheelbase of the 2+2. Some 80 per cent of Series 3 cars were exported to the USA, where the qualities of the E-Type were well appreciated, especially as it was now available with air conditioning.

The demise of the E-Type came in 1975. The very last 50 cars were painted black and included a special commemorative plaque signed by Sir William Lyons. The model was replaced by a very different creature, the XJ-S, which was far more of a grand tourer and less of a genuine sportscar. That made the E-Type the last great Jaguar sportscar.

A brand new sports model the XK8 was launched in 1996 and it took many of its cues from the E-Type. The XK8 became an instant hit, just like its forbearer.

As a classic, the E-Type is perhaps one of only half-a-dozen cars which are truly enduring and legendary. In the heady classic car boom years of the late 1980s, examples were changing hands for over £100,000, today they are much more affordable. The survival rate is quite high, since their classic status was recognised long ago,

The beautiful dashboard was a joy to view, if not to use. Also, the the seats in early models were criticized

and many examples have been restored to outstanding condition. The E-Type's enduring popularity has also meant that the choice is surprisingly wide. An E-Type may not be the most economical classic sportscar to own but it certainly is one of the most stylish and desirable.

FACTS & FIGURES

- **Engine:** 3781cc /4235cc/ 5343cc, 6/V12 cylinders, 171-272 bhp
- **Max speed:** 136-150 mph *(218-240 km/h)*
- **Years produced:** 1961-75
- **Numbers built:** 72,507

LOTUS
ELAN

The true depth of Colin Chapman's engineering genius is still being discovered. From his earliest days building Austin-based specials in a lock-up garage, he was always ahead of the game. He developed an unsurpassed reputation for designing race-winning cars and became pre-eminent among British race car constructors.

Chapman realised the need to develop road cars which would fund his true passion, motor racing. However, despite levels of performance and handling that led the field, Lotus road cars were almost always deficient in build quality. Ironically, Chapman's earliest true road car, the 1957 Elite, lost large sums of money for Lotus.

The Elan changed all that. By 1962, Lotus had become the dominant force in virtually all single-seater racing categories and there was a strong demand for a road car which embodied the Lotus principles of light weight and efficient engineering. After his experience with the glassfibre monocoque Elite, Chapman realised that what he didn't need was another difficult-to-make, expensive, raw semi-racing car.

So the Elan was conceived to be a true sportscar but one with practicality and ease-of-construction at the top of the

The Elan was years ahead of its time when launched in 1962. Drop-head models are most sought after due to their wind-in-the-hair thrills

agenda. Another glassfibre monocoque design was ruled out, so instead Chapman used a backbone chassis. This idea was not new (it had been seen in Edwardian times) but the method of its construction was. The Elan didn't use a steel tube type chassis but a folded pressed-steel sheet forming a single girder. The lightness and rigidity of this set-up so impressed Chapman that he began using it on his Formula 1 cars. Soon all F1 constructors had copied him.

The backbone split at the front into a two-pronged fork embracing the engine/gearbox and leading to the front suspension. A shorter fork at the rear carried a cross-member on which were mounted the rear Chapman struts. The suspension was by front wishbones, coil spring/dampers and an anti-roll bar, using proprietary parts where possible. The rear was independent by struts and coil-sprung wishbones. Disc brakes were fitted all round.

As for the body, this was a glassfibre open structure which contributed little to the rigidity of the chassis. It was a one-piece shell which bolted to the chassis and featured pop-up headlamps, which were a great novelty at the time. Overall dimensions were very compact and the first Elans were strict two-seaters. They were all initially open-topped, although an optional hard top was offered from May 1963.

The Elan was launched at the 1962 London Motor Show at £1,499 complete, although most buyers elected to save purchase tax and build their own car from a complete kit, priced at £1,095. Thus it was not a cheap car but it was certainly one of the most desirable sportscars of any description in 1962.

Lotus launched the Elan with a 1498cc twin-cam engine based on the Ford Cortina block. When the international racing class was raised to 1600cc, Lotus expanded the engine to 1558cc, recalling all the 22 Elans already built with the smaller engine. In this definitive form, the engine developed 105 bhp, enough for 115 mph and 0-60 mph in 8.7 seconds.

However, it was in roadholding and handling that the Elan excelled. It became a benchmark against which all others were judged and even today it has enough ability to raise the eyebrows of hardened road-testers.

There were many early problems, like flaking paint, poorly fitting trim and criticisms of the rubber doughnuts on the drive-shafts, which were quickly replaced with superior Rotoflex joints. Engine noise at high speed was also a concern, which was remedied in 1965 with the option of a higher final drive ratio.

In late 1964, Lotus introduced a Series 2 version incorporating larger brake callipers, a better interior and optional centre-lock wheels. The Series 3 of the following year had an extended boot lid, higher final drive and could be ordered as a fixed-head coupe as well as a drophead.

The 1966 SE (Special Equipment) became the best Elan to date, boasting a 115 bhp engine, close-ratio gearbox and servo-assisted brakes. The final Series 4 version (1968) had flared wheel arches, rocker switches and was available, from 1971, in ultimate Sprint guise, with a Tony Rudd-modified 'big valve' twin-cam

engine developing 126 bhp. The Sprint needed a strengthened differential and drive-shafts to cope with its performance (124 mph and 0-60 mph in 6.7 secs), and was easily recognised by its two-tone paint scheme. The two-seater Elan lasted until 1973.

Inevitably the Elan made it on to the track. Lotus built special racing versions with lightweight bodies and modified suspension to improve roadholding, which were called 26R. The drivers included Jackie Stewart, Stirling Moss, Mike Spence and John Miles, the latter achieving such great success he was given a place in Lotus' Grand Prix team.

There is a second chapter in the Elan story. Chapman launched another road-going Elan in the form of the 'Plus 2', or family man's Lotus. This was first introduced in 1967. The primary reason for the existence of the Elan +2 was to provide an extra pair of seats for children up to teenage years. In concept and layout it remained very much an Elan but it was larger in every way.

The backbone chassis idea was kept but it was bigger. To compensate for the increased bulk, holes were drilled in the steel to reduce weight. The bodywork was still glassfibre but it was substantially enlarged, gaining a foot in length and 7.5in in width. It was substantially redesigned, featuring a new sloping nose, much larger boot and fastback roof (all +2s were fixed-head coupes). The interior was also improved, having a more comprehensive dash.

Mechanically, the story remained much the same, although the +2 became the first Lotus to gain a standard brake servo. The same 118 bhp 1558cc twin-cam engine was used. Although the weight penalty over the standard Elan was considerable (16.8 cwt/850 kg to 14 cwt/710 kg), performance did not suffer too badly, probably because of superior aerodynamics: A +2 could reach 121 mph and 0-60 mph in 8.2 secs.

In 1968, the family Elan was uprated to +2S specification, gaining better trim and more equipment, such as fog lamps. It became the first Lotus that could not be bought in kit form, only being sold fully-built.

To return the Elan +2 to two-seater performance levels, Chapman introduced the +2S/130 in 1971, which had the 126 bhp big valve engine of the Elan Sprint.

Elan +2S/130s are easily spotted by their self-coloured silver roofs. The final metamorphosis came in late 1972, when a five-speed gearbox was offered as an option. By 1974, changing type approval regulations made it uneconomic to continue producing the Elan. In any case, by then Lotus had its brand new 2.0-litre Elite in a bid to move upmarket. The 90s Elan was a different animal and never quite rekindled the spirit of the original.

FACTS & FIGURES

- **Engine:** 1558/cc, 4 cylinders, 115-126 bhp
- **Max speed:** 115-124 mph
  (185-200 kmh)
- **Years produced:** 1962-74
- **Numbers built:** 12,224

GOLF GTI

In the early 1970s Volkswagen was becoming drastically out-of-step with the rest of the car world. While virtually every other manufacturer had abandoned rear-engined cars as second-best from the point of view of both dynamics and packaging, Volkswagen soldiered on with a range based entirely on the pre-war Beetle.

However, VW's new partner Audi was already ahead of the game with its range of smart-looking, well-built, front-wheel-drive saloons. Volkswagen took a leaf out of Audi's book and embarked on a spectacular, revolutionary rebirth. In the space of two years, from 1973 to 1975, it launched no less than four all-new front-wheel-drive cars: the Passat, Scirocco, Polo and Golf. Each one of them set new standards in their market sectors.

The most successful of the quartet was unquestionably the 1974 Golf. The name, incidentally, does not derive from the game of 18 holes but *Golfstrom*, the German word for the 'Gulf Stream'. In America, where the new car would also be manufactured, it was known as the Rabbit.

The Golf's styling was the brilliantly simple work of Giugiaro's newly-independent team, Ital Design. The packaging was exactly right, the hatchback tail made it extremely practical and the build quality endeared it to a generation of owners who had known only rust and breakdowns.

Some of the engineers at Volkswagen were convinced that the car Volkswagen had conceived as a bread-and-butter shopping trolley for the masses could handle much more power. Like the Mini 15 years before it, the balance of the front-wheel-drive Golf was so good that there certainly was plenty of potential to handle it.

The management at the Wolfsburg headquarters was not convinced and would not sanction work on what it saw as an uncommercial product. So, a dedicated band of technicians developed a rather special version of the Golf in their spare time, until the management finally liked what they saw and gave the project the green light.

This was destined to become the GTI. The most important changes happened under the bonnet. The largest engine in the intended Golf line-up was a 1588cc unit, due for launch in August

> *Golf GTI started a whole new automotive fashion combining sportscar performance with practicality. It's a recipe that's still popular today*

1975. It was to this unit (which developed 75 bhp in standard tune) that the engineers turned. They installed Bosch K-Jetronic fuel injection and boosted the power up to 110 bhp. The engineers also tweaked the suspension, adding a front anti-roll bar to stiffen it up, while fat wheels and tyres were specified to sharpen grip.

The marketing department decided on an understated style:

the simple, clean-cut lines of the Giugiaro original were left unmolested. Only a deep chin spoiler, discreet side stripes, a little bit of red trim around the grille and an unassuming 'GTI' badge made the car stand out.

Quite simply, the Golf GTI swept all before it when it was launched in August 1975. It caused a sensation with the motoring public who thronged to own one, even though it took almost a year for deliveries to begin.

In the first four years of the model's life, more than 100,000 were supplied to customers on the continent. In Britain the GTI was

only sold to special order, in left-hand form, for four years. It was not until 1979 that the GTI became available in right-hand drive, by which time the original four-speed gearbox had been replaced by a five-speeder.

British customers soon realised what they'd been missing. The GTI was a genuine firebomb, capable of over 110 mph and 0-60 mph in well under ten seconds.

Moreover, this power was delivered smoothly and reliably. Then there was the handling: it was pin-sharp, predictable and a revelation to a generation of drivers brought up on the Morris Marina

or the Ford Capri.

It immediately established a cult following. Other manufacturers could not ignore the rich business VW was doing and soon a swathe of 'hot hatches' came chasing at the GTI's heels: the Ford Escort XR3, Opel/Vauxhall Astra GTE, Fiat Strada Abarth and a dozen others. None of them ever quite matched the magic of the original Golf GTI and those three letters came to be synonymous with the new driving subculture: the hot hatch brigade.

Another significant newcomer in 1979 was the Golf Cabriolet. This was actually another brave and pioneering move, for at that

time convertibles were very much out of fashion. The engineering and construction work was done by the acknowledged masters of the convertible art, Karmann of Osnabruck. Their chop-top was typically Germanic in execution: there was a roll-over bar and a high-stacked hood to keep as much boot space as possible, although both luggage space and room in the rear seats was at a premium. There was a GTI version of the Cabriolet, which shared the dazzling dynamics of its hot-hatch brother, though the slightly compromised structure was not as rigid.

Another important derivative of the Golf was the Scirocco, Volkswagen's coupe which shared the Golf platform. Naturally there was a GTI version of this too, mimicking the specification of the Golf but adding performance through lighter weight and better aerodynamics, as well as offering attractive coupe styling.

A larger 1760cc engine became standard for the Golf GTI in 1982, which boosted power slightly to 112 bhp. More importantly, the engine had nearly ten per cent more torque, available much lower down the rev band. This made the GTI a much more tractable — and a less 'peaky' – car to drive than

many high-revving rivals. A hotter 139 bhp 16-valve version further cemented its desirability.

The Mark I Golf was replaced in 1983 by the second generation, and that in turn by the current Golf in 1991. All the time the GTI badge remained a stubbornly popular component of the Golf family. Amazingly, the original Golf Mark I bodyshell lasted right up until 1992 in convertible form, when it was finally replaced by the current Golf Cabriolet.

The Mark II is regarded as the best all-rounder, the latest Mk III was criticised for being too fat and heavy — the very opposite to the original. It needed the launch of a V6 engine in the sensational Golf VR6 and a new 16-valve 'four' to bring the fun back.

Few would deny that the Golf GTI has passed seamlessly from being the founder and benchmark of the hot hatch school to a widely-accepted classic. Even today it is still entertaining new generations with its delights.

Thousands were imported to Britain, which is good news for the bargain hunter today. The Golf

The hot hatchback Golf GTI only came about after VW engineers tinkered with an ordinary Golf in their spare time!

was so well built that many cars lasted the distance where other, more fragile performance cars bit the dust. Today, the GTI has a wide following and many examples have been restored. All models are desirable but it is the special edition Mk I Campaign model made after August 1983 which is currently the most sought after GTI. Those with simpler needs should head for the MK II.

FACTS & FIGURES

- **Engine:** 1588cc / 1781cc, 4 cylinders, 110-112 bhp
- **Max speed:** 110-116 mph *(117-187 km/h)*
- **Years produced:** 1976-92
- **Numbers built:** more than 350,000

AUSTIN HEALEY
100 & 3000

Donald Healey was a Cornishman who set up his own marque immediately after World War II to make a series of handsome Riley-engined sportscars, convertibles and saloons. Considering they were fresh designs in troubled times, they were amazingly advanced. In fact, the Healey was the world's fastest four-seater in its day, capable of over 110 mph.

In 1949, while travelling to America on the Queen Elizabeth, Healey chanced to meet George Romney, general manager of US car-maker Nash. They got on so well that a deal was struck, with Healey supplying complete body and chassis units to Nash, which

would install its own engines to create the Nash-Healey sportscar. This collaboration for the American market only did not prove to be a great sales success.

So in 1951, Donald Healey and his son Geoffrey began work on a new, cheaper sportscar, still with a firm eye on the American market. For his engine, Healey turned to another car which was British-built but plainly intended for American buyers, the Austin Atlantic. The

Atlantic saloon and convertible had not been a great success either, but its four-cylinder, 2.6-litre engine appealed to Healey.

Geoffrey Healey and Barry Bilbie designed the chassis, while ex-Rootes man Gerry Coker styled the bodywork. This was an undoubted work of genius; an elegantly curvaceous shape with a purposefully low stance and a lack of any unnecessary adornment.

Its essential 'rightness' was

proven when virtually nothing was changed for the subsequent production version.

The prototype appeared at the 1952 London Motor Show, where it was displayed as the Healey Hundred – it had a top speed of over 100 mph, as proven by a run of 106 mph at the famous straight Belgian road at Jabbeke. Donald Healey was unhappy about the styling of the grille, so he put the nose up against a pillar at the show but that did not stop the crowds thronging around it. The Healey was the undoubted star of the show and the salesmen on the stand took no less than 3,000 orders.

Austin's chief Leonard Lord had found out about the Healey before its show-stealing debut, but seeing this warm

reception it got there clinched the matter for him. Donald Healey was obviously not in a position to manufacture enough cars to meet demand and Lord saw an ideal opportunity for Austin. The car was rebadged Austin-Healey even while it sat on the motor show stand and Healey was engaged as a consultant on a 20-year contract.

The prototype was then whisked off to America for a round of shows. At the 1953 New York Show, it was voted International Show Car of the Year. Meanwhile coachbuilders Tickford built a batch of 20 pre-production cars in aluminium, though production bodies would be built in steel by another motoring legend, Jensen.

The Austin factory at Longbridge began assembling the Austin-Healey 100 in May 1953. Changes over the prototype included slightly raised headlamps and a revised grille (though still the recognisable Healey kite shape).

Mechanically, the Healey used the standard Austin Atlantic engine, a lumbering but torquey all-iron four-pot unit which developed 90 bhp. The Healey also took its four-speed gearbox from the Austin, though the bottom gear was blanked off to turn it into a three-speeder and there was overdrive on the top two ratios.

Since it weighed less than a ton (2015 lb/914 kg), performance was excellent. The top speed was 103 mph and 0-60 mph took a little over ten seconds. The Healey cost $3,000 (or £750) new, so Austin could boast that this was the cheapest 100 mph car on the market.

The Healey 3000 lasted until 1968. BMW is rumoured to be planning a revival of this classic sportscar

Even better performance was available from 1954, when the 100S was launched. This lightweight competition variant had a 132 bhp light-alloy cylinder head engine modified by Weslake. It had mostly aluminium bodywork and was the first production sportscar to have four-wheel disc brakes. Each example was high-speed tested by the factory and was easily identified by its shallow perspex wind deflector, oval air intake and knock-on wire wheels. The close-ratio four-speed gearbox allowed 0-60 mph in just 7.8 secs. Only 55 were made and, unsurprisingly, the 100S is a highly prized collector's car today.

A less expensive way to get better performance arrived in 1955, when the 100M was launched. This was a high-compression 110 bhp version with front anti-roll bar and bonnet straps.

By this stage the old Atlantic engine was definitely looking long-in-the-tooth. The Atlantic saloon had actually finished its production run in 1952 and its successors were a range of BMC saloons using a newly developed 2639cc six-cylinder engine. Healey was asked to modify his sportscar to accommodate it. He added two inches to the wheelbase, changed the grille to a prettier oval shape and installed a pair of rather marginal rear seats for children.

The result was the 100/6, first seen in 1956. It got a cool reception from buyers, who now regarded it as more 'touring' than 'sports'. Certainly, it was heavier and slower than the old 100, despite an increase in power to 102 bhp. This was not addressed until 1957, when a six-port head boosted power to 117 bhp and returned performance more to the original level.

Leonard Lord chose the 1959 New York Motor Show to launch the new Austin-Healey 3000, with its 2912cc engine. This brought the new 3000 the nickname 'Big Healey'. Standard front disc brakes featured on this more powerful (124 bhp) version, although overdrive was optional. The Mark II, from 1961, had triple SU carbs, a new gearbox and a vertically-slatted grille, while the Mk IIa got twin carbs, wind-up windows and a curved screen.

The final Mk III of 1963 was the most powerful and the fastest of all Healeys, with 148 bhp to play with. Although the Healey had really developed very little over its life, the car's death in 1968 was probably premature. Officially it occurred because of creeping US safety and emissions laws. That meant a prototype 4.0-litre Rolls-Royce engined Healey (to be called the 4000) never reached fruition. The vast majority of the 72,000 cars built over the model's 14-year lifespan were exported to the United States.

Although the Big Healey never had much competition success and was, in its day, viewed more as a good-value tourer than a full-blooded sportscar, it is today widely appreciated as one of the great classics. It has a brawny character, an extremely beautiful shape and evokes its period with faultless charm.

BMW is seriously rumoured to be reviving the Healey retaining its classic and traditional lines.

FACTS & FIGURES

- **Engine:** 2660cc / 2639cc / 2912cc, 4/6 cylinders, 90-148 bhp
- **Max speed:** 103-121 mph *(165-195 km/h)*
- **Years produced:** 1952-68
- **Numbers built:** 72,029

MARK II

When a luxury car-maker like Jaguar decides to expand its market into the cheaper compact saloon car category, other manufacturers should quake in their boots. Britain's established marques certainly felt the impact when a new 2.4-litre Jaguar was launched in 1956. The car simply was a huge leap forward from the expected standards of the day.

In the 1950s, Jaguar had already become Britain's leading high-class saloon manufacturer, being very successful with the Mk VII, which remains a very underrated car even today. What it created with the new, smaller 2.4-litre saloon was not only its first-ever chassis-less monocoque design, but an attractively modern-looking compact luxury car with searingly good performance and roadholding. That reputation was enhanced by the arrival of a faster 3.4-litre version in 1957.

These 2.4 and 3.4-litre saloons became known retrospectively as the Mark I up till 1959, and after that, the Mark II. The evolution between the two stages was subtle in most respects but in terms of the overall effect, the Mark II was a far more cohesive whole. Collectors and enthusiasts have recognised this fact and the Mark II has become the seminal classic Jaguar saloon.

Perhaps it is the elegance of its styling. Perhaps it is the thoroughbred responsiveness which made it such a favourite of contemporary racing drivers. Perhaps it is the old-world charm of its traditional leather-and-walnut interior, leaping cat mascot and oval chrome grille. Whatever, the Mark II's appeal is enduring.

Compared with the old Mark I, the Mark II looked much more balanced and delicate, having a larger glass area, slimmed-down pillars, more chrome and a wider rear track. The latter point meant that the full rear spats of the Mark I were replaced with cut-away ones. The interior was also superior, having exceedingly comfortable leather seats, masses of walnut veneer and a sporting feel to the dashboard layout.

The big news was the

The Mk II created a market for Jaguar and it is still trying to rejoin it with a new Mk II – expected to be launched in 1998

The famous grille is coveted as much today as it was when new

availability of three configurations of the six-cylinder XK engine: the 2.4 and 3.4-litre units which had already been used in the Mark I, and the spectacular 220 bhp 3.8-litre engine from the Mk IX.

The top-of-the-range 3.8 became legendary for its performance; it could reach 125 mph and do the 0-60 mph sprint in 8.5 seconds. That is the sort of performance which would not disgrace a sporting saloon car even today. In its day, it was easily the fastest production saloon car in the world.

Racing drivers certainly recog-

The classic feline style of the Mk II still looks good today, with the Mk II 3.8 the most desirable of them all

nised its worth. Jaguar's works drivers Mike Hawthorn and Duncan Hamilton were two of the more celebrated owners of 3.8-litre Mark IIs. Another profession that appreciated the pace and space of the Mark II was the British police force, making it a frequently seen pursuit and motorway patrol car.

Export markets were naturally targeted, the most important being America, where journalists had voted the Mark II 'Car of the Year'. The Mark II was given a spectacular showing at the 1960 New York Show, with an example having all of its exterior metalwork gold-plated, and a model on hand dressed in a gold-thread dress stitched with over 1,000 diamonds!

The Mark II remained largely unchanged throughout its

production life (1959-67) but there were a number of interesting derivatives. The first was the Daimler 2.5-litre V8 which was given birth because Jaguar had acquired the Daimler company in 1960 and inherited the fabulous Edward Turner-designed Daimler V8 engine. It was a natural fitment for the Mark II body shell and found favour with buyers less interested in sporting edge and more in luxury, refinement and pulling power. Ironically, it was actually a much better performer and handler than Jaguar's smaller-engined Mark IIs.

Another derivative was the Jaguar S-Type, which used the Mark II's hull and interior largely unchanged, but added a longer tail and slightly revised front end. This was in turn developed into another pair of identical twins, the Jaguar 420 and Daimler Sovereign, which had sharper front-end styling and 4.2-litre engines.

The Mark II officially died as a model in 1967, the last ones having cheaper 'ambla' instead of leather interior trim, in line with a general cost-cutting policy at Jaguar in the late 1960s. However, there was a pair of final run-out versions of the Mark II which were called the 240 and 340. They were made between 1967 and 1969. These were considerably less lavish models with slimmer bumpers and plastic interior trim. Officially there was no 380 version, either, although a handful were built to special order.

In the 1980s, the classic car market began to acknowledge the Mark II as a quality car with enthusiast value. Prices rose to extraordinary heights – beyond £30,000 in some cases – and, unlike many other classic cars, did not fall back dramatically in value after the price bubble burst in 1990.

However, all Mark IIs are not equally valued. The 3.8-litre version with a manual overdrive gearbox is unquestionably the best and consequently the most sought-after. The rather asthmatic 2.4-litre Mark II and down-market 240/340 models are at the opposite extreme, with automatic transmission also frowned on, since most potential Mark II owners – now, as in the 1960s – have a sporting inclination and love the overdrive option.

Likewise, the Daimler V8-powered versions are generally viewed with far less enthusiasm because they are not pure Jaguars and were conceived more for comfort than rewarding sports driving. As a result, Daimlers can make the best buys because they cost so much less.

A veritable industry has sprung up to support these cars and there are even businesses doing very well updating original examples to more modern specifications, for what seem enormous sums of money. More recently still, firms have set up offering Mark IIs on contract hire as an alternative to buying a brand new car. The attractions of running a classic as an everyday car have seldom been as powerful as they are with a Jaguar Mark II. It's all part of a mystique which will undoubtedly see the Mark II remain one of the great classic cars for as long as there are enthusiasts around to drive them.

FACTS & FIGURES

- **Engine:** 2483cc / 3442cc / 3781cc, 6 cylinders, 120-220 bhp
- **Max speed:** 96-125 mph *(154-200 km/h)*
- **Years produced:** 1959-69 (incl 240/340)
- **Numbers built:** 91,222 (incl 240/340)

MGB

What other car can claim to have introduced so many people to sportscar motoring than the MGB? Countless thousands of enthusiasts across the generations have enjoyed the pleasures of MG motoring, not only in Britain but in Europe – and especially in the United States.

The MGB is without doubt the most famous in a long line of sportscars made by MG. It was the most durable, lasting some 18 years in production, and the most popular, with not far short of half a million cars built. The MGB did more to establish the British sportscar as an institution than any other car before or since. In its heyday, it was one of the best sportscars around but, alas, in later life it became a jaded shadow of its former self.

MG began in 1922 as a contraction of Morris Garages, reflecting its origins as part of the Morris group. After the war, MGs were highly successful among traditionally-minded sporting drivers and became well-known in America (especially the TC, TD and TF).

The MGB grew out of MG's celebrated MGA, the most successful sportscar made up to that time, with 100,000 units sold. By the early 1960s, the MGA was looking decidedly old-fashioned. The new MGB would offer the same combination of speed, handling and good value, but would have modern styling and far more creature comforts.

An early decision was made to adopt unitary construction, as opposed to the separate chassis of the MGA. At that time, the idea was quite novel for sportscars. MG's Chief Engineer, Sydney Enever, began work on 'Project EX205' in 1959. All-independent suspension would perhaps have been the best system for the new car but Enever fell back on familiar territory by retaining the MGA's well-proven system of independent front suspension by coil springs and wishbones, with a live rear axle and semi-elliptical leaf springs.

The evergreen B-series engine (used in the MGA since 1955) was bored out for the MGB to 1798cc. The net effect of the expansion was a healthy increase in power of some 8 bhp to 94 bhp. Although this was less than the double overhead-cam engine used by the fastest MGAs, it was felt that the B-series represented a safer and more reliable choice than the troublesome twin-cam.

The MGB was launched in October 1962 at the London Motor Show and the response from press and public alike was extremely favourable. Here was a car which looked modern and felt modern – but was built on solid MG virtues. As *Autocar* said: "It is a forward step, in that the car is faster, and yet more docile and comfortable."

For its day, the MGB was a strong performer. The top speed was around 105 mph and 0-60 mph was accomplished in 11.4 seconds. The B-series engine's best feature

The MGB GT was dubbed a cheap Aston Martin, but it combined fun with a degree of practicality

was its wide-based torque band although it was never a particularly free-revving unit.

Out on the open road, the MG enthusiast felt at home; here was a car with solid roadholding and entertaining handling on the limit. The ride had improved by leaps and bounds over the rather harsh MGA. Indeed, there was some criticism from the press that the MGB suffered from too much body roll and that the suspension was too soft for a sportscar.

Compared to the model it replaced, the MGB was a paragon of comfort – it was easier to get into, had wider and more accommodating seats, winding windows, a modern dash and a leak-free hood. Options like the hard top and Laycock overdrive made it even more easy to live with. It cost just £950 and quickly became a sales success in Britain and the United States.

The MGB was immediately launched on a competition career. Its first outing, at the 1963 Sebring 12-Hour Race, did not go well, with both cars suffering main bearing damage. At the 1963 Le Mans, Paddy Hopkirk and Alan Hutcheson drove an MGB home to win 12th place overall, scoring a class victory at the same time. At the same event one year later, the partnership of Hopkirk and Hedges finished 19th overall. In the 1965 Le Mans, the MGB scored its best placing – 11th overall and second in class.

Back with the road car programme, the closed coupe version (the MGB GT) arrived in 1965. It was an attractive car, styled with help from Pininfarina, and its elegant fastback incorporated an opening hatch. The extra bodywork carried a small weight penalty, but this was offset by the

The roadster was by far the most popular MGB and became very popular in the USA

GT's shape which was more aerodynamic, allowing a slightly higher top speed of 106 mph.

The GT was described by MG as a "poor man's Aston Martin". It certainly looked the part, and it was much more practical than the roadster. There was a modest rear seat which could fit two small children, although luggage space was still limited. The GT immediately accounted for one third of all MGB sales.

The Mark II MGB arrived in 1967, with an all-synchromesh gearbox or the first chance to opt for automatic transmission. No external changes were made until 1969, when a matt black grille replaced chrome and the traditional wire wheels were replaced by Rostyle steel wheels.

There were also two attempts to fit larger engines into the MGB shell. The first was the MGC of 1967-69, an ill-fated attempt to pack the MGB with more punch. Into the engine bay went a 145 bhp Austin 3.0-litre straight-six engine. Despite its extra performance, the engine's extra weight made it unhappy in handling terms and under 10,000 were made in total.

The MGB certainly could handle more power, as was proven in 1973 when a 137 bhp Rover 3.5-litre V8 was shoehorned into the engine bay to create the MGB GT V8. The top speed rose to 125 mph and 0-60 mph came up in 8.6 seconds. Moreover, the alloy engine did not weigh much more than the B-series unit. The suspension did not need to be altered and handling remained as good as ever.

By the end of the 1960s, MG was part of an unwieldy industrial conglomeration of competing marques known as the British Leyland Motor Corporation. Slowly but surely, the MG name was strangled.

The most unfortunate changes were needed to bring the 'B' in line with American safety and emissions laws. In 1975, all MGBs suffered the ghastly fate of having black polyurethane bumpers fitted and their ride height raised by 1½in (to meet US headlamp height regulations). The body weight went up and the power output went down. This was controversial, to say the least, because performance and handling obviously suffered badly as a result.

The MGB limped on until 1980, with the final run, a batch of Limited Edition roadsters and GTs, emerging in 1981.

Today, the MGB undoubtedly has the strongest following of any classic car. More MGBs are on the road than almost any other sportscar and there are dozens of owners' clubs worldwide catering for tens of thousands of owners, who have remained loyal to the original embodiment of affordable sportscar motoring.

A whole industry has grown up to restore and service existing cars and supply spares. Well known B specialist, Heritage, even began making replica bodyshells in the 1980s. This formed the basis of MG's revived and much modified B of 1992, called the RV8.

FACTS & FIGURES

- **Engine:** 1798cc / 2912cc / 3528cc, 4/6/V8 cylinders, 62-145 bhp
- **Max speed:** 100-125 mph *(160-200 km/h)*
- **Years produced:** 1962-80
- **Numbers built:** 524,470

MINI

It is ironic that, after nearly 40 years in production, the Mini has become the very thing it originally bucked against: a motoring institution. The difference is, the Mini is a much-loved and much-respected institution. It was a pioneer in the art of transverse-mounted engines and front-wheel drive. It was a marvel of packaging and a testament to the conquest of technical barriers. It was, quite simply, a revolution when it was launched in 1959.

Five million Minis later, it remains in production, satisfying a loyal following of owners for whom its size, cost and above all character remain compelling even today. Over the years it has become a cult object across the world, from Carnaby Street in the 1960s to Tokyo in the 1990s.

Perhaps the most remarkable thing about the Mini is that it was the brainchild of one man: Alec Issigonis. The Mini was probably the last mass-produced car designed by one man alone; as such, it is unlike any other car seen since.

The birth of the Mini took place against the backdrop of the 1956 Suez oil crisis. For all anyone knew, there might be be an indefinite shortage of oil. British drivers were rationed to ten gallons of petrol a month. The popularity of bubble cars mushroomed.

The British Motor Corporation's chairman, Leonard Lord, realised there was a potentially huge market for a cheap small car which combined economy with large-car characteristics. To whom could he entrust the task of developing such a car? There was one obvious but brave choice: Alec Issigonis.

Born in Smyrna in 1906, Issigonis had come to Britain to study at the age of 15. When he had finished his education at Battersea Technical College, he worked for Humber. Then he joined Britain's leading manufacturer, Morris, in 1936. This was where he met Leonard Lord, on a team designing suspensions. After the war, he conceived the Morris Minor.

Then Leonard Lord asked Issigonis to begin development on a new small car project in 1957, which assumed the title ADO15. Assembling a small team around him, Issigonis created the Mini.

The essential factor for the new small car was that it should carry four adults in comfort, plus their luggage. Issigonis became obsessed with the need to save space. He was fervently in favour of front-wheel drive; this mechanical layout could save all the space needed for the propshaft and final drive by incorporating it at the front. From the start, he knew this was going to be right for the Mini.

As for the engine, on grounds of cost, the obvious choice was the A-series unit, as found in the Austin A35 and Morris Minor. The trouble was, this power train measured 38in from stem to stern and this, in Issigonis's view, would eat up too much space.

Then Issigonis had a leap of the imagination. What if the gearbox could be placed under the crankshaft, instead of behind? The engine and gearbox would effectively become one unit and could be mounted sideways, driving each front wheel. The lubrication problem could be overcome by plumbing the gearbox into the engine, so it could use the same sump oil.

The greatest car ever made? The revolutionary Mini can rightly stake its claim to the title

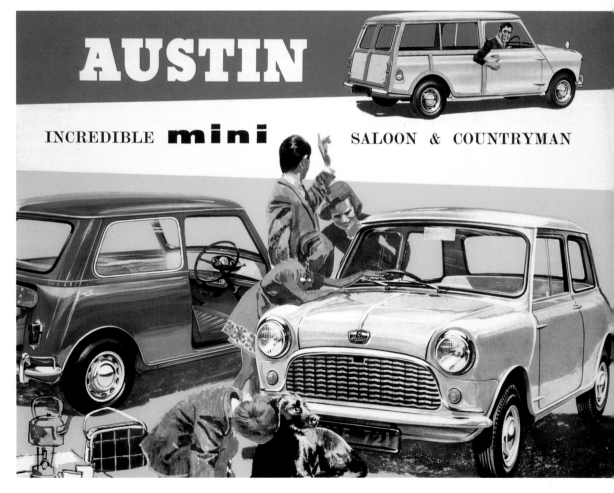

Issigonis felt that the A35's 803cc engine would not provide the performance and smoothness which the new car would require. So the decision was taken to expand the A-series engine to 948cc. On tests, the engine gave the little car too much performance – it was tested to beyond 90 mph with only 37 bhp on tap. So the engine was taken back down to 848cc and top speed fell to a less frenetic 74 mph.

Issigonis was always strongly in favour of small wheels; the 14in wheels of the 1948 Morris Minor were easily the smallest of any saloon of its day. The Mini went much further: its ten-inch diameter wheels were far and away the smallest used in any car, except for some tiny microcars which used scooter wheels. The sole reason for such small wheels was a sacrifice to packaging. They freed up more interior space by reducing the intrusion of the inner wheel arches.

The main disadvantage of ten-inch wheels was the harsh ride they gave over rough surfaces. Here again Issigonis was ahead of the objectors. From his days with Morris, when he had got together with Alex Moulton to build a rubber-sprung Morris Minor, Issigonis had become a convert to the idea of rubber suspensions, which Moulton was still working on. The Mini's rubber cone system was so effective that it is still used on the car today.

All the major components – engine, gearbox, suspension, steering – were mounted on one subframe at the front, with a further subframe at the back to carry the rear suspension. This eliminated a lot of vibration too, and would prove invaluable in the development of a wide range of Mini derivatives which could use these subframe assemblies completely unaltered.

Keeping costs to an absolute minimum meant accommodating such measures as exposed seams in the bodywork to allow easy spot-welding of the main body sections, exposed door hinges simply bolted to the main hull and a lack of winding windows or elaborate door handle mechanisms.

By August 1959, the most important car in BMC's history was ready to be launched. It arrived in two versions: the Morris Mini-Minor and Austin Seven (though the latter soon became just 'Mini' as the word pervaded the English language). Apart from the Ford Popular, it was the cheapest car on the market at £497. It caught on with city drivers who liked its park-ability and with the fashion conscious who thought it 'cool'. Widespread acceptance of the revolutionary Mini followed.

The Mini was also fantastic to drive: nippy, sharp-handling and manoeuvrable. Formula 1 World Championship constructor John Cooper realised its potential and persuaded BMC to let him develop a Mini-Cooper in 1961.

With a bigger 997cc engine, it developed 55 bhp and could reach nearly 90 mph – amazing performance for such a small car.

The Cooper's legendary reputation really grew with the 'S' version of 1963. This had an even larger engine (970cc, 1071cc or 1275cc), front disc brakes, wider wheels, even twin fuel tanks. In its most powerful 1275S form, it was capable of a top speed of up to 96 mph and 0-60 mph in 11.2 secs.

Coopers were all-conquering in rallying, their undoubted high point being three outright victories in the Monte Carlo Rally in 1964, 1965 and 1967. It could have been four wins in a row, but the entire Mini-Cooper team was controversially disqualified on a minor lighting regulation in the 1966 event.

They were pretty successful on the tracks, too. The Mini could humble the more powerful Jaguars and Ford Cortinas with its fantastic handling. The Mini Cooper S was not slow itself; on fast circuits such as the famous Belgian Spa track, Minis could top 130 mph.

The adaptability of the mechanical subframe package led to numerous Mini derivatives:

estate, van and pick-up, utility Moke, luxury 'booted' Riley Elf and Wolseley Hornet. It also became a popular basis for customisation and special bodyworks.

Mini became a marque in its own right in 1969 and settled into notching up spectacular sales,

Minis were, and still are, fantastic fun to drive thanks to its compact-ness and exceptional road-holding

reaching a height of 318,475 units in 1971. The Mini is easily the best-selling British car of all time.

Recently, the Mini received a new lease of life thanks to numerous special editions with names like Open Classic, Red Hot and Piccadilly.

Most exciting is the new generation Mini Cooper, launched in 1990, with its 63 bhp 1275cc engine and luxury trim. The popularity of the Mini shows no sign of abating, though Rover has announced plans for a brand new

Mini for 1999.

Sir Alec Issigonis summed up why the car has never been overtaken as *the* small classic:

"Small cars all look the same because they are designed by committees trying to copy the Mini."

That may sound arrogant but the Mini's brilliant and innovative formula of front-wheel drive, mechanical subframes and unique packaging certainly was the benchmark which others still follow today.

FACTS & FIGURES

- **Engine:** 848cc / 998cc / 997cc / 1071cc / 1098cc / 1275cc, 4 cylinders, 34-76 bhp
- **Max speed:** 70-96 mph *(110-154 km/h)*
- **Years produced:** 1959-date
- **Numbers built:** 5,300,000 to date

FORD

FORD
MUSTANG

Alongside the Chevrolet Corvette, there is perhaps no car more truly American than the Ford Mustang. In terms of sheer sales impact it is unrivalled among mass-produced cars. Mass-produced it certainly was, being the fastest-selling car in history, notching up a million sales in under two years.

The Mustang was a real trailblazer. In the US, coupes are even referred to as 'ponycars' in honour of the Mustang. It was the start of the craze for 'personal coupes',

The original and the best! The Mustang began the craze for coupes

affordable sports-type cars designed to reflect the individualistic tastes of Americans.

The man behind the Mustang was Lee Iacocca. He reasoned that there was a market for a sporty-looking four-seater that was cheap to build and could sell for under $2,500 (just over £600). The very first Mustang, seen at car shows in the early 1960s, was nothing like that: it was a small, two-seater sportscar made of fibreglass – not what Iacocca had in mind at all.

The real Mustang was created by Ford's styling studio and was the work of Joe Oros, David Ash and Gale Halderman. It was reported that they transgressed 78

official Ford design rules in arriving at the shape, which broke new ground with its long-nose, short-boot approach. Three body styles were conceived: a convertible, a crisp notchback hard-topped coupe and a pretty fastback 2+2 coupe.

If the styling was advanced, the mechanical package played it safe. Because the Mustang was meant to be a cheap car, the power range started with a basic six-cylinder 170 cu in (2788cc) engine, taken directly from the Fairlane compact saloon. It developed just 101 bhp, enough for a meagre top speed of only 90 mph. Optional was the 260 cu in (4260cc) V8, whose 164 bhp powered the car to over 100 mph.

Gradually, Ford introduced a policy of 'Total Performance', spiralling power outputs of its big block V8 engines up beyond 300 bhp (a high point of 390 bhp was reached in the 1968 line-up).

Ford sold the Mustang as a car 'designed to be designed by you'. In other words, the basic car really was basic, and the customer would then select options from a huge list of possibilities, like automatic or manual gearboxes, column or stick shifts, handling packages, disc brakes, power steering, bucket or bench seats, air conditioning, interior trim packages, GT packs with firmer suspension, and so on.

The Mustang arrived in April

1964, too late for the '64 model year and too early for '65. So Ford's marketing department pulled off a coup by calling the Mustang a 1964 '1/2 car'. The public went wild. Truck drivers crashed while looking through showroom windows and dealers auctioned cars off in the face of a 15-to-1 demand-to-supply ratio. One East Coast dealer sold a car this way and the owner slept in his car overnight

Successive designs diluted appeal, becoming bigger and flashier

to ensure it wasn't sold from under him until his cheque cleared!

It wasn't long before other companies realised what a jackpot Ford had scored and came up with their own 'ponycar' imitators. As a result, sales began to slip and Ford had to fight back.

After a minor facelift for 1967 (which included the dramatic SportsRoof fastback), the Mustang was extensively restyled for the 1969 model year. An extra four inches were added to its length, it gained an extra pair of headlamps, the sides were 'de-sculpted', the rear arches were smoothed out

and a new luxury version called Grande was added.

The most exciting news for 1969 was the launch of the Mach 1 fastback, which boasted a 250 bhp V8 engine, stiffer suspension, a special front grille and a black bonnet with an air scoop.

If buyers really wanted more power, though, the best place to turn was Carroll Shelby's Los Angeles factory. He took near-complete fastback Mustangs and fitted them with 306 bhp 289 engines with high-lift camshafts, four-barrel carbs and free-flow exhausts. They also got stronger

axles, fibreglass bonnets and were almost always painted white with blue stripes. The most fearsome models were the GT500 of 1967 with its 428 engine (for an advertised 355 bhp but probably more like 400 bhp), and the mighty GT500KR (King of the Road) with up to 425 bhp to tap into.

Ford responded to the success of the more powerful Shelby Mustang with its own version in mid-1969, and called it The Boss. Based on the Mustang which was successfully dominating the SCCA's Trans-American race series, these had 290 bhp small-

block V8 engines, chin spoilers and rear aerofoils. More powerful still was the Boss 429, sporting Ford's hemispherical combustion chamber and alloy-head Cobra Jet engine, whose power output went as high as a formidable 375 bhp.

A lack of interior space was addressed in the second major restyle of the Mustang, which was launched ready for 1971. This added yet more length and width, and significantly more weight, to the detriment of performance and fuel economy. Apart from the Mach 1 429 and the Boss 351, there was little of any interest in the new Mustang range. It was beginning to rely on fancy trim packages and colour options, like the Sprint package (white paint with red-edged blue stripes).

For the final year of production of this trail-blazing first edition of the Mustang (1973), federal law insisted on the fitment of 5 mph impact bumpers, rubber-covered switchgear and emissions-restricting equipment, which also strangled power outputs. The most potent '73 Mustang had just 156 bhp to its credit and the standard offering was a miserable 95 bhp straight-six power plant. Performance had plunged below the level of mediocrity.

In the last year of production, the original Mustang sold a paltry 135,000 units. It was looking increasingly out-of-place in the fuel-crisis ridden early 1970s, as it become bloated and lost much of its authentic appeal.

As Ford's design vice-president, Eugene Bordinat, admitted:

"We started out with a secretary's car and all of a sudden we had a behemoth."

The Mustang's 1973 successor, the Mustang II, was a very different car, no less than 20 inches shorter and 4 inches narrower than its predecessor, and some 500lb lighter. Also there was no V8 option to begin with, simply an 88 bhp four-cylinder or 2.8-litre V6. The third-generation Mustang arrived in 1978 and lasted for the next 15 years, and the current Mustang is still notching up a very successful sales record.

Nothing, however, could ever match that first 1964 Mustang. For the bravery of its lines, the 'must have' factor it inspired, and the dizzy heights of performance it reached, there really has never been an American car to match it.

That is very much reflected today in the high values placed on sound, original examples. If car enthusiasts want to own one of the Shelby Mustangs, they can expect to pay more than the price of a brand new Jaguar. However, it must be remembered that not all Mustangs have big-block Cobra Jet V8s under their bonnets; far more likely is a rather timid six or small-block V8 lurking in the engine bay.

For most people, it's the classic all-American shape of the Mustang which inspires such enthusiasm. Paint it white and add some blue stripes down the middle and anyone could imagine they're a NASCAR or Trans Am racer!

The Ford Mustang was not just a car; it symbolised the entire youth culture of America during the 1960s. Ford of Europe tried the same trick with the Ford Capri; it could go fast and looked a million dollars and scored a similar hit.

FACTS & FIGURES

- **Engine:** 2778cc to 7030cc, 6/V8 cylinders, 95-137 bhp
- **Max speed:** 90-137 mph (*145-220 km/h*)
- **Years produced:** 1964-73
- **Numbers built:** 3,120,100

ROLLS ROYCE
SILVER SHADOW

Although it sells a tiny number of cars in comparison to the world motor marketplace, Rolls-Royce has come to represent something quintessentially British. It trades off its reputation as the best car in the world, although in most respects it is nowadays outclassed by many

The Silver Shadow was Rolls Royce's most advanced car ever when it was launched in 1965

cheaper cars. But there is one thing which no-one does better than Rolls-Royce: the sheer crafts-manship of a Roller remains unparalleled.

It is difficult to identify the best Rolls-Royce of them all. The Silver Ghost was certainly the best car of its day; the post-war Silver Cloud was a resounding statement of elegance and the confidence of the old British Empire days; and the coachbuilt Phantom was the most opulent and expensive car in

production for decades.

If car experts judged a model's success by the numbers it sold, then the Silver Shadow was Rolls-Royce's greatest car, selling over 30,000 in its 15-year lifespan. In many ways, it was revolutionary for Rolls-Royce: it was their first car to do away with a chassis, it did not have the swoopy, antique curves of all the previous models, and its specification looked very modern by comparison.

Rolls-Royce claimed the new

car was "as revolutionary as the Silver Ghost was 59 years ago". *Autocar* magazine concurred:

"It possesses more individuality and advanced engineering than this company has ever displayed before in a new model."

The Silver Shadow cost £6,556 when it was launched in 1965 – three times as much as a Jaguar and just about the most expensive car on sale. There was also a companion Bentley model called the T Series, identical except for the

grille and badges, which cost slightly less at £6,496.

For their money, Shadow drivers were rewarded by a Rolls-Royce which broke new ground. There was more interior space, even though the overall dimensions were reduced. The body construction was monocoque, so the weight was reduced and the 6230cc V8 engine was able to deliver better performance. The company never discloses such figures but independent testers measured the new Roller at a 118 mph maximum with 0-60 mph coming up in just 10.9 seconds.

Just about everything on the Shadow was power-assisted, including the triple-circuit brakes, steering, seats and windows. There were disc brakes all round, too (the first time ever in a R-R) and standard four-speed automatic transmission with finger-light electronic control.

The legendary Rolls-Royce ride reached new heights of excellence, thanks to a new all-independent suspension system mounted on subframes. The biggest development in this department was an 'olio-pneumatic' self-levelling system, produced under licence from Citroën, whose DS was the best-riding car around at that time.

Naturally, passengers were cossetted with matched leather upholstery and woodwork, split-level ventilation (or optional air conditioning), cigar lighters (front and rear), folding picnic tables, adjustable arm rests and even little foot rests in the rear.

When it comes to luxury travel no car can match the unique quality and craftsmanship of Rolls Royce

The Silver Shadow may not have been the best-handling car around but it was certainly very respectable among large luxury cars of the time. It suited the owner-driver as much as the chauffeured tycoon. Perhaps its best quality was the effortless way it would travel long distances without tiring the driver. The silence inside the cabin was uncanny and the ride quality gave the impression of floating on air – which was virtually what occupants were doing thanks to the pneumatic suspension system!

The only problem concerned feeding it: 12-16 mpg was typical, so owners needed a fat wallet – though this was not a great concern for most Silver Shadow owners.

Rolls-Royce wanted to continue its tradition of offering coachbuilt bodies and asked Mulliner Park

Ward (which it had taken over by that time) and James Young to design their own two-door bodywork. James Young's route was to follow the lines of the Silver Shadow very closely, while MPW created a new style with a 'kick' in the rear wings. Alongside MPW's two-door saloon, there was also a two-door convertible from 1967; this pair would later make it on to official Rolls-Royce price lists as the Corniche model.

The limousine trade was not ignored, either. A long-wheelbase model was launched in 1969, which was distinguished by a full vinyl roof and optional glass division between front and rear passenger compartments.

More improvements followed: the engine grew to 6750cc in 1970 and there was a new Silver Shadow II (and Bentley T2) in 1977. The Shadow II included body changes such as rubber-faced bumpers and a chin spoiler, plus interior improvements (new seats, re-styled facia, and standard split-level air conditioning), while on the

mechanical side there were twin exhausts and rack-and-pinion steering. The limousine model was renamed Silver Wraith at the same time.

By the time the Silver Shadow left production in 1980, when it was replaced by the all-new Silver Spirit and Bentley Mulsanne, it had become easily Rolls-Royce's best-selling model. A total of 31,189 Silver Shadows and 2,436 Bentleys T Series had been made. It also formed the basis of two other Rolls-Royce models, the Corniche and Camargue, which shared the Shadow's floorpan and mechanicals.

In classic car terms, the large numbers sold have been good news for enthusiasts. With so many examples to choose from, prices have dropped dramatically – so much so that it became possible to buy one for less than an 'ordinary' new car. Private motorists began to cotton on to the fact that owning a Rolls-Royce was within their grasp.

They were attracted by the best build quality and the finest

materials in the world, unbeatable levels of comfort and refinement, enjoyable road manners, long-lasting mechanicals and, of course, the prestige of running a car with that famous flying lady mascot.

The negative side however, was the expense of servicing, the very high cost of replacement parts, the fuel bills, the complex mechanicals which are entirely unsuitable for DIY maintenance, and the 'jealousy factor' – Rollers are prime targets for vandals. In addition, contrary to popular belief, Rolls-Royces do rust. A lot of owners of second-hand Silver Shadows were tempted to run them on a budget. The cost of bringing them up to perfect condition could become prohibitive. The thought of owning a scruffy Rolls-Royce put off many.

One means of making a Silver Shadow pay for itself has been to hire it out as a wedding car or even include it on one of the directories of film and promotional hire cars. Plenty of owners make a decent living or at least a second income from this sort of work.

The Silver Shadow occupies a unique position as a classic car. It is dynamically much better than earlier Rolls-Royces, yet has less romance than the old-style coachbuilt carriages, so it falls between two stools.

The result is that it has become that rare ideal for the motorist – a genuinely affordable, classic Rolls-Royce; an ideal that is finding increasing popularity with those who thought owning a Roller was nothing but a pipe dream.

FACTS & FIGURES

- **Engine:** 6230cc / 6750cc, V8 cylinders, estimated 200 bhp
- **Max speed:** 118-120 mph *(190-195 km/h)*
- **Years produced:** 1965-80
- **Numbers built:** 33,625

TRIUMPH
TR4/TR5/TR6

The name Triumph has always been associated with sporting cars, from the glorious pre-war dropheads to the delightful, if slightly flawed V8-powered Stag of the 1970s. The pinnacle of Triumph's car building was the long run of true sportscars bearing the initials 'TR'... and in particular the classic TR4, TR5 and TR6.

The first TR, the TR-X of 1950, was to have been a handsomely aerodynamic, up-market two-seater, but only three prototypes were made before the idea was abandoned. The first production TR was therefore the TR2 of 1953. This simple and practical two-seater was very lively, and was the cheapest 100 mph car around in the 1950s, selling for just $2,500 in the USA, where enthusiasts lapped it up. Compared to the archaic MG TF which was its main competitor in those days, it looked smart and modern.

The improved TR3 brought the battle for American sales right to MG's door, vying for number-one spot with the MGA. The TR3 lasted from 1955 to 1962.

However, the Standard-Triumph group was in dire financial straits by the turn of the decade. It was losing £600,000 a month and might have died had not the British truck-maker Leyland stepped in and bought the company in 1961. It promptly fired most of the directors and embarked on a 'new era', targeting North America with a strong export drive which they hoped would turn the company around.

Spearheading that drive for exports was the new TR sportscar, the rebodied TR4 of 1962. The smart new set of clothes was designed by the Italian

coachbuilder Giovanni Michelotti. Triumph had formed a relationship with this leading Italian designer since 1958, when he had designed pretty new bodywork for the TR3A. This was the so-called Triumph Italia, built by Vignale and for sale only in Italy. However, Triumph was obviously impressed and asked Michelotti to style the TR4 and, as it transpired, every Triumph for the next ten years.

The TR4 was a foot longer than the old TR3, the 3in wider track made it look lower, while at the same time improving stability and handling. The 'hooded' headlamps were a distinctive feature.

With full doors and winding windows, the TR4 was also a lot more comfortable than the TR3, which had cut-away doors and simple side screens. The cockpit was certainly much more roomy and plush than the outgoing model, and featured face-level ventilation.

There was also a novel optional extra called a Surrey top. This was a half-hard top, where the rear section remained fixed and the central part of the roof could be lifted out and replaced by a canvas top. This in turn could be furled back for semi-open motoring. The system was a precursor of the Targa top which would later be popularised by Porsche.

Underneath the attractive steel bodywork lay essentially the same chassis as the old TR3. That meant a separate chassis, rigid rear axle

with leaf-spring suspension, front disc brakes and a four-speed manual gearbox (with optional overdrive). The main chassis advances for the TR4 were standard servo brakes and rack-and-pinion steering in place of the

cam-and-lever type.

However, perhaps the biggest change for the driver was an expanded version of the four-cylinder engine, which could trace its origins back through the Standard Vanguard saloon to the

Triumph's TR4 was aimed at American enthusiasts and featured an optional and novel Surrey top, which became the Targa top

days when it powered Ferguson tractors. In the TR4, it had grown from 1991cc to 2138cc.

The power output remained the same at 100 bhp, but the engine had a wider power band and much better torque. Compared to the old TR3, it was also faster, capable of reaching 110 mph and doing the 0-60 mph sprint test in just over ten seconds.

The smaller 2.0-litre engine remained available, however, because there was still a strong competition class for sub-2000cc

engines. The TR4 proved a popular choice for rally drivers. Triumph's works team scored a string of class wins through the 1960s and fielded TR4s with success in the Alpine Rally and at Le Mans.

Leyland's renewed vigour brought the desired increase in production. The whole group's output went up by a third. The TR sportscar scored a real hit: production trebled between 1961 and 1964, going from under 3,000 units to over 9,000. Export sales of the TR range were responsible for

keeping Triumph in the black throughout the 1960s.

An improved version called the TR4A arrived in 1964, whose main difference was the adoption of a superior coil-spring and trailing-arm independent rear suspension. This had a negative effect on overall weight (pushing it up by 100lb) but handling was much improved. Any performance loss due to the extra weight was countered by raising the engine's power output slightly to 104 bhp.

By this time, Triumph was also

experimenting with the idea of fuel injection – the first British manufacturer to try it. It decided to use the TR as its testbed for a new fuel-injected version of the six-cylinder engine from the Triumph 2000 saloon. The capacity was raised to 2.5 litres and, despite the larger capacity and extra pair of cylinders, the new engine was a comfortable fit in the TR engine bay – and no heavier than the old 'four'.

Lucas supplied the injection technology for what would become known as the Triumph TR5, which

Left: *The TR5 featured fuel injection and packed a 150 bhp punch*
Above: *The TR6 was a modernised TR5, but by its launch in 1968 the TR range was beginning to feel outdated*

was launched in 1967. Early examples were rather temperamental but the injection system was quickly sorted out and customers were soon enjoying the pleasures 150 bhp could bring – 120 mph and 0-60 mph in 8.8 seconds. Other mechanical improvements included bigger brakes and stiffer suspension. Since the TR4 had never been noted for the comfort of its ride, the TR5 felt fairly harsh on rough ground.

Fuel injection was discounted in America, where advancing emissions regulations had forced Triumph to fit plain Stromberg carburettors, and as a result power plummeted right back down to 104 bhp. The American market version was known as the TR250 and could be identified by its contrasting stripes over the car's nose.

The TR5 and TR250 were short-lived (lasting only one year) but they were good sellers, and three-quarters of the 11,431-strong production total went to the USA.

The model was replaced in 1968 by the TR6, basically a TR5 re-styled front and rear by Karmann of Germany. The seats were new and buyers got a front anti-roll bar, but underneath it was basically the same TR story as ever, now beginning to look rather antique. The power units were the same, too, with the 104 bhp version remaining in the USA (although European customers were subjected in 1972 to a drop in power from 150 bhp to 124 bhp).

The TR6 died as late as 1976, the last of a long string of 'real' Triumph sportscars in the traditional sense. By then the TR7 had already arrived, a radically different Triumph sportscar.

The TRs may not always have been very refined but their muscular character and handsome shape continues to endear them to tens of thousands of owners today. Apart from the MGB, the Triumph TR series is probably the most popular classic sportscar in the world, as burgeoning Triumph owners' clubs can testify.

FACTS & FIGURES

- **Engine:** 1991cc / 2138cc / 2498cc, 4/6 cylinders, 100-150 bhp
- **Max speed:** 107-125 mph *(172-201 km/h)*
- **Years produced:** 1962-76
- **Numbers built:** 257,930

A-Z
of
MARQUES

Over the 100 years that the car has been in existence it has seen many enthusiasts design and produce their own visions of how it should evolve. Some were more successful than others and have become major players in the industry while other have fallen by the wayside due to a variety of reasons. In many instances the demise was due to comercial acumen (or the lack of it) and this chapter amply proves that to succeed in this business you need more than just a great idea and burning ambition. Sadly, some of the car's greatest enthusiasts and inventors were poor businessmen and many great names could not survive the quickening pace of the 20th Century.

It is difficult to give an accurate figure on just how many car manufacturers there have been since Daimler and Benz laid down the original blueprint more than 100 years ago, but certainly the figure runs to over 4,000. To mention every one that has ever existed would fill this book easily. So, concentrating on a dedicated selection of the most significant players throughout the history of the car this chapter reveals the major marques from around the world charting their careers to date.

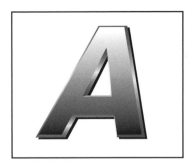

ABARTH

CYNICAL ENTHUSIASTS could be forgiven for thinking that the Abarth badge applied to a tuned Fiat became merely a marketing exercise, a ploy to get buyers to part with more cash for a car which may have enhanced sporting performance and some sporting trim but is nevertheless a Fiat underneath. However, it has not always been like that. The Abarth badge once meant a great deal more to car lovers.

Abarth's heyday was from 1950 to 1971 – that's when founder Carlo Abarth was at the helm. During those years a number of very interesting Abarths were made, including the 600 Convertible which was a Boano-bodied car using a 66 bhp, front-mounted engine. This was the first of Abarth's cars based on the small rear-engined Fiat 600. There was also a coupe which Abarth designed himself, even though it was also based on the Fiat 600. The secret was in the way Abarth tuned and developed the mechanical side of these cars, using stiffer engine crankshafts, reinforced clutches, lowered suspension and, from 1961, superior disc brakes.

Abarth produced models with beautiful bodies made by Allemano and Zagato. These cars were truly the first real Abarths, moving away from Fiat parts and becoming attractively individual in their own right. In the 1960s the Abarth name meant highly-tuned engines, sophisticated suspension systems which provided fine handling, and a cabin which was designed around the driver. In 1960 bigger coupes with all-round disc brakes and a 2.2-litre, Fiat-based, six-cylinder engine were produced. They were not available for long and were effectively the last of the true Abarth front-engined cars.

By 1961 the specialist-bodied models bowed out – they were too costly to produce – leaving the company with a number of mildly sporting coupes and saloons. The end result of this was the beginning of cars marketed purely on the appeal of the Abarth badge, not Abarth quality. Although these more modern cars are interesting, they do not hold the same cachet as the original delights that were produced during the late 1950s and early 1960s.

By 1971 the company was in financial difficulties, due mostly to the large amounts of money invested in competition cars which were not hugely successful. The writing was on the wall and, not surprisingly, Fiat stepped in and bought the name. Since then Abarth is the badge which has been applied to slightly sporty Fiats. Although the Italian company would claim these models are more than just a Fiat, they do not have the beautiful and distinct bodies with which Abarth made their reputation.

AC

THE FUTURE looks brighter for this great British sportscar maker, thanks to an eleventh-hour life saving takeover.

The name AC comes from one of the first vehicles built by this company which is based in south-east England. The Autocarrier was powered by a single-cylinder, rear-

AC Cobra *A 1960s favourite from a renowned sportscar maker saved by the American Pride Automotive Group*

mounted engine carried by three rather than four wheels. It had a boat-like tiller which was used to steer it. This was made between 1908 and 1914. In 1913 the company launched its first four-wheel car with an 1100cc single-cylinder engine and a three-speed gearbox placed in the rear axle.

In 1925, AC's own engines appeared and from 1921 to 1929 were raced in various competitions; in 1926 a six-cylinder version became the first British entry to win the Monte Carlo Rally. By 1930, the year the company was bought by the Hurlock brothers, the AC Magna was on the road, with a 2.0-litre version by 1933. All models were made to order, so trim and equipment levels varied. In 1939 performance increased again

when the engine was supercharged to give 90 bhp.

It wasn't until after the war that a new model was unveiled. This was the Ace, one of AC's most attractive two-seaters, a tubular-framed machine with an 85 bhp AC engine. The dynamics of the original Ace were so good that it could top 100 mph and was still being produced, with a V8 Ford Mustang engine, up until the company hit trouble in 1996.

AC hit the headlines in 1963 when they launched the Cobra, which was inspired by the American Carroll Shelby. The AC had a massive 4.7-litre, American-built, Ford V8 unit which developed 330 bhp, making the Cobra one of the all-time most desirable sportscars. Even today it does not look old fashioned. AC,

with the assistance of Shelby, also developed a 7.0-litre version of this car between 1965 and 1968. Although it carried the AC badge, the cars were actually constructed in the USA by Shelby American Inc. In 1966 the company also produced a luxury convertible, the 428, (with a hardtop option) with bodywork by Frua.

The AC ME3000 was launched in 1974, and was built in Surrey, England. This car used the 3.0-litre Ford V6 engine and AC's own five-speed gearbox, though due to several problems, models did not actually go on sale until 1979. This is a very competent machine, widely-acclaimed for its good

performance. Sadly, AC found it difficult to survive in the later years and early in 1996 the company went into receivership. It looked as though it was all over for the Surrey specialist, until the American company, Pride Automotive Group, saved the company with a £5.5 million takeover.

ALFA ROMEO

ALFA ROMEO, one of the most evocative names in the motoring world, began life in 1910 when it was simply called Alfa. The name was derived from the Italian initials of The Lombardy Motor Manufacturing Co. The real story began when the company was taken over by industrialist Nicola Romeo in 1915. The company then

became known as Alfa Romeo and entered a period of intense development which saw many of its cars winning international races. Almost as exciting were the road-going cars which came to the market thick and fast, a trend which has continued to this day.

One of the company's first successes was the 1750GS, a truly legendary piece of engineering, which first saw the light of day in 1924. This Zagato-bodied, twin-cam, supercharged sportscar managed to squeeze 95 mph out of a 85 bhp engine, a remarkable achievement in those days. This was followed by one of the most successful sports racing cars of the era, the twin-supercharged 2.9-litre P3 racer, which achieved notable success on the racing circuits of Europe.

In 1934 a supercharged six-cylinder, twin-cam, 2.3-litre car, the 2500, hit the roads. It was so successful it remained in production until the mid-1940s and became one of Alfa Romeo's most popular models. Easy to drive, with more than enough power, and looks to make even car-haters swoon, this beautiful piece of engineering must be on every car enthusiast's dream list.

A sea change in Alfa Romeo design began in 1950 with the launch of the four-cylinder 1900. This car is important because previous Alfas had been pretty exclusive and therefore expensive. The 1900, however, was of unitary construction, so costs were kept

down. This change in production methods spelt the end for Alfa's bespoke image but it also allowed more people to buy the company's cars, simply because prices came more into line with those from other mass car producers. Only four years after the first unitary construction models appeared the public first saw the original Giulietta range. Available initially in 1.3-litre form, the famed Guilia was developed from the Giulietta and arrived with a 1.6-litre engine.

Alpha Romeo

The Spider was in production for over 20 years and is still a much sought-after classic car

Soon after (1962), the six-cylinder 2600 was unveiled. The most exciting development was the launch of the Spider, the car which film-lovers will remember the young Dustin Hoffman driving flat-out to get to the church on time in *The Graduate*. The Alfa Spider is one of the longest surviving production cars in the world.

Originally unveiled in the mid-1960s, the many versions of the Spider have earned themselves a niche in the hearts and minds of drivers. Built in Milan, and only ever in two-seater, open-topped form, the Spider has played host to a variety of engines which all have one glorious thing in common – they beg to be driven hard.

In the 1970s and 1980s Alfa Romeo started to lose its shine. Now Fiat-controlled, the cars increasingly became re-bodied alternatives to unexciting Fiats with Alfa engines under the bonnet. The endearing little Alfasud saw the company move into the mainstream car market, with little success. Thankfully, in the 1990s Alfa Romeo is being given its independence with a batch of well-received designs, including a glamourous new GTV, although the company is still owned by Fiat. At last, things are looking up again.

ALLARD

CAR ENTHUSIASTS might not immediately think of Clapham in South London as a centre of automotive excellence, but for a few brief years it was – thanks to Allard Motor Co. From 1937 to 1960 a succession of very

interesting and very desirable cars poured forth, though poured is perhaps a little strong – trickle might be more appropriate a word. The Allard was born from a one-off trials special which itself had evolved from a 1934 Ford V8 originally carrying a Bugatti body. After some notable successes in hill climbs and various other events, Sydney Allard decided to offer his expertise to the public. The Allard Motor Company was born. Initially, Sydney made replicas of his successful trials car, however this time he used a 4.4-litre American Lincoln Zephyr engine. These were made up to the outbreak of World War II.

After the war, in 1946, the company resumed production. This was a very significant time, not only for Allard, but also for the buying public, because the new

Allard came onto the market. The Model K had a lowered chassis, sweeping two-seater bodywork and a very striking front grille – some have unkindly likened it to the type of grating that might be found in the road over a drain. However, flights of fancy aside, this grille was curved into the bodywork of the car and stretched part-way up the bonnet. The engine this time around was a Ford V8 in 3.6-litre form driving the rear wheels. As well as the K there was also an L, which was the four-seater version and the M, a drop-head coupe.

In 1950 the J2 arrived and proved to be one of Allard's most popular cars. This two-seater was light and very quick, came with a De Dion rear axle and used a 3.9-litre, overhead-valve Ardun-Mercury engine, once again

sourced from the USA. J2s sold well in the USA too. These export models used V8 engines, either a 5.4-litre Cadillac unit or an identical cubic capacity Chrysler power plant. Two years later saw the arrival of the P-type saloon which won the Monte Carlo Rally with Sydney Allard at the wheel.

However, this was nearly the end of the road for Allard: by then they were facing stiff competition from another marque – Jaguar. In any case, the P-type was not the best car of its era and by the time it was launched many rivals were able to produce cars faster, with better power and better handling, and in greater numbers, thereby keeping prices lower. The mid 1950s saw the beginning of the end for Allard and even the use of Jaguar's classic XK-engine couldn't stop the decline. Two years later the

Allard *For over 20 years Allard excelled in sporting saloons and sports cars, but had fallen from favour by 1960*

company sadly closed the doors of its Clapham factory and Allard became part of motoring history.

ALPINE

THE ALPINE CAR company has always enjoyed a close relationship with Renault, building individual sportscars with Alpine-designed and constructed bodies mated to Renault mechanicals. Alpine was founded back in 1952 and produced a variety of specialist sporting cars, the most famous being the A310. This was produced between 1971 and 1985, and is one of the most sought-after sportscars of all time. They are rare – just over 3,000 were produced in Alpine's factory at Dieppe but are still hugely popular with enthusiasts.

What made Alpines great were their prowess in motorsport and in particular rallying, where their design layout really came to the fore when traction was paramount, such as in snowy conditions. Made from GRP (glass reinforced plastic), bonded to a steel backbone frame and linked to Renault running gear, most of it on the 310s from the Renault 16 range. The engines were mounted Porsche-like at the rear, slung over the back axle. All 310s had a 1.6-litre, 127 bhp engine until 1976, when they were fitted with a V6 2.7-litre unit producing 150 bhp. In 1985, a radically redesigned, sharp-styled Alpine took over with a turbocharged engine, but retaining the same engine and gearbox layout.

Somewhat surprisingly, this value-for-money car never became fully accepted into the supercar market, despite its terrific acceleration and generally good handling. As many others have found to their cost, this market is dominated by names – Ferrari, Aston Martin, Mercedes-Benz, Jaguar – even the likes of BMW. This is unfortunate because the Alpine is still a thoroughly likable

Alpine *The ace Renault tuning and improving company also produced the classic 310 sports car that enjoyed rally success*

and impressive car, even if the build quality has not always been what it should have. And it must be said that because of the rear weight bias, one certainly needed to learn Alpine driving technique. It should also be stressed that no Alpine exhibits the tail-happiness which characterises the Porsche 911, a car with a similar mechanical layout. Of course, the body doesn't rust, but as with all cars made of

GRP there is a tendency for the paintwork to crack and craze.

Alpine added its touch of magic to various Renault saloons over the years, including the rear-engined Dauphine, the R8 and the front-wheel drive R16 hatchback. In 1976 it graced the Renault 5 Alpine – called the Gordini in the UK. This tuned and highly enjoyable car was arguably the first hot hatchback.

ALVIS

ALVIS IS one of those well-known British companies which thrived then died but along the way produced some of the most interesting cars ever seen. Built in Coventry, under a number of different owners, between 1919 and 1967, the story really begins in 1920 with the launch of the 10/30.

Alvis *One of the great British prestige car makers, they were taken over by Rover in the 1960s*

This used an extremely efficient four-cylinder, single-valve engine of 1460cc (the 30 part of the badge comes from the 30 bhp the engine originally produced). This car was available in several forms – a two-seater, four-seater and Super-Sports. The SS, as it was soon known, had the famous "duck's-back" sloping body which was to become an Alvis trademark. Though all versions of this car were very noisy and quite expensive, they became hot favourites with sporting motorists who applauded its strong body and robust mechanicals.

Perhaps the greatest Alvis of this period was the Silver Eagle with coachwork by Weymann and using a six-cylinder engine block. As was the Alvis fashion, a highly-tuned Super-Sports version was also added. The Silver Eagle continued in production, with regular updates, until 1936.

In 1928 Alvis launched a six-cylinder Super Sports model with front-wheel drive – the first British car to have this system. Unfortunately the front-wheel-

drive cars did not sell very well because they were complicated and temperamental. In 1932 the very handsome Speed Twenty was launched, combining the refinement of a 2511cc six-cylinder engine with speed, excellent roadholding, good brakes, stamina and a reasonable price.

In 1933 Alvis launched the Crested Eagle to join its brother the Silver Eagle. This new car used a 2511cc engine. The Crested Eagle chassis was the first Alvis touring car to have independent front suspension. Three years later the successful Speed Twenty was replaced by the Speed Twenty-Five which used a bigger 3.5-litre engine. This car was capable of smooth and virtually silent 95 mph performance in saloon form, and is justly regarded by many Alvis enthusiasts as the best Alvis built.

During the 1940s and 1950s the new Alvis models were the TA and TC, the latter designed by Alec Issigonis, the man who only a few years later was to launch the Mini. Alvis-guaranteed a top speed of 100 mph for the TC – no mean feat

in 1954. Following hard on its heels came one of Alvis's best-looking cars ever – the TD21, a Graber-designed saloon body on what was basically the TC21 chassis. This model was given a modified engine in 1959 which delivered 120 bhp. Disc brakes became standard on all four wheels for 1962. In 1964 the popular TD21 was replaced by the TE21. Unfortunately, soon after the launch of this car Alvis closed its doors, being absorbed into the Rover empire. It was a sad day, although Rover continued to market Alvis models until 1967.

AMERICAN MOTORS

AMERICAN Motors Corporation was formed in 1954 after the once great names Nash and Hudson fell on hard times and were forced to merge under a new umbrella name: Rambler. There followed a curious mix of model line-ups which even included the compact Metropolitan, built by Austin of

England for Nash.

The 1960s were good to AMC; its Ambassador was voted America's Car of the Year by *Motor Trend* in 1963 and it successfully launched itself into the 'muscle car' market with the stylish Rambler Javelin and the AMX sportscars. The Rambler name was dropped in 1970 to be replaced by Hornet while AMC relaunched itself into the compact market sector with the Gremlin and introduced the quirky-looking 'glasshouse' Pacer in the late 1970s.

It was AMC's acquisition of Kaiser Jeep in 1970 which stands out as the most significant development in the company's short history. In February 1970 AMC paid $70 million for the Jeep concern just as the trend for go-anywhere vehicles was taking off.

AMC's first move was to separate military production from civilian, the former based at the old Studebaker base. By 1972 AMC engines were fitted to all Jeeps including V8s, accompanied by a new slogan for the workhorse: "If a new Jeep vehicle can't take you there, maybe you ought to think twice about going!"

Throughout the 1970s AMC built up the Jeep range to such an extent that it was one of the few lucrative car brands around in the recession-bitten US automotive industry and was the main reason why the Chrysler Corporation bought out AMC in August 1987.

AMPHICAR

IN 1962 A MAN driving a car in Northern France headed straight for the English Channel. He did not stop at Calais but instead drove straight into the water and continued driving towards Dover. He came ashore safely some two hours later.

Not a tall story, but an effective piece of publicity to show what you could do with an Amphicar, the world's first amphibious car. It is

not clear just why designer Hans Trippel decided on this method of transport but what is interesting is that the Amphicar gained a loyal following, both in its native Germany and in the rest of mainland Europe. It was made between 1961 and 1968 and was a simple chassis-less convertible with a four-cylinder, 1.1-litre Triumph Herald engine mounted at the rear. The body was made of steel, with Trippel using boat technology to weld the body water-tight. In normal use, that is on the roads, only the rear wheels drove, but in the water two propellers at the back of the car were switched on, powering the strange little craft forwards. The driver continued to use the steering wheel which turned a rudder. On the road the Amphicar could reach almost 70 mph and when in the water, around six-and-a-half knots. Ideal transport for Venice!

ANADOL

HARDLY RENOWNED as a centre for automotive excellence maybe, but Turkey does have a car industry of sorts. Anadol, or to give the company its full name, Otosan Otomiobil Sanayii, is based in the Turkish city of Istanbul and it makes a 1.3-litre saloon. In fact, the Anadol is not Turkish in any sense other than it is made in Turkey, rather it is a collection of mechanical bits and pieces from other mainstream European car-makers, notably Britain's Reliant motor company from Tamworth in Staffordshire. The Anadol was at first known as the Reliant FW5 and it was built in Turkey from 1966 onwards. Reliant have never made their own engines, so the

Armstrong Siddeley *The stately AS belonged to a motoring era that died as the 1960s began*

original power unit for the Anadol was from the Ford parts bin, in this case the engine from the Ford Anglia Super, a 1.1-litre affair. In this form the engine was mated to an independent chassis and a fibre-glass saloon body, which of course Reliant had a lot of experience with, all their cars being made from fibre-glass. This approach was also ideal for a fledgling motor company like Anadol because it kept costs down. Such was the success of this simple formula that by 1970, just four years after production began, car-hungry Turks had bought more than 10,000 Anadols. In 1969 the engine had been changed for another Ford unit, this time the more powerful 1.3-litre, and there was a 1.6-litre option by 1974.

ARGONAUT

THE ELABORATELY named Argonaut Motor Machine Corporation of Cleveland, Ohio, USA, built cars between 1959 and 1963, though to be more accurate, it planned to build cars.

Argonaut's strategy was hardly a simple one – it wanted to build the world's first supercar. Called the Argonaut State Limousine, the first prototype was built on a Chrysler chassis. Argonaut didn't do anything cheaply and the intention was to use stainless steel as the main body metal with the addition of specialist metals such as magnesium, titanium and dural into the recipe. The engine for these monsters was a 12-cylinder, overhead-cam, air-cooled unit developing no less than 1,020 bhp!

It isn't clear whether any cars actually were produced, though the company did produce a luxurious catalogue which gave examples of several different cars and it was rumoured that a State Limousine version actually did get made, was driven on the roads and now belongs to a private customer. But where is it today? It would be interesting to find out because Argonaut claimed top speeds of 240mph which seems rather optimistic.

Perhaps one day the mighty machine will surface and we will know the truth.

ARKLEY

THIS IS A small British company, started by John Britten Garages of Barnet in Hertfordshire in 1971 and offering the Arkley SS two-seater sportscar. Like many of these small producers, the Arkley uses a range of different mechanical bits and pieces to produce an individual car. The SS was first seen at the Racing Car Show in 1970 and won praise for its very attractive period body and the high build quality. Originally the SS was placed on either an Austin-Healey Sprite or an MG Midget chassis. Those had to be in good condition before the engines could be fitted and the bodywork mated to the chassis and running gear. Some owners of these old original cars, if in poor condition, could take them along to Arkley and have the company take a look to see if the chassis could be used to hold Arkley's body. Basically any MG Midget or Austin-Healey could be converted at a reasonable cost to the new Arkley SS. The engine could, of course, remain faithful to the

original car. If buyers asked Arkley to make a car then the usual choice would have been the Triumph Spitfire 1.5-litre engine which provided very impressive performance. Initially the Arkley concept proved a very attractive and successful one with over 500 cars sold in the first five years of production.

ARMSTRONG SIDDELEY

THE ARMSTRONG SIDDELEY car company, another of those great names of the golden era of British car design, was born out of the amalgamation of Armstrong-Whitworth and Siddeley-Deasy of Coventry. The company concentrated on building family cars that offered first-class workmanship and superb comfort, as they believed that high-performance motoring was best left to other companies.

Up to 1939 AS's were easily recognised, thanks to their massive V-shaped radiators, multi-stud disc wheels and imposing bonnet-mounted sphinx mascots.

Armstrong Siddeley launched their first six-cylinder car in 1921, a 5.0-litre producing a rather meagre 30 bhp. In 1929 a smaller, but, for its day very efficient, 1236cc unit was unveiled which produced 12 bhp. At the same time a Wilson pre-selector gearbox was offered, first as an optional extra and then standardised from 1933 onwards.

Further changes came in 1930 with the addition of the mildly sporting 5.0-litre Siddeley Special with alloy engine and a top speed of 90 mph. Four years later AS brought out a very interesting new machine, the 1.4-litre sports coupe which it said was aimed at "daughters of gentlemen".

Production of AS's stopped during the Second World War as the company concentrated on building aircraft for the RAF, a fact reflected in the company's post-war automotive range which bore the names of famous World War II aircraft. In 1953 one of AS's most successful and endearing cars, the Sapphire, was introduced using a 3.4-litre engine. There was the choice of manual gearbox or an electrically selected pre-selector unit, the latter being quite advanced for that time, and very smooth in operation.

The base Sapphire was joined in 1954 by a twin-carburettor version which could top 100 mph. At last AS had entered the performance field, even if it was seeking to do so with a car which looked anything but sporty.

To many people it was most reminiscent of a large and somewhat cumbersome house on wheels. Nevertheless it proved popular with those who for whatever reasons did not want a Jaguar or Daimler. Development

continued throughout the 1950s; with 1955 seeing the option of an automatic gearbox, 1956 heralding the advent of optional power assisted steering, and the extension of the range to include a bevy of smaller models. The 234 had a four-cylinder, 2.3-litre engine based on the Sapphire, and the 236 used the old long-stroke six-cylinder unit of similar capacity.

Unfortunately, neither of the newer cars sold, or looked particularly attractive, and within a couple of years they were finally erased from the sales brochure.

Last but not least, along came the 4.0-litre Star Sapphire, available only in automatic form, though like the 3.4-litre cars which arrived soon after, the Sapphire was offered in both saloon and limousine forms. The final Sapphire left the works in the summer of 1960, a year after Armstrong Siddeley had merged with Bristol.

ASTON MARTIN

TO MANY THE Aston Martin will always be James Bond's car. The fictional British secret agent has had a long love affair with this most gentlemanly of sportscars. In fact, it is remarkable that Aston Martin is such a well-known name. After all, production, which began in 1922, has always been rather small scale. Of course, one could say the same about Ferrari or Lamborghini, and everyone has heard of them too. The key to these cars' success is their extraordinary performance and extraordinary performance is also Aston's vital ingredient.

The company began life in 1914, the Aston part of the name deriving from the Aston Clinton hill-climb where early Aston Martin's proved their pulling power, in more ways than one. The public first came to know of Aston Martin in 1947

when the company was acquired by the David Brown Group and the famous DB – the James Bond car – began its life. The origins of the road-going DB's can be found in the 1949 2.6-litre, twin overhead-cam, six-cylinder engine designed by W.O. Bentley for Lagonda (also part of the David Brown empire).

In 1952 a racing DB3 was unveiled and soon after that the company produced a DB3 for the road. The 1953 DB3S with 2.9-litre engine was produced in small numbers and today is much sought after. More common is the Touring DB2, so called because it was fitted with small rear seats when it was launched in 1954.

Aston Martin

A great name and a great reputation – saved by Ford's cash

A 140 bhp 2.9-litre engine was added in 1955. In 1959 a de-tuned 240 bhp version of the 3.7-litre DBR racing engine was installed in the DB4, an Italian-styled sports saloon. This is one of the most attractive Aston Martins ever built. By 1962 the 255 bhp Vantage engine was an option on the new DB5, giving this car particularly high performance.

The DB6 was a direct development of the DB5 and in many ways was a better car – more modern, better performance, and better reliability, but it never had the cachet of the earlier models. The launch of the exciting DBS coupe in 1968, distinguished by a four-headlamp arrangement and De Dion rear axle was a major turning point for the company. A new DBS

powered by AM's V8 unit, a quad overhead-cam, 5.4-litre engine developing 375 bhp, was announced in 1970, when a five-speed ZF or Chrysler Torqueflite gearbox was offered.

The V8 saloon and convertible (Volante) appeared in 1973 and became the archetypal modern Aston Martin. It gained Royal assent when Prince Charles bought

a British Racing Green V8. Originally these cars were available with fuel injection, but this was changed to carburettors in 1973 to

Audi

Revitalized by VW, Audi is now a technological tour-de-force

smooth out performance, which at times in the original injected versions, had been spasmodic.

Today Aston Martin is owned by Ford and it continues to make some superb sports cars, not least the beautiful DB7, the latest in the line, and the simply stunning Virage. Ford's intervention, back in 1987, was vital for the ailing company as, not for the first time, it was facing extinction.

AUDI

A MAN NAMED Horch started the Audi company in 1910, the name coming from the Latin version of Horch. The first Audi was the B10/28PS with a 2612cc engine. This was an immediate success and started Audi on the road to national and international recognition. Twelve years later Audi unveiled one of its most successful cars of the period, the overhead-valve Type K with a 3.5-litre engine developing 50 bhp. This was followed in 1924 with the launch of the Type M. This six-cylinder model launched a whole range of six, and later, eight-cylinder cars, truly putting Audi on the map. They were characterised by excellent build quality and durability.

The Imperator, officially called the Type R, appeared in 1928. This was an eight-cylinder car with a 4872cc, 100 bhp engine. Many enthusiasts believe this was the last true Audi, in that it was the last of the coach-built range. All of the models which followed were assembled, rather than crafted.

Launched in 1928, the year a certain J.S. Rasmussen became the main shareholder in Audi, the Zwickau was offered with a choice of two eight-cylinder engines, a 4371cc and 5130cc, and the Dresden with six-cylinder 3838cc unit. These became two of the best-selling cars in Germany and showed competitors and buying public alike just what German

Austin *The A35 saloon didn't look like a racer, but Damon Hill's dad Graham had success with one!*

engineering could produce when it put its collective mind to it.

After Audi's merger to form Auto Union at the end of the war, the Audi works were nationalised and no cars of note were built until 1949 when Auto Union re-established the car-making operation in Dusseldorf. These years then were something of an upheaval for Audi, but in 1965 the Audi name was resurrected to replace Auto Union on a new medium-sized saloon and sales began in earnest.

It was collaboration with Volkswagen which rebuilt Audi's reputation during the late 1960s as a name in its own right. Through the 1970s, the 80 and 100 ranges re-established Audi as a prestige car maker but the real landmark came in 1980.

Audi launched the car which took four-wheel drive out of the farmyard and on to the high performance circuit – that's perhaps the best way of describing Audi's technically-advanced Quattro. The original Quattro was a four-seater coupe which used Audi's own five-cylinder 2144cc engine coupled with turbocharging. Power output was a mighty 200 bhp and torque a mountain-pulling 210 lb ft. The gearbox was a five-speeder and brakes were all round discs with servo assistance.

Since then Audi has produced a competent range of cars. More recently this rather clinical German company has been showing its design flair in the shape of the superb A3 and A4 ranges, and the aluminium-bodied A8, a serious rival to BMW and Mercedes-Benz, and the soon-to-be-launched Roadster, an avant-garde open-topped racing machine.

AUSTIN

IF HERBERT AUSTIN had not had a disagreement with his bosses at the Wolseley Motor Company and hadn't walked out of his job as general manager in 1905, the Austin Car Company might never have existed. But he did... and Austin went on to become Britain's biggest industrial company. During its time, Austin produced some exciting new cars, then fell into the depths of depression. It became a by-word for all that was bad about strike-hit Britain in the 1970s. It eventually sank without trace in the reorganisation which saw Rover survive as the only passenger-car making member of the former BMC, the giant British Motor Corporation.

The story really begins just after the First World War when Austin unveiled the Twenty. This used a 3.6-litre mono-block, single-valve, four-cylinder engine.

One of the greatest of all baby cars, the Seven first appeared in 1922. It produced 13 bhp from a four-cylinder 747cc and, thanks to its keen pricing and four-wheel brakes (something of an innovation on a car of this period), it proved to be a top-seller. In 1929 a supercharged sports version was launched. The Seven was such a popular formula it was made under licence in Germany, France, Japan and the USA, making it the first genuinely world car.

At the end of World War II, Austin moved into the top rank of world car producers with a range of modern and very competent new ranges. In 1947 the company unveiled the luxurious and traditionally styled 4.0-litre six-cylinder Sheerline and Princess. These were complemented by the less expensive 1.2-litre Dorset and Devon saloons.

In 1952 Austin merged with Morris to form the British Motor Corporation (BMC). This marriage of convenience was an important turning point, not least because it heralded the launch of the company's first unitary construction car, the 803cc A30 and A35. This proved to be one of the company's all-time greats.

The really big innovation though, came in 1959, with the launch of the new Austin Seven, the first of Alec Issigonis's Minis. Morris sold the car as the Mini Minor and a legend was born. Austin, through its sportscar division, also offered the Sprite, an early rival to the popular MG Midget. The endearing Sprite offered sportscar enthusiasts a well engineered yet inexpensive package that made it a classic.

During the 1970s there were some horrendous Austins, not least being the Allegro – which originally came with a square steering wheel – and which earned the nickname 'Aggro', simply because it was so poorly built.

There were some minor successes during the late 1970s and early 1980s, chief of which were the Montego and Maestro. They provided good, basic family motoring, and while short on character, they were strong on value for money.

Today, Austin is not a badge seen on new cars, the company concentrates instead on upmarket, image-building products under the quality Rover badge.

AUSTRO-DAIMLER

FOUNDED IN 1899, Austro-Daimler lasted just 35 years but in that time produced some of greatest cars of that era. As the name suggests, Austro-Daimler was originally a part of the German Daimler car company. The founder's son Paul played a major role, with the company becoming independent in 1906.

They were known for their advanced engineering and none other than Ferdinand Porsche was one of the original designers, A-D quickly became known for making fast touring and racing cars. Porsche even developed one of the first electric-powered cars back in 1902, called the Electrique.

Austro-Daimler was one of the first manufacturers to extensively use overhead-camshaft engine designs, usually of straight six or eight cylinders. Its ADM III is rightly regarded as one of the world's best cars of the late 1920s.

However, by the end of that decade it became obvious that this specialist couldn't survive on its own against the might of Mercedes-Benz. In 1928 A-D went

Auto Union *Ancestor to today's Audi, Auto Union produced highly advanced Grand Prix cars*

Continental T

into decline, leading to a merger with fellow Austrian car-makers Puch and Steyer. This rekindled A-D's association with Porsche who worked for Steyer designing the sort of luxury cars Austro-Daimler had became synonymous with.

A-D's last milestone in design was its ADR 6 saloon which used a 3.6 six-cylinder engine good for 120 bhp and 90 mph – very impressive figures for the times.

However, in 1934 it was decided to kill off the Daimler link and one of the greatest names in the early days of the motor car had been consigned to the history books.

AUTO UNION

AUTO UNION WAS just that; a merger of four struggling German car-makers back in 1932. DKW, Horch, Wanderer and Audi joined forces to survive the tough times Germany was going through before the Second World War.

DKW was the strongest of the quartet thanks to its healthy motorcycle sales, although Auto Union became best-known in this decade for its fabulous mid-engine Grand Prix racer, designed by Porsche. It was also the only car to be simply called an Auto Union; DKWs became Auto Union DKWs, while the Audi name was effectively mothballed for 20 years.

After the Second World War, Auto Union became nationalised in 1945 by the East German government. This resulted in a brief disappearance of the marque until the 1950s when it was relocated to Ingolstadt and Dusseldorf, producing DKWs again but very much under the guidance of Mercedes-Benz, who virtually relaunched Audi as a modern car manufacturer.

However, in 1965 a major name change occurred when the Audi name replaced the old fashioned DKW brand label and with it came a new range of FWD cars. This attracted the fast-expanding Volkswagen company which was looking to build upon the success of the Beetle. VW took over from Daimler-Benz AG in 1964 after acquiring a 50 per cent stake in Auto Union, buying it outright in 1966. On 21 August 1969 the companies Auto Union and NSU were amalgamated to form Audi NSU Auto Union AG, with Volkswagen as parent to them all.

BENTLEY

W.O. BENTLEY, the founder of Bentley Cars, was a perfectionist. It was said that every day the great man routinely spent half an hour laying the pens out on his desk in perfect symmetry. Just such perfection applied to his famous racing cars.

The 1919 London Motor Show was the year and the place where the mighty Bentley 3.0-litre sportscar first appeared. This model had a single overhead-cam

Berkeley *A small but respected sports car maker that produced caravans in later life*

engine with fixed head and dual magneto ignition and produced 70 bhp in its early form. By 1927 this 3.0-litre had developed into a 4.5-litre, still with four-cylinders, but producing 100 bhp. Later it was further developed to give 130 bhp by the time production ended. This superb example of automotive power could crest 90 mph in standard form, which was no mean feat for any type of car of its era.

1924 was another important year for Bentley, as it introduced another model which was set to become famous, and virtually priceless – the Speed, with bodywork by Vanden Plas. This model is notable not just for its superb lines but also for the introduction of front brakes and four seats in a sportscar body. Interestingly, Bentleys of this era had different coloured enamel on their radiator badges – each colour gives a clue to the model – a convenient way for enthusiasts to easily label the cars.

In 1929, the Speed Six, considered by many to be the best of the old-school Bentleys, was launched, and in 1930 a

supercharged version was listed. It had 182 bhp but did not have the approval of W.O. Bentley himself. It was an excellent if somewhat thirsty car. Then, in 1931 with desperate cash-flow problems, the Bentley company sank.

In 1933 Rolls-Royce came to the rescue and in the same year the new owners unveiled their version of the great marque at London's Olympia. This was an entirely different type of car from those seen before. It was remarkable because, as well as being well able to reach 90 mph, it was also very quiet and earned its slogan 'the silent sports car'.

In 1951 Bentley became the first Rolls-Royce product to have a regular series-produced factory body, rather than the specialist coach-built bodies which had previously been the norm. The sweeping lines of the beautiful Continental became as popular as any car at this end of the price spectrum could be, and earned itself a reputation for fine build quality, silent running and the opulence of its interior. From this point on, however, the Bentley

individuality was no more. The Rolls-Royce and Bentley identities were merged.

Today Bentley, though still part of Rolls-Royce, is seen as the sportier side of the parent company, witness the Turbo R. But there is a distinction between the marques; today's Azure is a beautiful car and looks sufficiently different from any Rolls-Royce to fully deserve the Bentley badge.

BENZ

BENZ IS THE story of two companies. The first was founded by Karl Benz until he quit after a dispute with his business partners. The other car-maker was C. Benz Sohne, an operation run by his two sons and where Benz senior eventually worked.

Karl Benz was 42 when he produced his first car, a three-wheeler. Its subsequent designs found more favour in France than his native land. The Viktoria saw Benz move to four-wheeled designs and after the launch of the new Parsifal in 1902, Benz resigned

from the company he had founded after disagreements over who should receive credit for it.

The original Benz company thrived after his departure. The new regime produced fast, luxurious cars and also became involved in motorsport – something Karl Benz had resisted. The company built some huge capacity engines, the largest being more than 10-litres!

Although their founders never met, Benz and Daimler merged to form one company in 1926, to take the name Mercedes-Benz.

After his departure from the Mannheim factory, Karl Benz joined his sons Eugen and Richard at their new Ladenburg base, producing some fine big-engined quality cars from 1905 until 1926. Karl retired in 1912 and manufacturing after the war never took off in a big way. The company, C. Benz Sohne, closed the same year as the Daimler-Benz merger.

BERKELEY

IT MIGHT SEEM hard to imagine today, but Biggleswade was once as much a centre of car production as Detroit, Abingdon, or Toyota City – though not on the same scale, it must be said.

Biggleswade in the UK was where the Berkeley range of sportscars were made from 1959 to 1962. They were hardly stunning performers with their original 15 and 18 bhp two-stroke motorcycle engines. Later versions – the B95 and 105 – used a 700cc four-stroke engine made for Berkeley by the famous motorcycle company Enfield, and this produced a maximum of 50 bhp, giving this little two-seater respectable performance. Interestingly, the Berkeley was a front-wheel-drive car at a time when just about everybody else was using the more tried and tested rear-wheel-drive format. The Berkeley system was very basic – final drive was by chain and the drive shafts did not have today's universal joints – but it was a innovative design at the time, even if it did mean the wheels tugged quite violently when cornering.

With its convertible top the Berkeley certainly epitomised British sportscars of the period, but unfortunately the hood design was not the best, often letting in

BMW

From humble beginnings, this German car maker is now one of the world's most respected

copious amounts of wind and rain. The body was not taut enough either, even with the roof up, and because body sections were rivetted in place these often loosened and started to creak and groan. Sometimes this got so bad the car could start to sag in the middle! Partly, these body problems came about because of the use of a mixture of glass reinforced plastic and aluminium, which though technically innovative, did not give the car enough body strength and rigidity.

This problem was solved when the 95 and 105 versions were launched. They had a more orthodox steel body which gave

greater strength. The bad news was, this design allowed rust to take hold…

The rest of the package was quite straightforward, with front and rear suspension provided by independent coil springs, which actually managed to give the Berkeley a good ride and quite impressive handling. Vague brakes let the cars down, a result of using all-round drums, rather than opting for the more efficient disc system. As a number of Berkeley owners found to their cost, they were not good enough to stop the car quickly when travelling at its maximum quoted speed of 95 mph.

After the demise of Berkeley's

car-making in 1962, the name continued on caravans with considerable success.

BMW

IN A STRANGE twist of fate, BMW's first car was the Dixi, an Austin Seven built under licence by the German company. Today, more than 65 years later, BMW owns Rover Group which itself swallowed Austin back in the 1960s. Whoever would have believed it? Certainly not Herbert Austin back in 1928. His mighty company owned by this small German concern? Never.

BMW did indeed grow from humble origins. Founded in 1916 to make aeroplane engines, in 1922 the company became known as Bayerische Motoren-Werke (from whence the initials BMW) and production of engines for boats, lorries and motorcycles began. In 1923 the first BMW motorcycle appeared and five years later it produced the first car, the Dixi. The company learnt a lot from this car, so much so that in 1932 it felt brave enough to launch its own design, using an 800cc engine with a tubular backbone chassis and independent suspension. BMW has never looked back.

By 1933 BMW had launched its first six-cylinder model, the 303, the first of a whole range of Sixes which proved incredibly popular with buyers. The most successful of the lot, the 328, developed no less than 80 bhp – an amazing figure back in the mid-1930s. Unfortunately World War II then intervened and only a handful of the 335 model with its 3485cc 90 bhp engine were made. Interestingly, between 1935 and 1939 BMWs were imported into the UK and marketed under the name of Frazer-Nash-BMW.

And then up popped something completely different: the Isetta bubble-car. BMW started production of the three-wheeler under licence in 1955 and it actually proved rather popular.

Then came the car that was to turn BMW's fortunes around. At the 2002's launch in 1968 the German car company had reached something of a watershed, producing a range of worthy but often rather dull cars. The 2002 was the model which deservedly rescued the Munich car-maker's reputation. Many versions of the Two series were built – including Turbo and Cabriolet models – and production lasted until 1977 (the 2002 was made until 1975).

By the time one of the prettiest BMWs of all time came along in 1972, the CSi, BMW was into its stride, making cars that everyone aspired to. The CSi's body was built by Karmann and then mated with the 3.0-litre engine at BMW's factory. This six-cylinder engine produced 200 bhp and a mighty 200 lb ft of torque, or put it another way, identical power to the fabulous Audi Quattro which appeared a decade later.

Today, BMW is riding the crest of a wave. Rover Group has been bought, and a number of very interesting models have recently been launched. And in the eyes of image-conscious buyers, BMW can seemingly do no wrong.

BOND

FOUNDED IN 1949 by Laurie Bond, this Preston-based company established itself as one of the few UK manufacturers of three-wheeled economy cars which found favour in the 1950s. This particularly after the 1956 Suez

Bristol

Aircraft engineering with some quintessential 'Britishness'

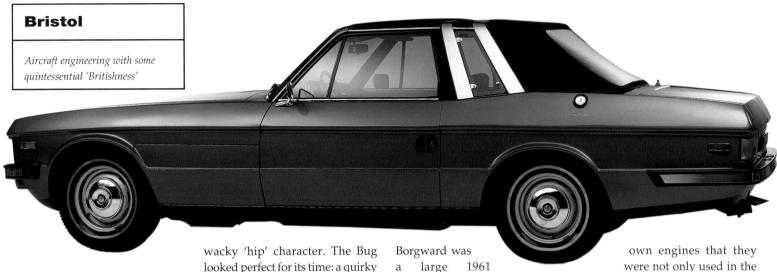

crisis, before turning the idea around as cheap, trendsetting transport for teenagers in 1970.

Bond's first Minicars used small motorcycle engines driving the front wheel via a chain. It even used a bike's kick starter! The ungainly looking Minicar continued in various themes up to the mid-60s by which time the company was more seriously involved in producing the Equipe, a two-seater sportscar based upon the Triumph Herald and Vitesse models of that era, including a rarer 'drophead'. The range was effectively killed off when fellow three-wheeler maker Reliant bought out Bond in 1969 and closed the Lancashire plant.

In 1970, Bond – or rather Reliant – took a bold decision to remarket the three-wheeler not as an economy special for frugal motorists but as a cheap fun car for the young. The idea was logical enough as three-wheelers were popular with motorcyclists because the law at the time dictated that they could drive these type of cars on a motorcycle licence. Bond wanted to tap into this market and tempt first-time drivers with its

Borgward

Impressive but little known German manufacturer that failed to survive increasing competition in the 1960s

wacky 'hip' character. The Bug looked perfect for its time: a quirky (usually orange) wedge-shaped wonder, and with its all-enclosing fold-forward cockpit canopy, quite radical too. However, its high prices and odd three-wheeled handling put paid to big sales.

BORGWARD

BORGWARD MADE cars in Germany between 1939 and 1961 and were the brain-child of Carl F.W. Borgward. His first car was called the Hansa 1100, but the bigger engined Hansa 1700 was first badged Borgward.

Then World War II intervened and Borgward shut up shop while hostilities raged. Come the end of the war, Borgward brought out two new cars, the Goliath and Lloyd, though the first really new post-war Borgward was the Hansa 1500 which made its appearance at the Geneva Motor Show in 1949. This was a very attractive car in its day and was the basis for a whole range of similar models, but with different engines. The 1800 four-cylinder and the 2400 six-cylinder soon followed the Hansa 1500 but by 1954 there was another model development when the Isabella was launched. This was one of the first cars of its era to be made without a separate chassis and it proved really popular with buyers, not just in Germany but across mainland Europe. The last

Borgward was a large 1961 limousine with a lusty six-cylinder engine. Owners could also specify air suspension, which was not at all common in those days. Unfortunately, this impressive car was only made for about eight months and then the company collapsed with big debts.

BRISTOL

STRANGELY ENOUGH, the very first of this most British of British makes was actually German. The 1947 Bristol 400, was Bristol's development of a popular 2.0 litre BMW. Bristol made many changes to the BMW recipe, including designing a dedicated independent suspension, bolting on a modern rack-and-pinion steering system, and including centralised chassis lubrication, again a fairly modern development for the time.

Bristol, part of the great aircraft company of the same name, has never made cars in large numbers, but the company has always been busy making sure that its cars provided buyers with the very best in grand touring elegance. This philosophy continued with the 401 saloon and 402 Cabriolet, cars combining the best in British engineering (the engines for these cars were made by Bristol themselves) with the very best of classic Italian styling for the bodies.

Such was the success of Bristol's

own engines that they were not only used in the company's own cars, but also supplied AC and Cooper, as well as numerous smaller specialist constructors. Developments continued throughout the 1950s and 1960s, with the Bristol growing into a four-door saloon in 1955 with the battery and spare wheel housed in the front wings and overdrive as standard. The 405 got disc brakes in 1958, while its successor, the 406, had a 2.2-litre engine and was very expensive.

In 1962 the old six-cylinder unit was replaced by a 250 bhp, overhead-valve, Chrysler V8 linked to an American Torqueflite automatic gearbox. By 1968 the 407 evolved into the 410 with minor styling improvements and a gear selector on the floor in place of the older push buttons. Further changes were made in 1978. A more streamlined 603 saloon had the choice of either 5.2- or 5.9-litre engines and the inclusion of air conditioning. One of the most attractive bodies was provided by the Zagato designed 412, a targa-type convertible. And finally, 1980 saw the launch of the mighty Beaufighter, with a turbocharged 5.9-litre Chrysler unit.

Today, the Bristol is very rare, simply because production is so small-scale. The cars have a loyal following, owners say once they've experienced the build quality and the performance, they never want to drive anything else.

BUGATTI

ONE OF THE most famous of all motoring names, Ettore Bugatti was a renowned racing driver who during the early 1900s rivalled Ferrari. He was only 19 years old when he designed his first car in 1901, a simple four-cylinder machine, which nevertheless won him a medal at the Milan Exhibition. The young Italian soon came to the attention of one Baron de Dietrich who took Bugatti under his wing and asked him to design cars for the Baron's new motor works. Unfortunately the three or four cars made during this period were not successful and Bugatti left de Dietrich and joined forces with another car-maker, Mathis.

This collaboration came to an end in 1906 when Bugatti went to work for the Deutz company in Cologne. However, while he was working for Mathis, Bugatti had produced his own car, working in his spare time. This became known as the Bugatti Type 10. By 1909 Ettore had moved to his own factory and started building the cars which would become world famous. The first model was a four-cylinder 1.3-litre car with overhead-camshafts. This was followed in turn by a wide range of attractive and powerful cars, including one destined to become a classic. The beautiful Bugatti Royale was launched in the early 1930s and is now arguably the world's rarest and most desired automobile. Bugatti died in 1947 and the name was effectively mothballed until 1993 when the exciting EB110 GT was launched. Sadly Bugatti, who bought Lotus at around the same time, have fallen on hard times and their future is in doubt.

Bugatti

The EB110 GT, one of the fastest cars ever, and the first Bugatti since 1947

BUICK

DAVID DUNBAR Buick's first car was built and offered to the public in 1903. It followed the conventional American wisdom at the time, having a flat twin-cylinder engine mounted under the floor of the car, coupled with a 'planetary' gearbox and final drive by chain.

Interestingly for the technically-minded, the Buick had mechanically-operated overhead-valves, a feature of all cars bearing the Buick name until very recently.

Buick, a Scottish plumber by profession, started churning out new cars by the thousand. By 1916 Buick was a member of the General Motors group and was producing the D47 saloon, or sedan as it was called in America, with a new overhead-valve, six-cylinder engine developing 45 bhp. This was followed in the same year by the D45 touring car which was essentially the same as the D47 but with a soft top which could be folded back to give full open-topped motoring. This car was offered at an amazing $1,020, a strong selling point. By 1918 Buick

was ranked fourth in the table of American car-makers, producing 77,691 new cars that year. By 1926 Buick had decided he'd had enough of four-cylinder cars and these were all ditched in favour of six-cylinder machines. These larger engined cars continued through to 1931 until they were joined by straight eight-cylinder units as well.

In 1929 David Buick, truly one of the great American automotive pioneers, died. Of course, the company had long since passed out of his control, but he is justly recognised as one of the great auto giants of the 20th century.

The problem for Buick, at least during the late 1920s, was that its cars could never make it to the top of the American new car sales league. That meant the GM division could not spend as much money on developments as some of its rivals could. For most of its life Buick has remained at fourth, or even lower, position in the production tables. However, in 1930 Buicks got more efficient engines – all straight eights. The same year a Buick-powered racing car qualified for the Indianapolis 500 Memorial Race and Buick's evocatively named Wizard Control made use of an automatic clutch to give fuel-saving free-wheeling ability.

Buick as a make is still routinely third in the sales charts, making is one of the US's most visible car makers. Successful models of recent years include the Riviera and the Roadmaster, which uses the mighty V8 engine from the Chevrolet Corvette GT, no less.

Legendary Marque

CADILLAC

IS CADILLAC the American Rolls-Royce? Some will argue that Cadillac are not only the match of Britain's finest but are superior. Not only has it always striven to maintain the highest standards of manufacturing but the company has also produced cars in much greater numbers than its British counterpart.

Cadillac was founded by William Murphy in 1902, the company name being taken from Antoine de la Mothe Cadillac, the French army officer who had founded Detroit some 200 years earlier. However, when originally established, the car giant traded as the Henry Ford Company. This title only changed after Ford was replaced by talented engineer Henry Leland. The former went on to achieve fame and fortune providing transport for the masses, whereas Murphy made Cadillac one of the finest marques in the world, adopting the motto: 'Craftsmanship a creed, accuracy a law' to denote the quality of his vehicles. To prove this point, he shipped out three totally dismantled cars to Britain and rebuilt them from the jumbled component parts to illustrate the firm's workmanship.

Cadillac's reputation for fine engineering quickly grew and the company was snapped up in 1909 by the rapidly expanding General Motors group. Cadillac was the first manufacturer to use an electric starter in favour of a cranking handle and also introduced the basis of the modern ignition and generating systems. Other firsts included the V16 engine, synchromesh gearbox and fully automatic transmission. Although Cadillac didn't invent the V8 engine, it was the first company to push it towards world acceptance, in its Type 51 of 1915.

The introduction of the Sixteen, with its radical V16 engine, marked a distinct turning point for Cadillac. With the appointment of new general manager Lawrence P 'Larry' Fisher in 1925, moves were made to establish Cadillac as America's premier car manufacturer. This meant that the company would have to spearhead an attack on the mass-produced luxury car market, as well as aim for the prestige sector.

Caddy's 'sweet Sixteen' was in the vanguard of this assault and the vehicle so impressed President Hoover – also a talented engineer – that he commissioned one for his own use, and took it with him when he left office. The presidential connection continued some 30 years later when in 1972 President Richard Nixon gave Soviet leader President Leonid Brezhnev a Cadillac Eldorado after a summit between the two superpowers.

Other famous individuals who owned Sixteens included Al Jolson, Al Capone, Marlene Dietrich, Gary Cooper and W.C. Fields, who had

Cadillac

The Als have it: both Al Capone and Al Jolson coveted their instantly classic V16s

two Sixteens, one of which had a built-in bar! Even the Vatican owned one.

This set Cadillac on the road to success. The Sixty Special of 1938-41 was one of the most distinctive-looking cars the company had produced up to that point in its history, and more radical design was to follow. In 1949 Cadillac received the ultimate accolade from America's *Motor Trend* when it won the magazine's Car of The Year award. The same year marked the production of the company's millionth car, a Coupe de Ville. This milestone had taken Cadillac almost 50 years to achieve, yet such was the motor car's growing popularity that the two-millionth Caddy rolled off the production line just nine years later.

By the late 1940s Cadillac, whose motto was now 'Standard of the World', had another first thanks to styling legend Harley Earl. It was the tail fin. Spurred on by fighter aircraft designs of World War II, Earl made these styling devices both his, and Cadillac's, trademark over the years. Throughout the 1950s the fins became more and more pronounced; the fad even started a booming auto accessory business, as add-on 'fins' could be bolted onto rival cars. Nothing was considered too outrageous!

Each year the fins and chrome work became bolder but in many ways the 'fin fuss' tended to overshadow the company's production of some highly-sophisticated cars. Power-seating, auto door locking, electric aerials, front and rear heating systems (with under-seat warming) and air-suspension systems were all Cadillac features of the period.

Cadillac

Left and Below *The Eldorado in all its finned glory* **Bottom** *After a shaky period in the 1970s and 1980s Cadillac is again producing the type of luxury Cars American buyers want, as in this 1992 Alanté* **Over** *The series 6.2 typified American cars of its era: lots of power, lots of creatures comforts and lots and lots of chrome*

By 1960 the marque's outward styling excesses were being restrained. The square-cut Seventy Five of 1966 was the first new design since the late 1950s. It was the 1967 Eldorado that was the most significant Cadillac of the decade, thanks to its front-wheel drive. This is still a rarity in American cars of the 1990s. By 1970 the Eldorado bore the largest engine yet fitted in a production car – a huge 8.2-litres – but the world fuel crisis three years later hit Cadillac hard. The cars became smaller, and Cadillac started to target Mercedes buyers with its homespun luxury Seville, which could even be ordered in diesel form. This didn't prove popular and after a long period in the automotive wilderness, Cadillac started to find its way again in the late 1980s through the revised Seville range. This car has been the catalyst for the company returning to what it knows best – building large, luxury, vehicles fit for princes and presidents.

CATERHAM

NOT SURPRISINGLY based in Caterham, Surrey, England, this company made a very wise move when they brought the production rights to Colin Chapman's Lotus Seven in 1970. This was Chapman's first major sportscar and it quickly proved popular with buyers, not least because of its terrific power, agile handling and real wind-in-the-hair motoring. Much copied but never bettered, the Caterham has remained true to its Lotus origins. It is considered by many to be the best spartan sportscar produced today – and it's not badly priced either.

This car, when known as the Lotus Seven, shot to instant fame when it featured in the cult TV show *The Prisoner*, and is still associated with that programme of some 30 years ago.

Interestingly, Caterham – who originally came to the market as a maker of kit-cars – can supply a Seven already built or it can be supplied in kit-form and built by a mechanically-minded enthusiast. There have always been a varied mix of power plants: the Ford 1.6-litre cross-flow unit, the Rover K-series fuel-injected twin-cam (this is the engine previously found in the Rover 400) which in Caterham's hands develops 130 bhp, or Vauxhall's Astra engine, again a double overhead-cam 16-valve unit but this time in 2.0-litre form and able to give 175 bhp. Such was the blistering performance that some models were only sold to enthusiasts on the condition that a special driving test had to be taken.

The Caterham's body is very simple, a combination of aluminium and glass reinforced plastic clothes the tube space-frame

Caterham

A back to basics sportscar maker that appeals to the true enthusiast

PPH 633R

Checker *As instantly recognisable as a red London bus, but Checker's attempt to sell its yellow cab as a private car met with little success*

chassis linked to double wishbone front suspension and a choice of a live rear axle or De Dion independent rear suspension.

The combination of light weight, good engine options and low stance means it really does fly along. The handling is legendary and in full-flight there is little that can touch the Caterham – all the more surprising therefore, that this is essentially a car which was launched 35 years ago.

Caterham has also been experimenting with completely different machines of late. The exciting new 21 is a Caterham for the 1990s, with its smooth, modern flowing bodywork (buyers don't have to have the wind in their hair, a hardtop will be offered). The 21 will appeal to those who like their creature comforts but still want to have the best of performance and handling. Don't worry about Caterham's background as a kit-car-maker. These are not low quality cars, they are built with as much, if not more, care than any mass production machine.

CHECKER

REMEMBER THE famous New York yellow cab? Who doesn't, it's as much a part of the American city as the black cab or the red double-decker bus in London. If it hadn't been for Checker Motor Corporation of Kalamazoo, Michigan, USA, who started making taxicabs as far back as 1923, the famous yellow cab might never have appeared.

Interestingly, Checker were not content with making just taxicabs; in 1949 they offered a car for private use – though this was actually just the taxi with some minor alterations. The company came to realise it had to broaden its range and in 1959 they began to make cars for private customers in larger numbers. There were two models, the Super and the Marathon, but they still owed much to the taxi design, with seating for eight. The original engine was a 3.7-litre six-cylinder Continental unit – the same as found in the taxicabs – but

from 1965 a new Chevrolet six or eight-cylinder was on offer. Strange though it may seem in the age of the sleek, sweeping lines of modern cars, the Checker changed very little in appearance, keeping its bulbous and hefty design. In spite of this it was regularly selling around 5,000 a year during the 1980s, and there was a choice of even more engines, including a 4.4 and 5.0-litre V8, and, unusually for the US market, a diesel.

CHEVROLET

WHEN RACING CAR driver Louis Chevrolet started work on a six-cylinder car back in 1909 he can have had little idea that his name would not only survive into the 1990s, but that it would appear on a range of cars which have been at the heart of the American obsession with the automobile.

Chevy, as it is colloquially known, is one of the largest of General Motors' divisions and it has given its name to some of the

most appealing cars we have ever seen.

In fact, Chevrolet didn't actually start the company which now bears his name, that honour goes to Billy Durant who recognised that Chevrolet's fame across America as a legendary racing driver should assure the success of the new company. This was important to Durant who had been ousted from General Motors, the company he had helped form. He hoped to use the Chevrolet Car Company as a lever to regain control of GM. The problem was, Chevrolet designed a prestigious upmarket car while Billy Durant wanted a cheaper car which could be sold in large numbers. Not too surprisingly, Louis soon left the company to build his own car, the Frontenac.

The first Chevrolet was, in fact, the 1911 Classic Six which was relatively large and used a cone clutch and three-speed, rear-axle-mounted gearbox. This was a successful car and two years later the profits allowed Chevrolet (now joined with the Little Car

Company) to set up a factory in Flint, Michigan, where the Chevrolet Model C was built. By 1916 Durant had achieved his goal, he succeeded Charles W. Nash as President of General Motors and Chevrolet became part of the growing empire. Nash, meanwhile, went off to set up another important American company, Nash Motors.

Chevrolet was a big success, until it hit a couple of problems. The biggest of these was the rear-engined Corvair of 1960. A sort of upmarket US VW Beetle, its quirky handling meant the Corvair fast gained a bad name. It was soon dubbed the car that was "unsafe at any speed" by safety campaigner Ralph Nader. Chevrolet retorted by producing some fine cars,

---

Chrysler

A chequered history was overcome with vehicles like the RAM pick-up

---

including the high performance Corvette Sting Ray in 1963 and various versions of the Camaro, as well as the Lumina mini-van which started the current trend in people carriers. Today, Chevrolet is rightly still one of the giants of the US car industry. And latterly, with the likes of the Seville STS, has started to produce cars with a European bias rather than cater for the US market alone.

CHRYSLER

CHRYSLER WAS BORN in 1925, and this was swiftly followed by its gulping down of Dodge, DeSoto and Plymouth, to form one large group. This became a rival to both Ford and General Motors, and the trio are often referred to as 'the big three'. Walter P. Chrysler was the man behind the new company and like many other early motoring pioneers in America he had cut his corporate teeth at General Motors, before retiring at the age of just 45

and setting up Chrysler.

Like Buick, Chrysler cars featured some of the new technologies which were flooding the American auto market at this time, notably power steering, electric windows and transistor radios, all of which were first found on Chrysler cars. All went well for quite some considerable time and Chrysler was routinely near the top of the new car production tables, usually through its Dodge marque. It also acquired AMC who owned Jeep and the British Rootes Group as well as the French company Simca. In the 1970s Chrysler experienced a severe downturn which saw the company heading towards bankruptcy.

The colourful Lee Iaccoca who had served as President of Ford from 1960 before being fired by Henry Ford II in 1978, joined Chrysler as President. He led a campaign against the Japanese who he blamed for Chrysler's misfortunes, saying they were flooding the market and seriously

affecting the American auto industry. By 1980 the situation for Chrysler had worsened and Iaccoca managed to secure federal loan guarantees from President Jimmy Carter's government in a last-ditch attempt to save the company.

It worked – at least for a while. Even as late as 1990 Chrysler was struggling, partly as a result of selling off most of its operations in Europe. Since then it has turned a corner and once again started to make money, partly because of its successful 'people carrier' which was proving incredibly popular.

Ironically, one of the cars which raised Chrysler's standing with customers was the 1991 Dodge Stealth which was a co-development with Japanese manufacturer Mitsubishi. Other cars which have sold well for Chrysler in recent years have included the Le Baron saloon with a standard V6 3.0-litre engine, the Dodge Caravan and the Dodge Viper which is a real monster of a car with its V12 engine and stunning performance. Chrysler is now trying to break into the European market, and there is every chance it will enjoy considerable success with its Neon family car, Voyager people carrier and New Yorker limosine.

CITROËN

"I WANT A CAR," said Andre Citroën, "in which a man wearing a top hat can drive across a ploughed field without breaking any of the eggs he might have on the seat beside him." And so the 2CV was born. The story is true (though the quote is paraphrased somewhat) and it highlights Citroën's sometimes bizarre approach towards car-making. Those who mock Citroën do so at their peril because today the company is one of Europe's most successful and still one of the most innovative.

Citroën began in 1919 when this

most imaginative of European companies launched the 1.3-litre, four-cylinder Type A. This was a simple single-valve machine and 10,000 were made by 1921. The following year Citroën launched an improved version, the Type-B with a 1.5-litre engine, and the similar 856cc 5CV. Though neither of these cars was a brisk performer, both were virtually indestructible and remained in production until 1925.

The big news came in 1934 when Citroën launched their first version of the 7CV Traction Avant, a revolutionary front-wheel-drive saloon with an overhead-valve, wet-liner engine and all-round torsion-bar independent suspension. The original engine was a 1.6-litre but in 1934 a new 3.8-litre, front-wheel-drive V8 was unveiled. The following year

Andre Citroën found himself in financial difficulties as a result of developing the new car and a special factory to build it, and was forced to sell the company to tyre-makers Michelin.

The 2CV (pictured above), launched in 1949 became a legend. Like its bigger brothers it had front-wheel drive but it also had inter-linked coil suspension, a four-speed gearbox and quick detachable bonnet, doors and front wings, for instant repairs to damaged bodywork.

Power originally came from a 375cc, 9 bhp, overhead-valve, flat twin engine, and the ugly corrugated grey bodywork finish attracted unkind comparisons with garden sheds.

In 1955 Citroën caused quite a stir with the launch of the futuristic

DS19. It had front-wheel drive and a four-cylinder engine. Self-levelling suspension was joined by power assistance for the brakes (discs at the front and drums at the rear), steering and gearchange. The DS was expensive and complicated and a year later a simplified ID19 version came out, retaining the advanced springing but doing away with the power assistance. This model cost less than the original car and Citroën sales leapt.

The SM, first mooted in 1969, came about thanks to Citroen's connections with Maserati and Fiat. Powered by a 2.7-litre, overhead-cam, V6 engine developing 170 bhp, this massive front-wheel-drive sports coupe was like nothing ever seen before. With a top speed of 137 mph, this was the most expensive and fastest Citroën ever offered –

Citroën

Individual and idealistic, Citroën has always been in a class of its own

and is still a desirable classic today.

Citroën fell under the control of Peugeot during the mid 1970s and it gradually saw a move towards more conventionally designed cars. The DS gave way to the CX range which in turn was replaced by the XM, the last of the idiosyncratic Citroens. However, the company hasn't totally lost the art of revolutionary design. In 1995 it launched the Xantia Activa using state-of-the-art computer-controlled suspension, just like contemporary Grand Prix cars, which is amazing the motoring world with its cornering ability. Founder Andre Citroën would have thoroughly approved.

CLAN

CONCEIVED BY ex-Lotus men Haussauer and Frayling in 1971, the Clan Crusader was a particularly bold attempt to unleash the potential of the Hillman Imp Sport with a purpose-built coupe body which could be bought as a complete car or built as a kit at home. The Crusader quickly found a niche market of enthusiasts looking for a neat looking, fine-handling car for road or competition use. In standard 50 bhp trim, the little Clan was good for more than 90 mph and made a useful base to build a circuit racer or rally car. However, the imposition of VAT in April 1973 coupled with the start of the energy crisis later that year killed off the charming little Clan in one swoop. More than 300 cars were produced but only a few survive. Dedicated attempts to revive the Clan, the most notable using an Alfasud engine and gearbox instead of the now defunct Imp unit, all sadly failed.

CORD

ONE OF THE most evocative names of American motoring history, the Cord was built between 1929 and 1937 and constantly impressed buyers with its grand looks and smooth performance. It was the also the first US car to be built in front-wheel-drive form.

The brainchild of one Erret Lobban Cord – who also owned Auburn and Duesenberg – the first Cord was the L29 which was home to a 5.0-litre straight eight-cylinder engine made by Lycoming. As was

Cord

Symbolic of the Roaring Twenties, Cord lasted less than ten years producing fine, expensive cars

often the fashion at the time, the L29 was made in both convertible and hard-top forms and also had a range of coachbuilt bodies which could be grafted on to the chassis. These cars were much sought-after at the tail-end of the Roaring Twenties but their high prices were a problem as the Great Depression spread across America. Nevertheless, even in a depression there seemed to be enough people willing to fork out the money for a Cord, a desire strengthened by

the 1936 launch of the famous coffin-nosed 810 and 812. This was like nothing ever seen before, or since, for that matter, and later models featured pop-up headlights, though the Cord's had

to be cranked up by hand. As well as this the car featured fingertip buttons to select gears in the four-speed gearbox. By 1937, the last year of production, the Cord 812 could be specified with a number of different bodies, and when supercharged it pushed out 190 bhp from its V8 engine.

COSTIN

FAMOUS RACING car designer, the late Frank Costin, also tried several times to break into the specialist car market with his innovative sportscars of the same name. A great fan of 'God's metal' Costin produced innovative wooden monocoque (a combined body/chassis unit) racing and road cars. His most notable efforts being a very competitive Formula 2 racer in 1967 and the Costin Amigo road car a year later.

Thanks to its lightweight construction with fibreglass outer panels, even when fitted with a standard 104 bhp Vauxhall Victor 2000cc engine the Costin was a particularly fast car for its time.

However, it was never a commercial success and only seven were made until when the company folded in 1972.

CUNNINGHAM

THERE WERE two Cunningham motor companies in the USA, one based in Rochester, New York

Cunningham
One name, two car makers, who tried to produce fast, unusual cars

State, making cars between 1907 and 1936, and another totally unconnected operation with its HQ in Palm Beach, Florida and making cars between 1951 and 1955. The earlier Cunninghams were made by James Cunningham and sons who had previously built carriages, then switched to car-making when these petrol-powered vehicles started to become popular. The first original Cunningham appeared in 1910 – before that they had been a collection of parts from other manufacturers, assembled by Cunningham – and powered by a V8 engine. This car was extremely popular, thanks to its good looks and excellent performance. It was bought by movie stars and business tycoons. It was so successful that it was still in production until 1933.

The second Cunningham company was started by Briggs Swift Cunningham whose main aim in life was to create a super American sportscar. The C1 model was a prototype but the C2 of 1952, with its V8 Chrysler engine, was meant for general production, though in the event only three were made!

The only Cunningham which reached the street in any numbers, and not many at that, was the 1953 C3 which was a large GT grand tourer. A total of 18 were sold.

DAEWOO

THIS SOUTH KOREAN industrial giant is relatively new to European shores. In fact, it has been an established car-maker for decades and formed a partnership with General Motors in the late 1960s.

However, it wasn't until recently that Daewoo cars became available in the UK. It quickly made a big impression with its unique sales strategy. This being to market the cars direct to the customer without the usual car dealer showroom and high-pressure selling. This sort of approach has been tried in the UK before when superstore giant Asda decided to sell cars direct to the customer in just the same way as they sold soap powder – pile it high, sell it at a competitive price. It did not work for Asda, and other supermarket chains who investigated this type of operation shied away from it.

Daewoo though is different. It does not sell soap powder or bread, it simply sells cars. The current UK range consists of two five-door hatchbacks, the Nexia and the Espero. Take a close look and buyers may experience a feeling of

deja-vu – these cars have been seen before. The Daewoo Nexia is based on the Vauxhall Astra or, to be more precise, on the General Motors Astra/Kadett. Likewise the Espero is a redesigned and re-packaged General Motors Cavalier.

There is nothing wrong with these cars but they are not exactly at the cutting edge of technology. For many bargain-hunting buyers that most probably doesn't matter because prices are keen and equipment packages are high. Daewoo has also ensured customer loyalty by handing out of free cars to motorists so that the company can find out just what customers think of their vehicles. The motoring 'establishment' is becoming worried about this customer-friendly approach which could revolutionise car retailing as we know it. Watch out also for some revolutionary cars as Daewoo firmly establishes itself.

DAF

DAF WAS HOLLAND'S only major car-maker and they came up with something very clever indeed. Variomatic automatic transmission system was the simplest, most straightforward automatic ever seen.

The transmission system worked via a large and robust rubber belt. This was connected to the front-mounted engine – originally a flat twin-cylinder, 600cc, overhead-valve, air-cooled unit. In its original form it produced 22 bhp, which was not a lot, but this was compensated for by the ease with which this car could be driven. This first car appeared in 1958 and four years later new versions were launched, the Daffodil and the 750, both of which used a 750cc engine. This was such a successful package that within a few years 20,000-a-

year were being sold. By 1967 there were further developments with the launch of the 44 which was based on the 750 but with a larger, roomier body.

The 55 was launched in 1968 and this time used a water-cooled, 1.1-litre Renault engine. Two years later the performance got another boost when a 1.4-litre engine with twin-choke carburettors was launched. Cars fitted with this uprated set-up proved to be very popular on the rally circuit.

In the mid-1970's, DAF was bought by Volvo. Interestingly, DAF also bought troubled Leyland Vans in Birmingham, England in the early 1990s, but later sold it to a management buy-out team.

DAIHATSU

BY JAPANESE standards Daihatsu is a relatively small-scale producer,

which first saw the light of day back in 1930. The first Daihatsu engine, however, dates back to 1907. It's comparative size does not make it any the less important on the international market. Originally renowned for its three-cylinder engines when most manufacturers routinely used four, the Daihatsu has always impressed with its lusty nature, high equipment levels and good build quality.

In 1951 the Hatsudoki Motor Company was re-named Daihatsu Kogyo Company. In 1965 a Daihatsu won its class in that year's Japanese Grand Prix and two years later the company signed a business tie-up with Toyota.

The beauty of Daihatsu's 1960s three-cylinder engines was their lively character. Easy revving, they had more in common with a good motorbike engine than with more sluggish motor car units and they not only performed well but they also provided exceptionally good fuel economy.

As well as a range of saloons and hatchbacks, Daihatsu has also had the Fourtrak four-wheel-drive vehicle in its range for many years, treating it to regular trim and engine up-dates. Today the Fourtrak is best known as a 'farmer's friend' because it has a rugged, no-nonsense character which is more at home crossing fields than climbing pavements outside fashionable high street stores. In comparison to most rivals the Fourtrak lacks a 'lifestyle' image, but it will go anywhere.

In fairness to Daihatsu, they have equipped the latest 2.8-litre models to an impressive specification level, and prices are competitive – it is possible to buy three Fourtraks for the price of one Range Rover!

Daihatsu is no stranger to high tech designs. In 1987 a special development two-seater, code-named the ZA-X80, using only a 996cc engine was shown at the Frankfurt Motor Show and was claimed to have a top speed of 155mph. Four years later a Charade turbodiesel drove itself into the Guinness Book of Records as the UK's most consistently economical car, by achieving an average of no less than 103.1 mpg.

DAIMLER

THIS IS NOT the company which is now part of England's Jaguar but rather the original German company, named after Gottlieb Daimler, inventor of many of motoring's most useful innovations. In fact, Daimler himself was a director on the board of the British concern for several years but then went his separate way, eventually joining forces with Mercedes-Benz to create Daimler-Benz, the name by which the German company is officially known today.

Daimler, together with Karl Benz, is credited with producing the world's first cars powered by the internal combustion engine. The two Germans were working independently of each other (they didn't even know the other existed) so it is somewhat ironic that eventually the two names should be intertwined, as they are today.

The interesting fact about this early development of the car is, as it turns out, many inventors around the world had seized on the idea of creating a horseless carriage, as they were known, and work was going on in all the industrialised nations of the time. None of them knew of each other. Benz and Daimler both formed their early cars by developing a principle which had originally been touted by Nicholas Otto. By 1886 two German motor vehicles appeared, Benz's three-wheeler, and Daimler's side-wheeler cycle.

In 1886 Benz, quick to spot a miracle when he saw it, patented his plans for the petrol-powered Motorwagon (a German patent only, it must be said).

This did not stop Daimler, or any of his contemporaries carrying on with their own designs, which is just as well, otherwise there might not have been so many cars to choose from today!

DATSUN (NISSAN)

WHEN THE JAPANESE company Datson was first formed the name soon had to be changed. The word sounded too close to the Japanese word for 'ruin'. The new title 'Datsun' gave the company a whole

Datsun (Nissan) *The 240Z was a 1960s classic that helped Datsun become a major player in making the Japanese a real force in automotive manufacturing*

Delahaye *One of the oldest names in automotive history, Delahaye couldn't sustain its early promise, and became truck makers*

new meaning along the lines of 'invocation to the powerful sun'. Whatever, as it now stands the company is known as Nissan which apparently means nothing and will never offend anyone.

In the early days of the Japanese automotive invasion into North America and Europe, the cars, and this included Nissan, were not seen as too much of a threat. Datsun first stated producing cars in 1931, making Austins under licence before designing and building its own ranges. Datsun (Nissan) were one of the very first car-makers to enter European and American markets, but its first attempts at contemporary designs were nothing special. They were mechanically conventional, tended to rust quite badly, and the styling was all too often not acceptable to European tastes.

What the Europeans and the Americans failed to take into account was the Japanese penchant for niche marketing – in other words, spotting a gap in the market. In this case it was a battle of equipment. European cars in particular in the 1950s rarely came with radios. All Japanese cars of this period had one fitted in the dashboard, even if it was hardly the latest in high technology. Potential buyers were impressed – they wanted good equipment levels.

The Japanese revolution had begun. Next Nissan tackled the problem of looks, starting up a major design studio in California to tap into the American way of doing things. Similarly, they opened a modern design centre in Holland and another in the UK, where designers produced more European-style cars.

Today all this hard work and forward-thinking investment is paying off, and not just for Nissan, also for their customers. Today's Nissan buyers get competent, well designed, attractive and yes, well equipped cars. It must be said however, that the Americans and Europeans have learned the hard way, and most of their cars are well equipped now, too.

Nissan has offered some very impressive cars during its relatively short history, including the sporty 240Z, one of the few Datsuns which can be considered a true classic car. Around the early 1970s it was a world-beating rally car.

The company now has production plants across the world, including England, while an upmarket offshoot appealing to luxury car-buyers is popular in the United States.

DELAHAYE

ONE OF THE oldest of French car-makers, Delahaye built its classic cars in Paris and Tours between 1894 and 1954. In the first years the company concentrated mostly on stationary engines for engineering purposes, then they started making commercial vehicles. It was not until four years after the Paris factory had opened that they made their first car. It was a 1.4-litre vehicle with a choice of single or twin cylinder engines.

Emile Delahaye had come to car-making late in life and he retired in 1901. Three years later the company was turning into one of France's most prolific auto manufacturers and was producing a range of cars, including a huge 8.0-litre beast which proved popular with the wealthy. Customers included the King of Spain, who must have been kept busy because this big Delahaye had two handbrakes and two footbrakes – one for front and one for rear brakes – and a foot-operated decompressor.

After World War I Delahaye really didn't produce any exciting cars, preferring instead to concentrate on worthy but rather dull machines which nevertheless remained popular with those French buyers who did not demand the latest in fashion. It wasn't until 1935 that Delahaye showed some more promise with the launch of two six-cylinder sports models, the 3.2-litre Coupe des Alpes and the 3.5-litre Type 135. Delahaye had earlier merged with Delage but the duo could not retain decent sales figures and in 1953 they were amalgamated with Hotchkiss; eventually they stopped making cars altogether, concentrating instead on trucks.

DE LOREAN

THE DE LOREAN car company has an interesting history which is all the more surprising considering it only made one car, the DMC12. John Z de Lorean, the colourful former Chief Engineer of Pontiac in the USA started to plan his 'safety sportscar' as far back as 1976, though it took four years to get into production. It crossed the Atlantic in the process, before eventually being built at a new factory in Dunmurry, County Antrim, Northern Ireland with the help of British taxpayers' money.

Safety was definitely a major quality of the DMC12, the car being designed to give protection against lateral as well as end-to-end collisions. Today this sort of protection is hardly remarkable but, when the DMC was launched, it was. The DMC had a rear engine, Lotus-designed all-independent suspension, servo disc brakes and a Giugiaro-styled two-seater coupe body finished in unpainted stainless steel. The original prototype's transversely-mounted Ford V6 was changed for production, replaced with a 2.8-litre fuel-injected Volvo V6 unit mounted back-to-front and linked with a five-speed Renault gearbox. Automatic was an option. A four-door model was under development in 1981 but was shelved after the firm ran into financial problems early in 1982.

There then followed some curious episodes, including an operation by the American FBI which caught De Lorean on secret film allegedly discussing the sale of illegal drugs. When the case came to court De Lorean was completely cleared of any wrong-doing but the company did not survive. Be that as it may, the DMC is an interesting car with modern gull-wing doors which opened up and outward. While this looked good in the brochure it was wise to remember that if an owner parked in a tight space in car park, it is impossible to get back in the car if other cars parked either side. It also had quite a claustrophobic feel inside because the side windows only had a small portion which could be opened.

Practicality was not a strong point either, there was very little room inside, though in fairness this applied to any compact sportscar of the period. As far as performance was concerned, the De Lorean was no ball of fire, despite that reasonably potent engine at the back. Handling though was very good, with a stability on the road which few other rear-engined sportscars could provide. Reliability was fairly good, though few cars were eventually built and even fewer delivered so it was hard to quantify. Suffice it to say, build quality was never brilliant, and this often left the few owners endlessly tinkering with bits and pieces of loose trim. However, it is now a modern classic car and its appeal boomed after its appearance as a time machine in the successful film *Back to the Future*.

DE TOMASO

ANOTHER OF THE great Italian sportscar companies, De Tomaso was actually founded by an Argentinean. Alejandro de Tomaso, a successful South American racing car driver, bought the world-famous Ghia design studio in Italy in the late 1950s, aided by his wife Isabell, who was also an ex-racing driver. Small wonder then that De Tomaso cars were always fast!

His first road-going model was the Mangusta which came out in 1969. This two-seater sportscar was powered by a 4.7-litre Ford V8 engine, coupled to a five-speed ZF gearbox and servo assisted four-wheel disc brakes. Capable of 155 mph, which is a fast enough by today's standards, let alone the tail-end of the 1960s, and with high equipment levels, the Mangusta

De Tomaso

Revitalised Italian supercar maker, founded by an Argentinian

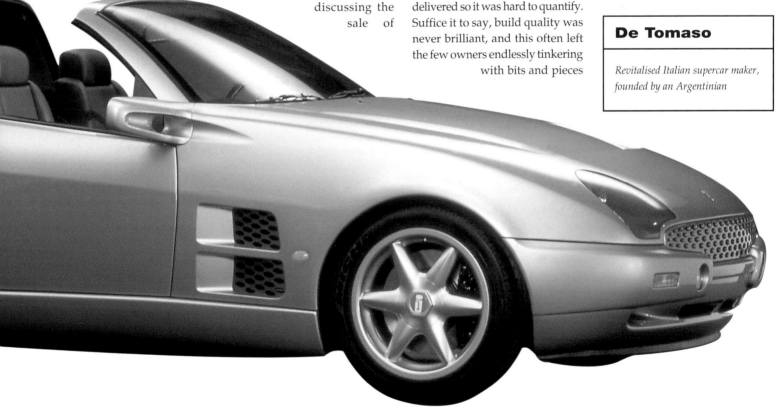

Dodge

Known as 'dependable Dodge' for its rather average cars, they also created the fearsome Charger (above) and the awesome Viper

was much sought-after. This car was important not just as a racing car for the road but also because it led to a close association with Ford who later distributed De Tomasos in the USA.

The Mustela GT coupe appeared in 1969, using a British Ford 2.9-litre V6 engine converted to overhead-camshaft design with fuel injection. Thanks to 230 bhp of

power there was plenty of performance. Then came the Deauville, an important development when it appeared in 1970 because it was the company's first front-engined touring saloon.

The previous cars had been out-and-out racers but this was advertised as a luxury four-door. Automatic transmission was standard and there was a choice of engines, either a double overhead-camshaft American Ford V8 with a capacity of 4.7-litres, or the same engine but re-bored to give 5.8 litres. Interestingly, the bigger engine, in 330 bhp push-rod form, powered the next car produced by De Tomaso, the 1971 Pantera, effectively this was a Mangusta

development which could top 162 mph. There was also a two-door version of the Deauville, known as the Longchamp, launched in 1973.

Neither the Deauville or Longchamp were particularly successful sellers, proving the old motor trade maxim that makers of two-seater sportscars seldom produce good saloons.

It was back to basics again with the launch of the exciting high performance two-seater Pantera. Part of the reason for its success may well have been the decision by Ford to sell the Pantera in the US through its Lincoln-Mercury dealers. The trouble was, this relationship did not last long, ending in 1974 when it proved

unprofitable for the dealers. Nevertheless, despite Ford's eventual about turn, De Tomaso continually developed the Pantera, launching the GT5 and 5S versions in 1980. It was still being sold up until 1994 though its relative success did not stop the company eventually being put in the hands of the receiver. However, De Tomaso is still in business and has released its latest creation called the Guara (shown on previous page) which uses BMW V8 power. Just 70 a year are expected to be produced. This 304 bhp, 170 mph supercar could be the car to launch De Tomaso back into the big league. It deserves to, even with its £90,000 price tag.

DODGE

DODGE BECAME part of Chrysler early on in its life only a few years after it was formed by the Dodge brothers, Horace and John in 1914. Dodge suffered along with Chrysler when things were not going well for the parent company but Dodge's strength has always been in its bread-and-butter cars. They have earned the company a good reputation for long lasting reliability. 'Dependable Dodge' as the company's cars were known and it was this quality which saw Dodge and Chrysler through the leaner times.

This strength can be testified to by some hard-pushing Dodge owners. For example most American police forces for years used the 1980s Dodge Diplomat which was developed out of the Dodge Aspen of 1976. By 1986 this car was still being used by many police forces and taxi companies, due as much to its reliability as its 140 bhp V8 engine.

By 1986 the Dodge Daytona coupe (the successor to the mighty Dodge Charger of the 1970s), had got Chrysler's 2.5-litre four-cylinder engine as an option but the real news was the Turbo Z, which not only had the up-rated engine but was also home to a handling package – called the CS in honour of Carroll Shelby – which transformed a quite ordinary car into a real fireball.

Meanwhile the very compact Omni GLH (which owners took to mean 'Goes Like Hell') came to the market for just one more run, and still proved popular with buyers, even if sales did dip when the new turbocharged Shelby GLH-S arrived and stole the Omni's thunder.

The following year – 1987 – Dodge carried out much restyling and repackaging of its products, including the launch of the Grand Caravan which was a lengthened version of the company's best-selling people carrier. Also new was the Shadow which was to replace the Omni and the America – which was actually an Omni (in fact, it was actually a European Talbot Horizon – also owned by Chrysler) – a super-value version of the car with a low price tag.

The Daytona, a famous Dodge sportscar, got a major restyle and stretched the range to include the turbocharged Shelby Z model, though even this did not stop Daytona sales plunging by 11,000 units for the year.

Dodge, continues today of course, generally making good, reliable, value-for-money cars. However there is one exception among their more predictable output : the Dodge Viper. This is now on sale in Europe as well as North America, and what a huge success it has been. Powered by a 400 bhp V10 engine, this brutish but beautiful piece of machinery is fast and very rare.

DUESENBERG

THE DUESENBERG Model A, launched in late 1920, has the distinction of being the first American production car with all-wheel hydraulic brakes and a straight-eight engine, in this case a single overhead-cam design. Technological prowess was always a feature of this company, as were high prices and high quality.

By 1929 Duesenberg was in top gear, even though the Roaring Twenties had gone and the Great Depression was just around the corner. Duesenbergs were always costly and all of a sudden few people could afford them. This didn't stop the company launching the massive, and massively expensive, Model J with a 265 bhp dual overhead-cam, straight eight-cylinder engine. Not surprisingly this unit gave this large car some very impressive performance and once again Duesenbergs were in demand – among the very wealthy.

By now the company had successfully planted their slogan 'It's a Duesy!' into the American psyche and they were somewhat immodestly claiming the title: "The World's Finest Motor Car".

Of course, at this time many cars were still coachbuilt and Duesenberg made much use of this craft. Companies like Murphy built some beautiful versions including the Model J Torpedo Berline and the Town Car, the latter even included a stop-watch and altimeter in its comprehensive standard set of dials. This is not as silly as it sounds, for the Model J could reach an impressive 116 mph, with 90 mph of that in second gear.

The next major engine development came in 1932 when Duesenberg introduced super-chargers to its cars, giving the Model J a top speed of 130 mph. It could accelerate to 100 mph in 17

Duesenberg *A victim of hard times and over-indulgence, nothing symbolized star status as well as a 'Duesy'*

Edsel *One of the biggest automotive blunders or a good car given a bad press? Edsel was designed to fill a market niche that didn't exist*

seconds, no mean feat for a car of this period. By 1935 power was increased once again with the launch of the SJ which was clearly identified by its four exterior exhaust pipes, flowing out of the engine and down the side of the car. Supercharged power hikes were often an option on a Duesenberg – no less than 400 bhp was possible on the SJ. By this time Duesenbergs had become the preferred transport of movie stars and royalty, including the Maharajah of Indore, India, who bought a SJ Speedster-Roadster in 1935. Red and blue running lights signalled whether the Maharajah or his wife was driving.

In 1936 Duesenberg breathed its last, unable to compete in a world where cars were mass-produced. Before its factory doors closed though, it produced the supercharged SSJ Speedster. Only two were built, one for Clarke Gable, the other for Cary Grant.

EDSEL

NAMED AFTER Henry Ford's son, Edsel, this range of cars has gone down in history as being real lemons. This is not strictly true. Today we might look at the distinctive front grille and wince, but back in 1957 when the first Edsel was launched there were plenty of people willing to go out and buy one – some 35,000 in fact, though by US standards at the time this was hardly a major success.

Ford launched the Edsel range to fill what they saw as a gap between Ford and Mercury

models, the latter being part of Ford's Lincoln-Mercury division. However, buyers did not seem to believe there was a gap, despite the fact that Ford's market research suggested otherwise. The Edsel was certainly competent enough with its coil and wishbone independent front suspension, and the choice of two engines, a 5.9 or a 6.7-litre, overhead-valve V8.

Within the division Edsels were also offered in Pacer and Ranger form which were cheaper and therefore, so Ford thought, more likely to appeal to buyers. There was also the Corsair and Citation which had push-button automatic gearboxes, while the Ranger and Pacer could be specified with manual, overdrive or automatic gearboxes. There was a choice of convertible or hard-top Edsels and, in 1958, the Bermuda stationwagon which could be specified as either a six or nine-seater. Edsel production ceased in 1959.

FACEL VEGA

FACEL VEGA BUILT some of the most beautiful French cars ever seen, though under the metal most of the components were bought from American companies. The company's products were fast, expensive and luxuriously equipped and were available in both saloon and coupe form. They were rather in the same tradition as the great Delahaye concern, which floundered around the same time as Facel Vega founder Jean Danino's dream began.

Before deciding to build its own

cars, Facel Vega had made good money out of building bodies for Panhard, Simca and Ford, so it certainly had plenty of expertise in crafting attractive-looking cars before launching the first original design in 1954. This model – the FVS – had a boxed chassis frame, coil and wishbone independent front suspension and hydraulic brakes. The engine was a 4.5-litre hemispherical head Chrysler V8, producing 180 bhp, and giving the FVS respectable performance in spite of the relatively heavy bodywork. The magnificent Coupe bodies were welded on to the frames, and the instrumentation was similar to those in light aircraft.

These early Facel Vegas were available with either Pont-a-Mousson manual four-speed gearboxes or with automatic transmissions. As the models were improved they gained bigger versions of the Chrysler V8, taking capacity and output up to 5.8-litres and 325 bhp by 1958, and ultimately to 6.3-litres and 390 bhp, giving a top speed of 135 mph. Power steering was available from 1957, and in the same year the company launched the long chassis Excellence four-door saloon. From 1960 all Facels had disc brakes.

In 1960 the smaller Facellia was launched and, although this too was a really good-looking car, it did not have the best engine. The mistake Facel Vega made was to use its own engines, rather than American units which had previously proved so reliable. This new twin overhead-cam, 120 bhp, 1.6-litre, four-cylinder unit proved terribly unreliable and also cost a lot of money to produce in the small numbers Facel were making. By 1962, faced with complaints from owners, Facel Vega changed to the tried and trusted 1.8-litre, push-rod, 108 bhp, Volvo engine.

Had Facel Vega done this earlier the company just might have survived and indeed a new Facel using the Austin-Healey 3.0-litre engine was ready for transplant into the Facellia in 1964, but the firm went bankrupt before these could be made in any numbers.

Fagel Vega

A latter day Delahaye, Facel was lost to the same fate, but remaining models are blue-chip classics

Legendary Marque

FERRARI

ENZO FERRARI WAS a true car enthusiast, a fact which showed through in all his designs. A former racing driver, Ferrari had some illustrious wins in the immediate post-World War I years, but never quite made it at the top-flight. By 1929 he had retired from the track to form Scuderia Ferrari, which duly ran the Alfa racing team for whom he had earlier driven.

An agreement with Alfa Romeo meant that Enzo couldn't use his own name on the cars that he built for the team in the 1930s. The first machine to wear the now famous 'prancing horse' Ferrari badge (presented to him by the parents of Italian World War I flying ace, Francesso Baracca) was not unveiled until 1940.

Success on the track came fast

and easy to Ferrari cars after World War II – in 1947 they were consistent winners on the sportscar circuit, while Grand Prix and Le Mans victories all fell to drivers at the wheel of a 'prancing horse' before 1950. Ferrari scooped the first of many Formula One World Championships in 1952, followed by the World Sportscar title a year later – a remarkable achievement.

The manufacturer has since gone on to become the longest survivor in Grand Prix racing, and it was only recently that McLaren overtook Ferrari's total number of wins. The team still hold the records for the most racing constructors' titles and the number of Grand Prix contested. With so much success on the track, the world market for racing-bred road cars boomed, but Ferrari couldn't keep pace with demand – a situation deliberately engineered by Enzo Ferrari, who was first and foremost interested in motor racing. Indeed, it wasn't until the late 1950s that sales broke the 100 cars-a-year barrier. One of the reasons for such limited market supply was that Ferrari relied upon outside coach builder Scaglietti to construct the glorious flowing panel work that graced his sporting chassis. With demand showing no

Ferrari

The F40 and (overleaf) F512M typify the shape and style of the modern Ferrari

sign of abating, Ferrari eventually took control of the specialist company.

A famous old saying about Ferraris is that buyers paid for the engine and the rest was thrown in for free. Certainly Enzo Ferrari had a love for beautiful sounding, and even sweeter performing, V6, V8 and V12 engines. Every Ferrari made became a classic – the 250 and 250 GTO (Gran Turismo Omologato), the 275 GTB and the 365 GTB Daytona being just some of the wonderful creations from the 1950 and 1960s. Ferraris were, and in the main still are, only fun for two, and it wasn't until 1960 with the launch of the specially adapted 2+2 250 GTE, that Ferrari started to cater for young families.

The advent of the little Dino in the late 1960s was a breakaway from traditional Ferrari practice. Not only did it feature a mid-mounted transverse engine (thanks to the Dino being designed for racing purposes) but was also the first ever Ferrari not

to wear the prancing horse badge. Instead, it was simply badged 'Dino' as a tribute to Enzo Ferrari's young son, who had died in his early twenties from cancer. The engine for this car also powered the Fiat Dino, which gave rise to

the rumour that the motor wasn't actually a Ferrari unit at all. However, despite lacking a prancing horse on its sleek bonnet, the beautiful little Dino was indeed a true Ferrari.

The production career of this car also coincided with the sale of Ferrari as a company. Although a successful exotic car manufacturer in the 1960s, Ferrari's true desire to compete in all major motor racing formulae without large-scale outside sponsorship was proving a big drain on the company purse – so much so that Ford moved in and tried to buy Enzo Ferrari out.

The board room battle with the American giant was successfully fended off, however, and instead spilled onto the race track. Ford launched its GT40 in an all

out assault on the Italian legend's sportscar racing crown. Following this expensive tussle, Fiat had to step in and acquire 40 per cent of Ferrari in 1969 to secure its future.

Although Fiat was now a major shareholder in Ferrari, it still kept the company as independent an entity as possible. The former's intervention came just in the nick of time as the Yom Kippur War of 1973 sparked a global oil crisis that hit the exotic car market hard. With its Fiat

connection, Ferrari was able to weather the storm far better than many of its established rivals. Under the parent company's guidance,

and with the founder allowed to concentrate fully on his cherished motor sport, car production dramatically rose. For the first time more than 1,000 cars were made in 1971 – a figure that had trebled by the

mid-1980s.

In August 1988 at the age of 90, Enzo Ferrari succumbed to deteriorating health and the car world lost one of its all time greats. As if it was preordained to mark the sad occasion, his Formula One team scored a rare one-two victory at the Italian Grand Prix at Monza a month later.

Although the founder of Ferrari has gone, his spirit has remained very much alive in the company's products of the 1990s – the F40, built to mark Enzo Ferrari's 40 years of car manufacturing; the brutal F1-based F50; the 348 tb; the four-seater Mondial t; and the F355 and 456 GT. All these cars still epitomise the beliefs of Enzo Ferrari. No other constructor can evoke such emotion amongst car lovers, or possesses such charisma and romance. The name 'Ferrari' says it all.

Ferrari

Left *The mighty F50 is based around a Grand Prix racer and is one of the fastest cars ever produced*

Right *The classic 250 LM of the mid-1960s scored a memorable victory in the 1965 Le Mans 24 hour endurance race. The car featured special rear bodywork to improve aerodynamics*

Over *The beautiful Dino was not badged as a Ferrari but sole named in honour of Enzo's son, who died tragically young due to cancer.*

FIAT

ONE OF EUROPE'S largest industrial companies, Fiat is still a family business, run by Gianni Agnelli, a direct descendant of the founder Giovanni. Fiat stands for Fabbrica Italiana Automobili Torino. Today it also owns Ferrari, Lancia and Alfa Romeo, some of the most important names in the history of motoring.

One of the founders of the car industry, dating back to 1899, Fiat certainly made its mark in the early days of motoring, being involved in racing and rallies of all kinds and winning some spectacular successes. During the 1950s and 1960s it produced a range of thoroughly delightful cars, high both on style and performance, not least being the Ferrari-powered Dino and Spider. Not to be confused with the far more exotic

– and somewhat more expensive – Ferrari Dino, the Fiat of the same name is one of the most elegant cars ever built by the Turin-based company. The Fiat Dino came about because Ferrari – at the time an independent company – needed a V6 engine in ordinary production road-going cars in order to qualify for certain race categories.

Ferrari asked Fiat to make one and the company seized on this opportunity to make their own Dino sportscar using this engine. Such was the success of the Fiat Dino that nearly 4,000 were built between 1966 and 1973. The double overhead-cam engine had a capacity of 2418cc which gave it a top speed of 130 mph and magnificent acceleration too.

Originally there was a short-wheelbase Spider (convertible) version designed by Pininfarina, soon followed by a longer, very elegant four-seater coupe by

Bertone. All are desirable classics.

The 124 Spider was another hit from Fiat. Shrewdly, the company took many of the parts already used in their much more mundane but very popular 124 and 125 saloon models of the 1960s. This meant the Spider was cheap to make and yet it had head-turning style and proved incredibly popular with buyers. Built firstly in Turin, and then by specialist body-builder Pininfarina between 1966 and 1986, the Spider used a variety of different engines, including a twin-cam 1.4-litre, 1.6, 1.8 and 2.0-litre. Unfortunately for UK buyers, this model was not sold in Britain. Fiat decided not to because of the cost of conversion to right-hand drive. It did sell well in the USA however, over 6,000 miles away.

A true global automotive giant with interests in all sectors of the industry – and beyond, Fiat bought

Fiat

A car industry giant, Fiat were revitalized during the 1990s, producing cars full of flair

Ferrari and Lancia in 1969, and two years latter acquired the Italian tuning wizard Abarth.

Fiat's more recent history is mixed. It produced the cracking X19 sportscar in 1972 plus one of the very first superminis, the 127. But, by the end of the decade, Fiat was starting to lose its way, producing mundane machinery like the Strada and the 131. However, the 1990s saw Fiat bounce back with a vengeance. The Coupe, Brava, Cinquecento (pictured above), Bravo and the Barchetta all look wonderful and perform brilliantly, taking Fiat back to the cutting edge of auto design.

Legendary Marque

FORD

Model T *The car which set Ford on the road to international success*

IF MR AND MRS FORD had had their way, young Henry would have taken over the family farm, but their son was fascinated by the idea of producing cheap, reliable, cars for the masses. Instead of farming, he moved to Detroit and built his inventions in a small garage behind his modest suburban house. The first 'Ford' was the Quadricycle of 1896.

Putting his $5,000 life savings

Ka

Billed as one of Ford's most radical designs and its first mini car

into the Detroit Automobile Company just before the turn of the century proved a false start for Ford. He was soon bought out and the company name changed to Cadillac. Undeterred, Ford was on the road again by 1903, forming the Ford Motor Company. He followed this up a short while later by becoming the fastest man on earth when he set a new land speed record of just over 91 mph behind the wheel of his '999' car.

Ford is best known, however, for his desire to produce transport for all. This fixation for a cheap car led to the Model T, which took the world by storm through the production of a million vehicles in just 16 months. It was the sheer success of the 'Tin Lizzie' which

caused Ford to devise the modern factory production line.

The 'T' was produced between 1908 and 1927 and was almost reluctantly replaced by Ford with the more sophisticated Model A.

In 1911 Ford came to Britain to produce its cars, following Percival Perry's successful establishment of the first Ford sales organisation in the UK eight years earlier. Ford rapidly expanded outside the

American continent after World War I and by 1925 had set up bases in Germany and Australia, as well as establishing the huge East London plant on the banks of the Thames at Dagenham. Throughout the 1930s Ford's famous flat-head V8 underpinned the company's fortunes in the States, but in the UK it was the introduction of the Model Y Popular which cemented its success. Billed as the country's first

£100 car, it took over from the 'T' as the definitive cheap family vehicle and gave rise to the highly successful Anglia, which in turn made way for the Escort in 1968.

During World War II, Ford turned its might to producing military hardware, while the company faced its own crisis when company head, Edsel Ford, died prematurely. This forced its 80-year-old founder out of retirement – a move resented by many – until his grandson, Henry II, took over at the ripe old age of 28.

In 1947 Henry Ford died. That same year Ford-France was founded, but its Vedette car came at the wrong time as the country was looking for economy rather than luxury vehicles and Ford quickly sold the plant off to Simca in 1954. American influence on its European product increased with the launch of the Consul, Zephyr and Zodiac in 1950, while in the US models like the Galaxie, Fairlane and the immortal Thunderbird kept the company a best seller.

Then in 1957 disaster struck in the ungainly shape of the Edsel. The car was the brainchild of Henry II who, tired of seeing the vast choice of upmarket cars offered by arch rival General Motors, assembled an entirely new marque within Ford to cater for the prestige buyer, even though it already produced the Lincoln and Mercury range. However, Edsel was an unmitigated flop, with the entire range being dropped just after its second birthday at the cost of more than $300 million to Ford – a huge sum even today. Its looks were its downfall, compounded by the timing of its launch at the end of the 1950s. US buyers' tastes were changing with the coming of a new decade.

Meanwhile, in Europe more co-operation between Ford's German and British companies was demanded for future cars; the first joint venture was actually the eternal Transit van launched in 1965. Three years earlier one of Europe's most significant cars had been launched in the shape of the Cortina. This vehicle was not simply just another model range but a car which introduced a completely new market sector as it bridged the gap between small and large family saloons. The Cortina is credited with being the first modern car designed using aircraft stress calculation methods to retain strength but reduce weight. The job of styling the Cortina fell to Roy Brown, who had also been responsible for the later Edsel models. Thankfully the Cortina looked far more appealing. The vehicle's name came from the venue of the 1956 Winter Olympics, and soon became synonymous with the British family and company car markets. It remained a best-seller right up to 1982 when it was finally replaced by the Sierra. With the release of the latter, a mini-Edsel crisis seemed to be in the offing as conservative British buyers didn't take kindly to the vehicle's aerodynamically-optimised 'jelly mould' shape nor its odd name – the Sierra took a while to find favour.

Ford

The GT40 was built as a result of Ford failing to buy Ferrari

On the other side of the Atlantic no such problems had faced the Mustang when it was unveiled in 1964, the car becoming both a cult classic and a fashion icon. A simply-designed, yet stylish fastback or drophead based on the Fairlane saloon (but with a multitude of options), the Mustang took the young US car enthusiast by storm. When the car was originally launched Ford had predicted selling 100,000 in its first year – it did so in just four months. In 1966 Mustang sales passed the million mark.

That same formula was adopted in Europe some three years later when 'The car you've always promised yourself' appeared in the shape of the Capri – it also started a similar fashion trend. The Capri also became one of the few European cars of its era to

Fairlane *This average family car also provided the backbone for the colt Ford Mustang*

find favour with American drivers, remaining in production for nearly 20 years. It did much to put Ford firmly on the map in the international motor racing world, together with the far more specialised GT40. This came about after Henry Ford II tried unsuccessfully to buy the cash-strapped Ferrari concern in the early 1960s, in an attempt to bolster the prestige of the Ford marque in Europe and also give it the edge in world motorsport. As a result of Ferrari's defiance, Ford went and built its own world beater in the low-slung shape of the GT40 – its name reflected the height of the car in inches.

The 1970s saw the parent company introduce its line of compact cars to fend off the increasing spread of foreign imports, with the Maverick and Pinto ranges flying the Ford flag in this market sector. A further reaction to the oil crisis of 1973 was the re-release of the Mustang in its Mk II guise. Sadly, the car was a mere shadow of its former self through a combination of downsized engines and woeful suspension set-ups. It is only in the last decade that the Mustang name has regained some respect through a thorough overhaul of the car.

During the 1970s, Ford acquired specialist car-maker De Tomaso and the prestigious Ghia and Vingle styling companies.

Ford 'caught a cold' when it bought Jaguar in 1989 after a battle of bank balances and egos with General Motors and the company reported heavy losses as a result.

However, it still had enough in the coffers to purchase that other great British institution, Aston Martin, in 1991, thus saving it from extinction.

After wide collaboration in Europe, Ford started to look towards producing a truly world car for the 1990s. Specially-adapted variants of the front-wheel-drive European Ford Escort started the trend but it was only partly successful. The answer lay in designing a global car that differed only in details. Ford came up with the Mondeo, first instigated in 1985 – eight full years before its European launch.

The Mk 5 Escort introduced in 1990 was ill-timed and Ford of Europe found out the hard way since the Mk III of a decade earlier. It cost a lot of money to revamp both the Escort and Fiesta ranges to bring them up to the best European small-car standards.

Thirty-seven years after decreeing it wouldn't produce a rival to the Mini because of profit margins, Ford ventured into the mini-car sector with its Ka, based on the Fiesta but even smaller. Then again, no global market would be complete without Ford.

Ford

Top *The Model T was not only a car for the masses but also instigated mass production techniques.*

Right *The mighty Thunderbird, an American classic*

Frazer-Nash *Much respected specialist sportscar maker which is still involved in manufacturing engineering*

GILBERN

FRAZER-NASH

CAPTAIN A. FRAZER-NASH has an important place in motoring history. He was the genius who opened the doors of one of Britain's most famous car-making companies in 1924. Frazer-Nash started out by making quite traditional family cars with a shaft-drive system and simple water-cooled, four-cylinder engines.

Before long Frazer-Nash started building the sporting cars which were to make the company's name.

In the early days of Frazer-Nash the cars were named by their engines, and the Plus Power, a big seller in the mid-1920s, was no exception. It featured a dog-clutch gear change, separate chains for the three forward speeds, a solid rear axle and high-ratio steering. This car was popular with enthusiasts because of its good performance.

The Anzani Sports used the well-known single-valve, water-cooled, four-cylinder 1.5-litre Anzani unit which initially produced 40 bhp. The secret of this car's huge success was a combination of a simple design with a strong chassis which was also quite light. The price was right too. Such was the success of these early machines that Frazer-Nash was being compared with Aston Martin, and increasingly being seen as Britain's answer to imported sportscars like the renowned Italian Bugatti. The Sports proved so popular it remained in the catalogue for 15 years.

From 1934 Frazer-Nash also offered a 1.5-litre single overhead-cam engine known as the Gough, after its designer. This engine was also available supercharged in either the Shelsley or TT Replica chassis. The model names referred to the chassis and these could be fitted with any engine.

In 1934 Frazer-Nash linked up with BMW to provide the BMW Type 319 engine in the Frazer-Nash chassis. After the Second World War Frazer-Nash took the pre-war BMW Type 328 engine, modified it, and placed it in the High Speed Model. In 1948 the High Speed Model was developed into the Le Mans Replica.

In 1954 Frazer-Nash launched the beautiful Sebring 2.0-litre two-seater sportscar. Not long after this it bought the BMW 2.6-litre V8 engine which was eased into the Competition, and a new two-seater coupe, the Continental.

By 1957 this unit had proved so popular with buyers that it was the only one on offer to Frazer-Nash customers. Unfortunately Frazer-Nash then suffered the fate of many a British company of this era – it went bankrupt and an illustrious motoring chapter closed. However, Frazer-Nash is still involved in the engineering industry, and its cars highly sought-after classics.

IN THE EARLY 1960s there was a thriving Welsh motor company called Gilbern which was very successful for a time. Today it's called niche-marketing, back then it was simply the company's ability to spot a gap in the market.

Gilbern's first offering, in 1959, was the GT four-seater. There were no less than three engines on offer at first, a Coventry-Climax 1098cc or an MGA unit. By 1962 the MG engine was standard. From 1963 the slightly bigger MGB 1.8 litre was used. All of this was clothed in a glass-fibre body and the build quality was very good. Such was the success of the GT that Gilbern was soon able to launch a second car, the sporting Genie.

The Genie appeared in 1966 and was basically a larger version of the GT coupe, with bigger and more potent engines. These were Ford V6 units of either 2495cc or 2994cc capacity. The chassis remained a BMC unit which was further developed by Gilbern. The Genie was one of the most popular of Gilbern's cars, despite quite a high asking price, simply because it not only performed well but it also looked good, and again, quality was very impressive.

Three years later, though, Gilbern felt they needed a new car on the block and they launched the Invader. Power was once again courtesy of Ford, using the same strong Ford V6 seen in the Genie, but with a number of improvements to increase performance and keep fuel consumption at a reasonable level. Again, the Invader was very successful and well built. In 1971 this sales success prompted the company to launch the Mark II model. The significant point about this development was that the Invader was also available as a sporting estate. Ironically, this is when the problems began.

It seemed Gilbern was on to a winner, and with sales increasing steadily, decided to expand its operation by moving into new, bigger premises geared for increased production.

Sadly, this was a mistake. The Mark III version of the Invader was launched in 1972. It featured a number of significant improvements, including a stronger box section frame, Ford Cortina front suspension and, from Germany, a Ford Taunus rear axle. A 3.9-litre version of the lusty Ford V6 engine, as used in the Capri, developing 140 bhp was fitted. It should all have gone according to plan. The car was good, the build quality was good – but the buyers were not there.

Gilberns had become rather too costly, the company asking several thousand pounds more for one of its cars than similar competitors. By the mid 1970s the receiver had been called in. Another enthusiastic and innovative car-maker had closed its doors. Gilbern had deserved better.

GINETTA

GINETTA IS one of the rare specialist car-makers which, since its inception in 1958, has remained not only solvent but also independent.

The company was started by the enthusiastic Walklett brothers, Trevor, Bob, Ivor and Douglas, and based in Essex before moving with new owners to Scunthorpe in 1989. Later they moved on to Sheffield and also Sweden. Early Ginettas were best known for their successes on the race tracks using proprietary components from various car-makers.

Ginetta started to concentrate on specialist glassfibre-bodied road cars, initially powered by Hillman Imp and Sunbeam Rapier engines

with the G15 coupe (1967-74) and the G21 respectively. The 2+2 G21 was launched in 1971 and production ran for seven years with a total of 150 being built. A much more powerful 3.0-litre model was produced using a Ford V6 engine and a superior chassis but its high production cost resulted in limited demand.

The G32 was the first car to come out of the company's change of ownership, using Fiesta XR2 power with a short-lived open-top version appearing a year later.

The 1990s saw Ginetta face its bleakest times, even spending a short period in receivership. But Ginetta rose from the ashes with its monster Rover V8-powered, 4.0-litre G33, which spawned the G34 that was fitted with a Volvo turbo.

Ginetta is now thriving. With its Ford Zetec-engined G27 and development of new mid-engined successor to the G32 under way, the company even went as far as launching its own one-make racing series in 1996 for its G27 – taking Ginetta firmly back to its roots and winning ways.

GKN

Better known for its engineering excellence, automotive component company GKN decided in the 1970s to develop a high-tech sportscar to act both as a test bed and flagship for the firm. It was really a Jensen in disguise, for at the heart of the FFF100 was a 7.0-litre, 600 bhp Chrysler V8 engine, mated to four-wheel-drive running gear from the 1960s supercar, the Jensen FF, and finished off with Maxaret anti-lock brakes. It was all very advanced for its time and the GKN car had blistering performance, capable of blasting to 100mph from rest in just 6.5 seconds – as quick as a contemporary Grand Prix car! The FFF100 was launched in 1972 and enjoyed considerable press coverage – as intended – but never materialised as a production car.

Gilbern

The Invader, one of Gilbern's best

GENERAL MOTORS

"WHAT'S GOOD FOR General Motors is good for the USA", so said GM President Charlie Wilson in the early 1950s, and most people would still agree with that. Today GM is the world's biggest company, let alone biggest car-maker (though Japan's Toyota is snapping at the General's heels).

The automotive giant produces an incredibly wide range of diverse cars under various brand names. Just such diversity was claimed by analysts to be one of the reasons why the mighty giant nearly crashed to its knees in 1992-93 with staggering losses. By 1993 GM had an enormous deficit of $18 billion. Shareholders obviously wanted to know why and in 1992 they ousted the company's leaders and replaced them with their own chosen people.

Today GM has turned the corner and once more its divisions worldwide are making money. Ironically they partly have the Japanese to thank for this because the ballistic rise of the yen against the dollar made Japanese cars very expensive. American buyers began to turn once again to home-grown products. Hand-in-hand with this came a new kind of quality at General Motors, and this too tempted buyers back into the fold.

When GM began life Americans needed little tempting to turn to the General's products. General Motors was founded by William C. Durant, more commonly known as Billy, who soon took Buick into the growing company. Durant was later ousted from the company and set up Chevrolet which he used as a weapon to fight himself back into control at GM. He succeeded and Chevrolet became another name in the GM list.

Today General Motors owns Vauxhall in Britain, Opel in Germany, had brief ownership of Lotus sportscars in Britain, a recent tie-up with Saab in Sweden (the latest 900 is based on the Vauxhall Cavalier) and Holden in Australia. It also has a large interest and stock-holding in Izusu, one of Japan's largest industrial groups. In its native USA, GM is once again the top producing car company, investing more money in research and development than any other American company.

GORDON-KEEBLE

THERE HAS TO BE something special going on when a car-maker who is only in production for seven years becomes one of the great names of British motoring. And so there was. Gordon-Keeble only built two car ranges between 1960 and 1967 but they made an indelible mark on the world motoring scene.

The secret of Gordon-Keeble's success can be seen in the shape of the GT coupe. This potent little machine had a fibre-glass body designed and built by Williams and Pritchard and was home to a beast of an engine, the American Chevrolet 5.4-litre unit. This mating of a large and lusty engine with a light body ensured the car had terrific performance, and this was at a time when buyers could buy inexpensive fuel and there were no worries about escalating oil prices.

A good number of these cars were made and proved to be immensely popular with buyers. Unfortunately, as happened to so many British companies of this era, the sales were not sufficient to save Gordon-Keeble from financial ruin in 1965. By this time only 93 cars had been made – but this was not to be the end of the story.

A company like this would not go quietly. Two months later, after frantic negotiations, the Gordon-Keeble was revived by a knight in shining armour in the form of London motor dealer Harold Smith. He wasted no time in re-opening the company and that meant they could unveil the 300 bhp GK1. Once again, this was a much-sought after car offering terrific performance, superb handling and brutish good looks too. The trouble was the small production run was not sufficient to keep money flowing into the company as overheads escalated. Harold Smith found that he too could not keep the concern going. In 1968 Gordon-Keeble closed its doors finally and the motoring world lost one of its most promising talents.

Gordon-Keeble *A great but short-lived company with a talent for innovative car making*

HEALEY

DONALD HEALEY was a busy man during the 1950s and 1960s, producing a whole range of sporting cars. Many of these were for Austin where they bore both his name and that of the British company. Healey also had his own car-making concern in Warwick,

England, from 1946 to 1954, and he later worked for Jensen Cars too.

Healey opened the doors of his factory in 1946. The first car he produced used a Riley engine of 2.4 litres in four-cylinder, overhead-valve form. He mated the engine with a separate chassis and at the time of its launch it was the world's fastest production saloon. Only a few were made until 1954 but several versions were produced. These included the two-seater Silverstone sportscar, as well as some bigger saloons and a number of convertibles, the latter being produced hand-in-hand with coachbuilders Tickford, who later worked with Aston Martin. Nash also got involved in the series,

producing a similar car but with Nash's own 3.8-litre, overhead-valve, six-cylinder engine. The Nash model was destined for overseas markets where it sold just over 500 cars, but another version was made for the UK, this time with a 3.0-litre engine from Alvis. The last Nash-Healeys were made in 1954, after which Healey became involved with Austin in a big way, making the Austin-Healey sportscar which proved such a major success. The Austin-Healey's, including the charming little Sprite, typified British sportscars of that era. The Healey 3000, with its muscular looks and performance, was a success both on the road and in competition.

Healey

One of the great British motoring names, Healey may return as a result of BMW's takeover of Rover

HEINKEL

LONDONERS AROUND during World War II will remember the German company Heinkel. Their planes were among the scores of German Luftwaffe bombers that visited the capital and dropped their deadly loads. After the War, Heinkel turned its hand to the rather more peaceful operation of car-making, using their technical

expertise and knowledge to design a range of vehicles which appealed to post-war Germans who were generally short of money.

Initially Heinkel concentrated on two-wheel scooters and static engines. It wasn't until 10 years after the cessation of hostilities, in 1955, that Heinkel presented their first real car, a rear-engined bubble-car with two front wheels and one at the rear. This gave it superb manoeuvrability but not a lot of interior room. The driver opened a wide door at the front of the machine and climbed in. The engine for this small car was a single-cylinder, four stroke design which was air cooled and had a capacity of 175cc. There was another version which gained an extra rear wheel and a bigger engine based on the same air-cooled format, this time of 198cc. Heinkel disappeared from the motoring map in 1958 when the company was sold to an Irish

company, Dundalk Engineering. Dundalk continued to make the four-wheeler for some years before selling the design rights to Trojan in England who marketed the car under its own name.

HILLMAN

HILLMAN IS ONE of those British companies which was eventually swallowed up by bigger groups, in this case firstly by Rootes in 1926, itself later taken over by Chrysler, which gulped down the group, name and all. During the glory days in the late 1950s and early 1960s this British company produced some worthy, dependable machines before it died a rather unceremonious death.

William Hillman was a cycle-maker and in 1907 started to produce good, if ordinary cars. One of the most interesting was the Hillman Minx Convertible which

was altogether more beguiling than the staid Minx saloon. Like all other Minxs, the Convertible had a charm all of its own with a comfortable and well-trimmed interior, and a decent level of equipment. These were attributes common to all Hillmans of this era. Built in Coventry between 1956 and 1962, some 500,000 Minxs of all types were produced, though few of these were convertibles. The car may have been a straight-ahead piece of Rootes engineering but the bodies for the Minx convertible were actually made by Thrupp and Maberly.

The engine was a simple four-cylinder – various power units were used over the Minx's life. There were also Manumatic and Easidrive automatic transmissions, however, it must be said, they were rather unreliable.

By 1963 the company was after a more modern image and they achieved it with the launch of the

> ## Hispano-Suiza
>
> *True car lovers will know this company for its innovative yet classic-looking designs, forward thinking and superb craftsmanship*

Imp, one of Britain's all-time great designs. It continued to be built until 1976. As radical as the Mini ever was and perhaps more in tune with modern times, the Imp was however, a commercial disaster.

Looking back experts say the Imps were not as popular in their day as they should have been, due mostly to a lack of on-going development of the original idea. When production ceased only 440,000 had been built.

Hillman would never be so bold again, preferring to go back to what it knew best, producing rather predictable, conventional cars like the 1970s Avenger and the Arrow range of Minxs and Hunters. By 1976 the Hillman name was replaced by the parent company Chrysler's badge which in turn was replaced by Talbot, before Peugeot took control.

Now French Peugeots are built at the old factories and proving a real sales success.

HISPANO SUIZA

THIS SPANISH COMPANY – though it also opened a factory in France – not only produced some of the most beautiful cars of all time but thanks to Hispano's boss, Swiss designer Mark Birkigt, the company also produced many motoring innovations which are still with us today. Companies like Rolls-Royce have regularly used Hispano inventions to improve their own cars, which must be the ultimate in compliments.

Hispano Suiza originally designed and made aero engines, hence the stork emblem which adorned these Spanish cars. In their heyday – the cars were built in Spain between 1904 and 1938 and in France between 1911 and 1938 – they quickly became a by-word for all that was excellent in automotive design.

In the early 1920s, Hispano Suiza was up there with the best of them, competing directly with the big names like Alfa Romeo, Mercedes, Fiat and Peugeot, and took part in many gruelling pan-European races.

In 1924 Andre Dubonnet, heir to the family fortune made from the famous drink which bear's his family's name, drove a Hispano Suiza Tulip Wood (so named because the gleaming body of the car was quite literally made out of tulip wood) against the top teams in Europe. He participated in the annual Targo Florio, one of the most torturous races in Europe. Despite lacking the large and well-resourced back-up teams of his rivals, Dubonnet showed the Hispano's power and performance when he came in a worthy sixth.

In fact, as was common at this time, the bodies were made not by Hispano but by specialist coachbuilders.

Nieuport were one of Hispano's chief suppliers and produced a large range of delectably beautiful bodies which were both aerodynamic and roomy.

The engines were Hispano units, typically straight six-cylinder units of overhead camshaft design with alloy pistons. The wooden-bodied versions were made using aircraft technology, clearly something Hispano could identify with, by using a wooden ribbed frame and then coating it with several layers of wood veneer which was then attached to the ribs by thousands of aluminium rivets. The whole ensemble was then sealed and veneered again to give an ultra-smooth and relatively light finish.

Today any Hispano, wooden or steel, is much sought after and, of course, they are very, very rare. It is well worth the trip to see one (most are in US auto museums), because they represent the pinnacle of the motor craftsman's art.

HOLDEN

THE AUSTRALIAN ARM of the mighty General Motors, Holden produces its own range of cars, but they are based on GM products sold elsewhere in the world. Based in Melbourne, Holden produced its own cars from 1948. Before that, in the 1920s, the company made its own bodies which were fitted to British-made Morris cars. By the early 1930s, and under GM ownership, Holden was an assembly plant, putting together British and American GM cars.

After World War II Holden offered what it called "Australia's own car" but this was not strictly an individual effort, rather a Buick design which strangely enough did not go into production in the USA itself. This was officially called the model FX and came with a 2.2-litre, four-cylinder engine linked to a three-speed gearbox. Australian content was over 90 per cent and the strong body and tough mechanicals ensured good sales – at the height of its success the FX accounted for no less than 50 per cent of all Australian car sales. This car survived until 1956 when the FE was launched. This was a bigger car – able to seat six – and used a 2.3-litre engine. The FE was replaced in 1964 by the Premier series with 2.9-litre engines, and the Standard and Special which had a 2.4-litre engine. The Torana appeared in 1969 and was loosely based on the British Vauxhall Viva. From 1974 there was the LH which could be specified with a big V8 engine. Later models included the Gemini, Sunbird, Starfire, Monaro sports coupe and Commodore.

HONDA

Often referred to as the BMW of the East, Honda has an interesting past and many believe it is likely to have an interesting future too. Honda's medium saloon, the

Holden *The Australian division of General Motors*

Accord, was top of the American new car charts for seven years. The selling points for this most cultured of Japanese cars are that build quality is second to none, reliability is among the very best and the cars have not suffered from the traditional Japanese weakness of failing to offer European buyers European-looking cars.

Many in Europe will be more familiar with Honda as the company which teamed up with Rover Group in the UK, helping the British company which was at the time ailing, turn an important corner. This arrangement produced the Triumph Acclaim, which was

Honda

One of Japan's most technologically advanced car makers, Honda is also successful in Grand Prix racing

a Honda with a Triumph badge on it, the first Rover 200-series, which was a Honda with a Rover badge on it, and the Rover 800, which again is based upon the Honda Legend, its flagship model.

All good things must come to an end – and the parting of Honda and Rover was not very pleasant. When BMW came up with the money to buy the Rover Group, which by this time had developed into a very enterprising and successful company, Honda was unceremoniously left out in the cold, much to the annoyance of the normally retiring Japanese management.

Be that as it may, Honda do not have too much to worry about. It has for some years now been building the Accord estate in the USA from whence they are shipped to Europe. Honda has been especially good at this policy of

expansion outside Japan. It allows them to circumvent import restrictions on Japanese cars and has given them unfettered access to both the European and North American markets – the two biggest markets in the world.

Honda's origins can be traced back to 1962, when this motorcycle-maker turned its hands to cars, first with mini designs such as the S500. The 1973 Civic marked the real turning point. A front-wheel-drive supermini, it surprised the motoring world with its all-round ability – something which was to become a company hallmark.

Today Honda offers the latest version of its Civic in hatchback, saloon and coupe form with a choice of 1.4, 1.5 and 1.6-litre engines, the sporty CRX, the Accord which is virtually identical to Rover's 600, the executive Legend with a V6 engine, the

sporty Prelude and the creme-de-la-creme, the NSX, with a Formula One based power unit, looks and goes like a Ferrari, but without the bills or the reliability fears.

HOTCHKISS

THE AMERICAN Benjamin Berkeley Hotchkiss had a factory in St. Denis, France, where he made military arms from 1867. Business was tapering off and so Hotchkiss decided, as did many industrialists of this period, to start making cars. From 1903 the first Hotchkiss appeared with a choice of either 4.6 or 7.4-litre engines and by 1906 there were no less than five different models on offer, including a 4.2-litre saloon in four- and a six-cylinder form. Just before World War I, Hotchkiss had effectively established itself as a serious auto manufacturer, producing a whole range of cars including the AB with 3.7-litre engine, the 4.7-litre X6 and 5.5-litre AC6, the 2.6-litre AG, 4.0-litre AF and the six-cylinder AC6.

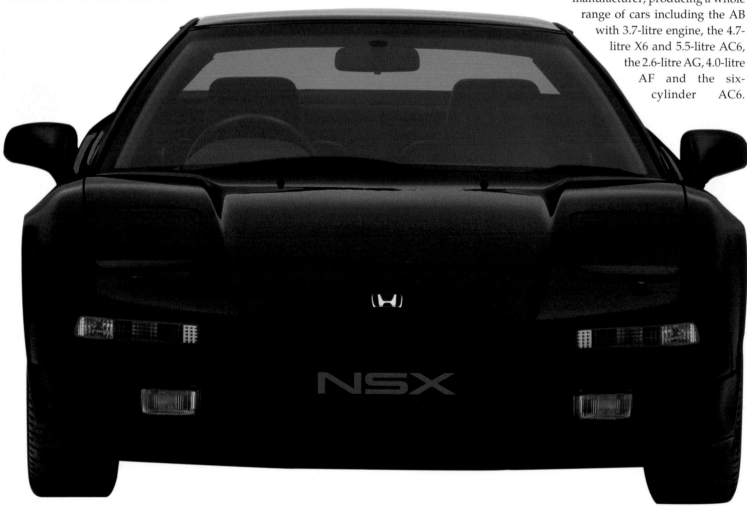

After the war, the 2.4-litre 12CV AM appeared. This proved to be a very popular car right through the 1920s and only left the brochure in 1932. Right up to World War II, Hotchkiss continued to produce some interesting cars which were very much sought-after.

Unfortunately the war brought the nail in Hotchkiss's coffin. The company never relived its pre-war glory days, its cars failed to capture the public's attention any more and it staggered from one financial crisis to another. By 1952 the company had closed its doors; it was only a rescue package from fellow French car-maker Delahaye that saved the Hotchkiss name. Unfortunately, Hotchkiss only continued with truck production.

HUMBER

THOMAS HUMBER made bicycles and a very lucrative business it was too. After all, how else did people get around at the turn of the century? This was exactly the question forward-thinking Thomas asked himself. And then, on a trip to Germany, he saw one of the first Mercedes models. He came back, enlisted the support of business colleagues, and soon he had set up the Humber Car Company.

The Humberette was Britain's first popular light car; it sold well, at the right price, and lasted for years. It used a De Dion engine of 613cc, though by 1904 this had been increased. At this time there were two Humber factories, one in Coventry, the other in Beeston. Both built the same car but the Beeston-built models were slightly more expensive. Not too surprisingly, financial problems led to the closure of the Beeston factory in 1905.

After World War I Humber started to build a range of side-valve engined cars. It created a whole collection of popular family cars but this was not enough to stop

Hotchkiss *A grand old marque that was consigned to producing commercial vehicles by the 1950s*

a take-over by the Rootes Group in 1929 and a fresh injection of capital. The first cars produced by the new owners were the 2.1-litre 16/50 and the 3.5-litre Snipe and its long chassis brother, the Pullman. By 1939 there was the Super Snipe, a compact saloon which saw the large 4.1-litre six-cylinder engine placed in a smaller chassis.

When World War II was over,

Humber resumed production and, like their competitors, post-war austerity meant the same old cars but with new bodies.

There was one newcomer, the 1.9-litre side-valve Hawk based on Hillman's Fourteen of 1938-40.

By 1964, the year Chrysler bought out the Rootes Group, the Sceptre was launched. Humber was another of those once proud

British companies which now saw its badges on the bonnets of a range of cars, many of which were not Humbers at all. The Sceptre was just such a car, based on the Hillman Super Minx but with overdrive as standard. From 1968 the only Humber was the 1725cc Sceptre, a prestige edition of the Hillman Hunter. In its final 1976 form it had twin carburettors, 82 bhp and a choice of automatic or a four-speed manual gearbox with overdrive, plus a classy estate, a popular theme today. Like Sunbeam, Humber disappeared in the 1970s as American giant Chrysler tried in vain to stop the slump. The end of Humber prefigured the end of the British car industry in general in the 1970s.

HYUNDAI

HYUNDAI IS A South Korean company which has quickly established a niche in Britain and in the United States. When the company first came to the international market the marque was no match for sophisticated European hardware. Its cars were based on old-fashioned Mitsubishi engines and transmissions, with a dated rear-wheel-drive format. Within a decade, however, Hyundai has been able to produce some very impressive cars that are competitively priced, with an enviable reputation for high equipment levels and long-term reliability. They are becoming a force to be reckoned with.

However, buyers of Hyundais face the same problem today as buyers of Japanese cars face – the regular and complete model changes. The names may remain but every three years or so a completely new model will come out, lowering the value of previously prized specimens. However, South Korean cars do tend to be revolutionary – the new model will be a quantum leap ahead of the old one.

The Pony was Hyundai's and

> ### Hyundai
>
> *Korea's largest car maker has come a long way since the Pony*

Korea's first car, originally shown at the 1974 motor show circuits. Their cars have improved in both style and quality since then.

The Pony, although rather staid and conventional, was the perfect springboard for future success. In just over 20 years since its launch, Hyundai now offers the Accent in Europe, the first car from this company that is Hyundai's own design – it does not owe anything substantial to Mitsubishi. Available in four-door saloon and five-door hatchback form, the Accent is Hyundai's best-selling car.

The new Lantra is another in-house design that has surprised many with its quality, especially the striking Coupe (below).

Top of the Hyundai range is the Sonata, a large executive car which uses Mitsubishi V6 power. Like the company which produces it, the Sonata is a surprisingly capable car and one which rivals are taking very seriously.

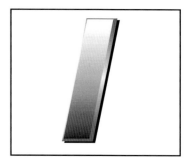

INNOCENTI

BASED IN MILAN, Italy, Innocenti is perhaps best known for making the Lambretta scooter. They have always, however, had a thriving car business too. Born in 1961, and still going strong today, Innocenti bases all its cars on those made by other manufacturers, either using the base units of other cars and grafting new bodies on, or making best-selling cars under licence. The company has strong links with the British motor industry – their first car was the Austin A40, built under licence, from 1961. In the same

ISO *Bubble car maker turned supercar specialist who couldn't survive the depressed 1970s*

line-up Innocenti also made a Ghia-bodied Austin-Healey Sprite.

By 1963 Innocenti were offering a model called IM3 which was actually the Morris 1100 but with servo-assisted brakes, a smarter looking front end and a relatively powerful 58 bhp engine. Two years later they unveiled the J4 which again was a modified Austin 1100.

The big news came with the launch of Innocenti's version of the Mini which proved to be one of the Italian company's top-selling cars. Innocenti even launched their version of the Mini Traveller, and both these Mini models sold exceptionally well in Italy. Such was the success of the company that in 1972 the then British Leyland, forerunner of Rover Group, bought the company. As with many such mergers of the time, this resulted in some bizarre cars, including an Innocenti version of the Austin Allegro, the Regent.

Thankfully the Mini design continued and in 1975 Innocenti produced a three-door hatchback version. By December, BMC had decided not to continue ownership

of the Italian company and closed the factory. A heroic saviour in the shape of De Tomaso rescued the company and they began making Bertone-styled Minis, the BMC versions being dropped.

ISO

ISO IS AN Italian company that have provided some of the best sporting cars ever made. ISOs were built between 1962 to 1979 and at the time were often seen as an attractive and affordable alternative to other Italian sportscars. The ISO may not have had the cachet of Ferrari or Maserati but they could often perform just as well and many looked just as good too.

ISO started from small beginnings – quite literally. The name stems from Isetta who were best known during the early 1950s for making economical 'bubble' cars. These were even considered good enough for BMW to build under licence.

The first performance ISO to

see the light of day was the Rivolta which coupled Italian design flair with tough old American mechanicals, in this case an overhead-valve, V8 Chevrolet Corvette engine. With a capacity of 5.4-litres and producing 260 bhp this was clearly no slouch. The body was designed by top Italian automotive artist Bizzarrini and the car had all-wheel disc brakes (in-board at the rear), coil and wishbone independent front suspension, a De Dion rear axle coupled with a limited-slip differential, and centre-lock wire wheels. The gearbox was a four speeder, though automatic was optional from 1966. The Rivolta was a real ball of fire, easily able to reach 142 mph, the sort of performance that is normal for supercars today but which was quite outstanding 30 years ago. Not only did the Rivolta go well, the bellowing exhaust note sounded terrific too.

Surprisingly, ISO were not content with such performance and so the company designed something new, the Grifo, which

was even faster. It reached a top speed of 162 mph in its 410 bhp form. This two-seater convertible first emerged in 1963 and originally it was available with a 365 bhp version of the Chevrolet V8. Essentially the Grifo was a version of the Rivolta but placed on a shorter chassis which gave it even better handling. In its final form the engine was up-rated again, this time by using a Ford engine of 7.0-litres. This car was clearly one of the most alluring ISOs and even today buyers try to track them down, such is their enduring appeal.

The Fidia was a four-door saloon, launched in 1968, with coachwork by Ghia. The following year ISO brought out another saloon, the Lele, which was a direct descendant of the Rivolta. Perhaps ISO made a mistake turning from out-and-out racers to slightly more staid saloon cars. It's certainly a path not often resulting in success for other sportscar-makers. The company found it was just not making enough money and in 1975 bankruptcy forced its closure.

ISUZU

THE JAPANESE company Isuzu was initially better known for making trucks. Its car-making started when they began building Wolsleys in conjunction with the Tokyo Gas and Electric company in the late 1930s before moving on to Hillmans during the 1950s.

The Japanese car industry started to blossom in the 1970s and the giant American corporation General Motors, looking for a foothold in the lucrative Asian markets, bought just over a third of the growing company.

Unlike its some of its home-spun rivals, Isuzus were traditionally more advanced in design, with twin-camshaft engines and Ghia bodywork found on some models.

It was not until 1985, however,

that the brand became known to the UK with the introduction of the stylish Piazza Turbo Coupe.

First shown as a design exercise by leading stylist Giugiaro, it became a production car in 1981. With a 150 bhp, 2.0-litre turbo engine, the car certainly had speed, but the Vauxhall-sourced suspension was easily taxed.

It required the expertise of Lotus to refine the package, turning it into the car that was originally intended. However, the Piazza's life in the UK was short-lived and

it was discontinued in 1990, by which time Isuzu had tilted itself towards the flourishing four-wheel-drive off-road market with its sturdy Trooper 4x4.

Increasing influence and cash from General Motors saw moves to re-badge the Trooper as a Vauxhall or Opel for the European market. This resulted in a messy inter-company fight.

Of course, General Motors got its way and Vauxhall introduced the Monterey, a more upmarket Trooper clone, for the UK market.

Despite this, owner loyalty to Isuzu remained strong, and it continues to consistently outsell the more popular branded model.

Although the Trooper is Isuzu's best known car, it also produces the Charade and applause ranges of family cars.

Isuzu

GM's Japanese arm markets large 4x4s and compact family cars

JAGUAR

STRANGE THOUGH it may seem, Jaguar has not always been the household name it is now. Before the Second World War this greatest of marques did not actually exist. The company we know today as Jaguar started life called SS (for Swallow Sidecars). At the time of Hitler's Nazis, SS was quietly dropped and the company re-named Jaguar.

The marque was the brainchild of Sir William Lyons. Jaguars have since become legendary over the years for their English style, their driving ability and their value for money. The same is still true today.

Just after the war, however, from 1945 to 1948, Jaguar cars were really the 1940 SS models with the addition of hypoid back axles and the big cat's badge on the bonnet. They were available in 1.8-litre four-cylinder, or 2.7- and 3.5-litre six-cylinder forms with beam axles, push-rod operated overhead-valves, four-speed gearboxes and mechanical brakes. The four-cylinder engines were actually made by Standard but all post-war six-cylinder engines were Jaguar's own. From 1949 only six-cylinder cars were made and the new push-rod Mark V saloons got independent front suspension and hydraulic brakes.

One of the most beautiful Jaguars of all time, the XK two-seater sports, first saw the light of day in 1948, and was an instant hit with its 120 mph performance from its brilliant new XK twin-cam engine. Less than a tenth of Jaguar owners at this time were British, the rest of the XKs made up to 1954

were shipped to the USA, where demand was very strong.

Jaguar was making luxurious saloons too and in 1951 had launched the big Mark VII saloon with the company's advanced twin-cam engine. This car was a successful attempt to ally American roominess with traditional British build quality. So successful was the formula that this large car won the Monte Carlo Rally in 1956. Around this time the Coventry cats were making a name for themselves in racing too, winning a brace of Le

Mans races. Jaguar's biggest success story though was the Mark I and Mark II saloons, which were available with 2.4 and 3.4-litre, straight-six engines which continued right up until 1969 when they were superseded by the XJ6.

The E-Type rewrote the sportscar rule books when it was unveiled in 1961. The S-Type saloon, which appeared in 1963 as an 'improved Mark II', was never as successful. It was more powerful, had better handling and offered more cabin space too, but

it simply did not have the same compact shape.

Jaguar was another British company snapped up by BMC in 1966 before becoming British Leyland in the 1970s. It was during this period that the XJS sportscar was launched – and Jaguar lost its way. Intended as a replacement for the hugely successful E-Type, the XJS never had the earlier car's looks or reputation. The 1970s were truly bleak times for the famous Browns Lane concern. Under British Leyland's control, quality and

Jaguar

After a troubled recent past, the Coventry cat is back with the XK8

desirability slumped and by the early 1980s it looked the end of the line for Jaguar.

Thankfully the cat was saved by an ambitious privatisation plan under John Egan who turned Jaguar's fortunes around. Now Jaguar is enjoying something of a

Jeep *A descendant of the troop carrier, Jeep's reputation is built on the original's initials, GP – General Purpose*

rebirth. True, it needed the intervention of Ford to secure its future but has gone from strength to strength since. The XJ220 was an expensive but sensational sign that the company was back to its best. Now, more than 35 years after the fabulous E Type was unveiled at the Geneva Motor Show, Jaguar launched its spiritual successor, the XK8. Stunningly beautiful and seriously powerful, it continues the tradition of 'space, grace and pace'. In 1996 the XK8 was voted the most beautiful two-seat luxury car in the world.

A successor to the Mark II, the X200, is set for launch in 1999, based on an American Lincoln floor with Jaguar mechanicals.

JAMESON

OUTLANDISH engineer Paul Jameson may have only produced a handful of specialist cars in Surrey, England... but then not everybody uses Rolls-Royces for the donor parts!

Jameson leapt to fame in the 1970s when he designed a fibreglass-bodied special, based around a 750 bhp Rolls-Royce engine with a Corniche radiator grille. This car became surrounded in controversy and myth.

Jameson sold the car to John Dodd who enjoyed much of the car's fame. It was claimed that this 200 mph monster used an engine taken from a Spitfire fighter plane. In fact, the engine came from a Meteor tank, so it was still very powerful. The car was virtually destroyed by fire but has been rebuilt on a variety of bodyshells.

Jameson did build the ultimate supercar in 1976, powered by a 1,760 bhp Rolls-Royce Merlin engine. With this mighty power-pack mid-mounted, the Jameson Mk II required six wheels – with four of them driven by the engine.

JEEP

THE NAME JEEP comes from the initials GP – for General Purpose. This was the simple name given to the rugged and robust little four-wheel-drive machine which American forces drove during World War II. So successful was it on the field of operations and so popular with those who drove it, that the company decided to make it for the public. And so a legend was born.

Jeep is now built by Chrysler, and is a world away from that first utilitarian machine which was dropped by parachute to help the fighting forces. Today's Jeep is a luxury machine with a good choice of powerful and lusty engines. Yet it shares a simple philosophy with its much humbler forerunner – it can be asked to go just about anywhere. In fact, today the Jeep Cherokee or Grand Cherokee are more likely to be seen climbing the kerb outside Harrods than plugging across a muddy field or up a mountainside, but that is not to say it couldn't do it if asked.

After the war, the Jeep was produced by Willy-Overland, forming with the Kiaser Corporation in the mid 1950s. However, it was AMC who really turned the Jeep name around. It bought out Willys-Overland in 1970 and expanded and refined the ranges before Chrysler bought AMC in 1987. Now a full range of working or luxury Jeep designs are offered and are fast gaining the level of popularity in Britain that they have enjoyed in the United States for decades.

JENSEN

BROTHERS Richard and Allan Jensen were British through-and-through, yet they turned to

America for the technology to power their range of powerful saloons and coupes. The Jensens cut their automotive teeth designing bodies for the likes of Standard and Wolseley before embarking on their own creations... and what creations they were!

Always renowned for their

Jensen

Another specialist car maker that couldn't survive the 1970s recession despite offering exciting models like the Interceptor and the FF

innovative streak, the Jensens launched their 3.5-litre model in 1937. This car was powered by an American Ford V8, but it had other exciting features. The chief of these was a Columbia two-speed back axle which gave the car six forward gears, 50 years before rivals adopted a similar design. Later versions used either a 2.2-litre Ford V8 unit or the 4.2-litre, straight-eight, overhead-valve Nash engine, or Steyr and Ford's Lincoln Zephyr power units.

In 1950 Jensen launched its first Interceptor in saloon and cabriolet form. This time a British engine was used, the six-cylinder Austin 4.0-

litre. One of the most beautiful Jensens appeared in 1954, the big 541 saloon. This could reach 115 mph but its light weight meant it was economic to run too.

It was back to American V8 power in 1963, when the CV8 got Chrysler's 5.9-litre, 305 bhp unit with a choice of manual or automatic gearbox. The biggest innovation came in 1966 with the FF, fitted with a revolutionary Ferguson four-wheel-drive system plus anti-lock brakes. The FF's system of hypoid final drive to all four wheels was not revolutionary when compared to the Audi Quattro's system – but Jensen

launched the FF more than a decade before the four-wheel-drive German car.

For all its revolutionary skills, the FF was overshadowed by the simpler and cheaper Interceptor range which also included a good-looking drophead. By 1968 Jensen was taken over from the Norcros Group of merchant bankers (who owned the company since 1959), by William Brandt.

This restructuring saw Donald Healey of Healey sportscars fame at the helm as chairman. This lead to a change in direction in 1972 when the Jensen-Healey two-seat sports was launched. Powered by

a Lotus 16-valve engine, this cut-price Jensen was a good idea at the wrong time. There was also a GT version which had an estate car body, but only 500 were made before the company got into financial difficulties and folded in 1976. All efforts to revive the company have since sadly failed.

JOWETT

YORKSHIRE IN ENGLAND may seem an unlikely place to produce world-beating motor cars, but from 1906 to 1954 it was a centre of automotive excellence, thanks to Benjamin and William Jowett. The brothers started out making V-twin engines for cars and stationary work. They were also the geniuses behind the first Scott two-stroke motorcycles.

As with many pioneering engineers of that era, the Jowetts then turned their attentions to the car and from the early 1920s the little Flat-Twin saloon went on

sale. The secret to its success, and of the Jowetts that followed, was a light body, good performance and first class reliability.

After World War I, production began in earnest with the launch of the Jowett Seven. It was not perfect – its fixed-head engine made maintenance difficult, the suspension was hard and the brakes were poor, but because the engine gave most of its power at low engine speeds, flexibility and acceleration were superb. There was a change in direction in 1923 when the big Long Four was announced, with its more roomy four-seater body. Like the Seven this was hugely popular.

In 1929 the Jowett engine was given a detachable cylinder head so maintenance was easier. At the same time the low-cost Chummy appeared. More modern was the Black Prince saloon, which had a fabric body with a high waistline, shallow windows and attractive wire wheels. At the time it was the height of fashion.

In 1934 one of the very best Jowetts, the Kestrel sports saloon, was launched, followed a year later by the twin-carburettor Weasel sports tourer. By 1936 the Jowett factory was in full-swing and the brothers launched the Ten saloon with a modern and efficient flat-four engine of 1166cc.

After World War II, Jowett produced some of its most successful cars, again the emphasis was on value and reliability. The first of these newcomers was the Javelin, a small family car with independent torsion-bar suspension, a rigid unitary body-chassis construction, smooth aerodynamic lines, light weight and high gearing. It was capable of 80 mph and had class-leading acceleration. All this, despite a flat-four engine of only 1.5-litres.

In 1950 the Javelin was joined by an even more advanced car, the two-seat Jupiter (shown below). This model could crest 90 mph, but even this was not enough for Jowett. In 1954 it launched the R4

Jupiter. Lighter than its brother, it could top 100 mph. Sadly only a handful were made before the company went out of business late in 1954. A great loss to motoring.

KAISER

AMERICAN SHIPBUILDING millionaire Henry Kaiser wanted to break into the luxury car market just after the Second World War. With a partner, Joe Frasier, he commissioned two cars, suitably named the Kaiser and the Frasier, to be built.

Kaiser used some quite advanced thinking with his cars, like the introduction of a novel safety windscreen which 'popped out' when subject to a 35lb force.

Kaisers comprehensively outsold any Frasier models and in its prime the company reached 12th place in the US. This still fell well short of Kaiser's expectations.

The ultimate Kaiser was the 1953 Hardtop Dragon, which featured automatic transmission and even a gold-plated interior. However the company had already reached its zenith and later that year merged with Willy's Jeep concern. This did little to halt the slide and Kaiser production was shipped to Argentina before its ultimate demise in 1955.

KIA

KIA MOTOR CORPORATION has come a long way in a very short space of time. From its humble beginnings as a Korean bicycle-maker after the Second World War, to a major global automotive player

Jowett *Yorkshire-based Jowett built a reputation for engineering excellence with superb small sportscars and saloons*

in 50 years is no mean achievement. Especially when its taken into consideration that the company's first car, the Brisa, wasn't produced until 1974.

Before this Kia busied itself making motorbikes and commercial vehicles. In 1979 Kia started making its own version of the then discontinued Peugeot 604s and Fiat 132s, after buying their production lines. By the 1980s, however, Kia was beginning to be taken more seriously.

The Japanese manufacturer Mazda bought eight per cent of the growing company and Ford (who has a stake in Mazda) took a further

10 per cent slice of the action.

By 1988 Kia had sold its millionth vehicle and moved into Europe in 1991 with the Kia Pride, a re-badged Mazda 121, sold through Mazda's importers.

From producing other car-maker's cast-offs, Kia steadily began to create its own designs with the Sephia (called the Mentor in Britain), the 4x4 Sportage off-roader and various commercial vehicles from Asia Motors Corporation, which was purchased back in 1976.

Kia recently took an interest in the ailing Lotus concern, eventually buying the latest front-wheel-drive Elan from the company to make and market it as its own in Korea.

Exporting to over 120 countries with dedicated production facilities in more than 10 countries, Kia's dream of becoming a major automotive player looks well on course to becoming a reality.

LADA

THE RUSSIAN car-maker Lada first started to produce Fiat-based vehicles, with aid from the Italian giant, back in 1970. Incidentally, Lada is the name given to the cars when they are sold in countries outside Russia. The company's proper name is Zhiguli.

Using Fiat's trusty 1960s 124 and 125 as the base stock, Lada pitched in at the economy end of the market with its Riva range, diversifying in 1978 with its tough little 4x4 Niva off-roader.

Amazingly, these ranges still sell to this day, the only addition to cater for modern times being the front-wheel drive Samara cars, introduced in 1987. The Samara was a promising enough car at the time but Lada has since let slip the opportunity to move forward and is fast being outclassed by other budget-based car-makers from further East.

LAGONDA

WILBUR GUNN, an American, arrived in England in 1897. A year later he built an air-cooled motorcycle in a greenhouse at Staines in Middlesex. Lagonda was born. Gunn got the name from the French for the American Indian name for Buck Creek, a stream near his home town in Ohio, USA.

The Torpedo was Lagonda's first successful car, launched in

Lagonda *British-based but founded by an American, the right to the Lagonda name is now owned by Aston Martin*

1906 with a 20 bhp four-cylinder engine. This was soon joined by a six-cylinder version.

Lagonda has Russia's Nicholas II to thank for its success, because after the Tsar saw the car cruise to victory in the 1910 Moscow-St.Petersburg reliability trial he liked it so much, he bought it. From then on Lagonda was recognised as a maker of highly desirable cars.

The Torpedo – so named because of its sleek lines – was a saloon, but in 1925 it was joined by Lagonda's first sportscar, the 14/60. The engine was a modern 1954cc, overhead-valve, twin camshaft design which gave good performance. This was eclipsed by the 1928 launch of the Speed, a 2.0-litre engined sportscar with twin carburettors. By 1930, with speed the goal, the chassis of the 2.0-litre was lowered and a higher performance supercharged model was also offered.

Three years later at the London Motor Show Lagonda showed-off two new models, the 1104cc Rapier with twin overhead-camshafts and the 4.5-litre M45. Both were fine

performers, but they were heavy due to the increasing weight of the tailor-made Lagonda bodies. In spite of this both these cars became very popular with buyers.

By 1935 Lagonda became another British motor company facing bankruptcy and though the company launched the Rapide and LG45, this was not enough to stop the inevitable. Ironically, this could be said to be one of the best things to have happened to Lagonda, because new owner Alan Good appointed W.O. Bentley as Lagonda's chief designer.

By 1938 the company was ready to launch Bentley's 4.5-litre Lagonda, the LG6. Its V12 engine is reckoned to be the best of Bentley's designs and it allowed the LG to reach a top speed of 130 mph. For a decade Lagonda prospered, helped by the 2.6 and 3.0-litre models, again designed by Bentley. They were to be his final work. These Lagondas were a superb piece of engineering, mating a cruciform chassis to independent rear suspension and a twin overhead-cam, six-cylinder

engine. The top speed was more than 100 mph. Just after the Second World War, Lagonda was taken over by the David Brown Group who also owned Aston Martin.

By the 1960s Lagonda was using other people's engines. In 1961 the Rapide appeared with an Aston Martin DB4 unit of 3996cc. A beautiful streamlined aluminium body by Touring of Milan helped the car to a top speed of 125 mph.

Today Lagonda is a name used as a trim level for top Aston Martins and a four-door DBS was produced in 1975 in small numbers. Also a sharp-styled, high-tech Lagonda did briefly appear in the late 70s.

LAMBORGHINI

STRANGE though it may seem, in Italy Ferruccio Lamborghini was best known for producing tractors. This was a business he started in 1949 and which is still successful today. But Ferruccio had a passion... and it wasn't for four-wheel-drive agricultural vehicles. He wanted to build sportscars.

In 1963 he achieved his ambition with the launch of the stunning 360 GT. This was powered by a 3.5-litre, four-overhead-cam, V12 engine fitted with no less than six Weber carburettors. The 360 got its name from the terrific amount of power this unit developed – 360 bhp. Specification was state-of-the-art, featuring a five-speed ZF gearbox, self-locking differential, all-round independent suspension by coils and wishbones and servo-assisted disc brakes. The body was beautiful with a large single windscreen wiper and pop-up headlamps. The top speed was approaching 150 mph, which in the mid-1960s was something indeed. Not only that, this car also handled incredibly well, giving its driver a Grand Prix-type experience in the shape of a well made and well equipped road-going car.

The 400 GT was next off the Lamborghini production line in 1966. This was essentially a development of the 360. As its badge suggests, the 400 had more power than the 360, even though the engine was the same. Careful tuning extracted better acceleration and a more flexible character. There were two versions, a two-seater and two-plus-two.

The same year as the 400 GT appeared Lamborghini launched the now classic, Miura, which was a different car altogether. Judged by enthusiasts to be one of the most exciting Lamborghinis, the Miura had its 4.0-litre engine mounted sideways at the rear. This power unit gave the car a top speed of 180 mph with excellent traction and roadholding to match.

By 1968 Lamborghini had become a well known name, sales were strong and the cars were gaining a well deserved reputation not only for performance but also for reliability. It was the perfect time to launch the Espada, with a V12 engine. A two-plus-two version, the Jarama, was launched in 1970.

It seemed as if hardly a year

Lamborghini

*From tractors to exotica: the
Muira, a classic from the 1960s*

went by without a new Lamborghini appearing. In 1971 yet another new model was unveiled. The Urraco used a V8 engine of 2.5-litres producing 220 bhp. This was a clever development of the Miura but with MacPherson strut suspension replacing the coils and wishbones of the earlier car. Three versions were available, the P250, the larger-engined (3.0-litre) P300, and the targa-topped Silhouette.

The most amazing Lamborghini of them all, the Countach, first appeared in 1974. Its six carburettor, 4.4-litre, V12 engine was mounted longitudinally at the rear and its five-speed gearbox further forward. This car was capable of 190 mph.

Lamborghini was bought by Chrysler in 1987 and the Countach is still built, though in very small numbers.

LANCHESTER

IN 1895 THE Lanchester brothers built the first all-British car. So advanced was its design, with innovations such as counter-balancing shafts for engine smoothness (latterly used by Mitsubishi and Porsche), that great things were expected from this Birmingham-based engine company. It never quite happened, and by 1931 Lanchester was taken over by fellow British firm, Daimler. With that, any semblance of individuality died.

Quite simply, Lanchesters were too far-sighted for their own good. Their complexity put off many buyers who feared these new-fangled horseless carriages anyway. Even when the company looked to more conventional

Lancia *The delightful Fulvia showed Lancia at its best, but rusting Beta models killed off the company's UK sales in the 1980s*

designs, the cars couldn't net the sales their quality fully deserved.

The splendid 4.4-litre, straight eight-cylinder engine (with an advanced overhead-camshaft design) produced in 1928, is regarded as the last 'true' Lanchester. When the company was taken over three years later they merely became Daimlers by another name.

While Lanchester's engineering excellence was used to the benefit of both companies, the name was dropped in 1956. Purists still mourn the loss to this day.

LANCIA

VINCENZO LANCIA might have followed his father into the soup business and we might never have seen a car bear his name if he had not got a job at Fiat. Vincenzo eventually rose to the office of

Chief Inspector at Fiat where he learnt much about cars. His real passion was motor racing and by 1906, after a couple of seasons in the Fiat racing team, he had formed his own company. A year later he brought out his first car, the confusingly-named Alfa. Greek letters were used as badges on all Lancias until 1929. By 1908 there was a brother model, the 3.8-litre, six-cylinder Di-Alfa, but only 23 were made.

The Beta, Gamma, Delta, Eta, Theta and Kappa ranges arrived in 1909 and Lancia still uses several of these original names to this day. The Beta had a 3.1-litre engine; capacity was increased to 3.5 litres for the Gamma of 1910, and to 4.1 litres when the Delta appeared in 1911. Full electrics were available on the 4.1-litre Eta by 1914 – the first such installation standardised by a European manufacturer.

After World War I Lancia

launched the Kappa, which was an improved 90 bhp development of the Theta. This was eventually replaced by the overhead-valve Dikappa and the Trikappa which used a 4.6-litre, overhead-cam, V8 engine.

By 1923, and with sales rising, Lancia launched the revolutionary Lambda. This used a space-saving narrow-angle V-type overhead-camshaft engine, which meant there was plenty of cabin room for the driver and passengers.

For 1929 the Lambda appeared with a V8 engine. In 1931 Lancia launched replacements for the Lambda, the 1.9-litre, 54 bhp Artena and the Astura, a 2.6-litre, 73 bhp, V8-engined car, which by 1934 had grown to 3.0-litres.

In 1937 Vincenzo Lancia died and in that same year his last creation, the 1352cc Aprilia, was launched. This model had a streamlined saloon body, low

weight, a top speed of 80 mph and fuel consumption of 30 mpg. The Aprilia is rated as a classic and judged decades ahead of its time.

The Lancia family lost control of the company in 1953. Three years later the new Lancia company launched the Flaminia, a 2.5-litre V6-engined car with a rear-axle gearbox. The saloon bodywork had been developed from the Aurelia-based Florida, exhibited by Pininfarina at the Turin Motor Show in 1955. By 1958 a short chassis GT version was available, producing 125 bhp.

One of Lancia's all-time greats, the Fulvia, was unveiled in 1964, replacing the Appia. The new car had much in common with the earlier Flavia, though it used an 1100cc V4 engine rather than a flat-four unit.

The truly exciting Montecarlo was built in Turin in two periods: from 1975 to 1978, and from 1980 to 1984. This two-seater, rear-wheel-drive coupe used a four-cylinder 1995cc engine with a top speed of 120 mph. An earlier 1.8-litre engine was simply not powerful enough. Interestingly, the Montecarlo was penned by the same team which developed the pretty Fiat X1/9, and was seen by many as a more powerful, upmarket version of that car.

During the 1980s Lancia did not have a good time. After newspaper stories about the perils of severely rusting 1973 Beta models, British buyers turned their backs.

In the latter half of the 1980s the company limped on with the Thema, which was actually a top-flight car – it was even Ferrari-powered. Eventually Lancia's owners Fiat, decided that dwindling sales were reason enough to withdraw the Lancia sales operation in the UK. Perhaps one day Lancia will rise again in Britain. True enthusiasts and lovers of Italian flair can only hope.

LEA-FRANCIS

LIKE MANY OTHER pioneering British car-makers, Lea-Francis of Warwickshire started in business by making bicycles. Although it turned to cars in the post World War I years, Lea-Francis never ditched its bicycle operation. They preferred instead to make cars, at least in the early days, more as a hobby than a major business.

It wasn't until 1922 that the company launched a car which was to earn decent money and prompt Lea-Francis to concentrate more on four than two-wheeled transport. This original model had a 1.0-litre, four-cylinder engine in a light car body and was made

Lea-Francis

A low output maker of classic small cars, now sadly missed by enthusiasts

until 1928. In 1925 a wider and larger car, the J-Type was launched, aimed much more at family motorists. This had a 1.5-litre Meadows engine and a four-speed gearbox, the previous models had three-speed 'boxes. In the same year the L-Type, which was the company's first sportscar, came to the market. By 1931 Lea-Francis had also launched a six-cylinder engined car, the Ace of Spades, with a 2.0-litre, single overhead-cam engine. From 1928 a powerful new car was added to the list, the Hyper Sports with a Cozette-supercharged Meadows 1.5-litre engine, low bodywork and two seats. This quick convertible could reach nearly 100 mph and there was also a coupe version available. A model called the Leaf was built just before World War II and was thoroughly modern. When hostilities ceased this car was launched again. By 1960 the company was in some financial trouble, due mostly to their small production output, and though there was a model called the Leaf-Lynx it never entered series production. In 1980 the company was taken over by A.B. Price of Warwickshire.

LINCOLN

LINCOLN AND CADILLAC have been slogging it out for years, each claiming they produce the best luxury American car. The irony being that Cadillac, in a manner of speaking gave birth to Lincoln. Caddy's founder, Henry M. Leland, formed the Lincoln Motor Company in 1917. Unfortunately the company did not do well, its products were too expensive because they were luxurious. The company simply opened its doors at the wrong time – just before American entered World War I. If Lincoln could have held on a little longer and made it intact into The Roaring Twenties it might have survived, but in 1922 it went into receivership.

It had to be rescued by Henry

Ford, who paid $8 million for the privilege. Ford decided to develop Lincoln as its own luxury car division. By the end of the 1920s there were several versions of the Lincoln Town Car being offered, most of them more luxurious versions of the Ford Model A, itself a top-seller.

Interestingly, Henry Ford's son, Edsel, (who would later have a specific and not too popular car named after him) was the man who created the Town Car concept. Unfortunately it was not an instant best-seller. This could have had something to do with the fact that the Town Car, though well equipped, was typically twice as much to buy as the best-equipped Ford Model A!

In 1931 Lincolns were one of the few cars in America which actually increased in price. Despite their prices, however, they sold reasonably well through the depressed 1930s. The Model K, as this version was known,

---

Lincoln

Ford's luxury car division will also provide the basis for a new Jaguar

Lotus

Design and packaging brilliance rarely resulted in commercial success: Proton now own Lotus

sheet-steel, box-sectioned backbone chassis was used. It branched at the front to hold the engine, also branching slightly at the rear to house the Colin Chapman-designed strut suspension.

The Elan's superb handling and performance could not be beaten. With dual twin-choke Weber carburettors, 105 bhp was produced in standard form.

In 1965 a pretty hard-top coupe version, the very successful Series Two was launched, as well as the longer, family-sized Plus 2 two years later.

had a long wheelbase so it was roomy inside. By 1940 the marque had made a name for itself, thanks to its beautiful new bodies and the willingness of potential owners to choose something different from the crowd. At this time the range included sleek coupes and what Ford called the club coupe, a large five-passenger Lincoln. By 1941 Ford had launched another great motoring name – Continental. The first Lincoln Continental proved popular thanks to a 120 bhp V12 engine, even though it had to haul around a massive body. Today, the Lincoln range continues and

Ford has announced another re-launch of this most venerable car, with a V8 engine under the bonnet.

LOTUS

COLIN CHAPMAN, founder of Lotus Cars, was a characterful automotive entrepreneur of the 1960s who seemed to strike gold every time he turned an ignition key. Not only did he design and make a whole range of very attractive sporting machines, but his and his company's expertise were regularly sought out by the

world's car-making giants.

Chapman's first car for public use was the Seven, a highly-tuned two-seater which used the engine from the staid old Austin Seven. The Lotus Seven showed just what could be achieved with a little bit of imagination and the right skills. The very basic and light body allowed the Seven to roar along and soon sales were climbing.

By 1962 there was whole new Lotus, the Elan, which used a twin overhead-cam version of the 1.5-litre Ford Classic 116E engine. Unlike the beautiful but unreliable and unprofitable all-fibreglass Elite, launched a few years earlier, a

The Europa was destined for export and used a reversed Renault engine which was mid-mounted. This arrangement gave the Europa terrific road-holding and handling and the aerodynamic fibreglass body, designed by Frayling, ensured amazing performance. A move to Lotus power in 1971 increased its appeal and this car stayed in production until 1975.

By 1974, with sales booming, there was a move up-market with the launch of the Elite as a four-seater sports saloon using a 2.0-litre 155 bhp version of the Lotus twin-cam engine, a five-speed gearbox, retractable headlights and electric windows. The Elan was killed off a year earlier to make way for the Elite, a move the company must rue to this day.

The 1976 Eclat was a development of the Elite, had a two-plus-two cabin, and again offered first-class performance and handling if suspect built quality.

A number of early Lotuses were kit-built, and sometimes even the factory-built models felt that way, but the after the introduction of VAT in 1973 all Lotus cars were factory built. As a replacement for the Europa, the Esprit was introduced and is the only name to survive to this day.

When Colin Chapman died in December 1982 the company lost its founder, and it seemed, its way. Bought first by General Motors, then sold to Bugatti who in turn sought a buyer – the unlikely Malaysian budget car company Proton moved in. A move to relaunch the Elan name in 1990 was short-lived due to its high cost. The car was sold to Korean maker Kia, but the new Elise and mighty V8 Esprit now show promise.

MARCOS

AN UNLIKELY car-producing town perhaps, but Bradford-on-Avon in England's leafy west country is nevertheless the home to Marcos, one of the UK's most interesting ranges of sportscars.

Marcos was a mix of its founders' names, Jem Marsh and Frank Costin. Production began in the early 1960s with the launch of the GT, a two-seater sportscar which was built until 1968.

Over those four years some 370 were made, not a bad number for a small operation. Originally this Marcos was fitted with a 1.8-litre Volvo engine which hardly sounds a recipe for sportscar performance. However, the Volvo unit was no sluggard in the very lightweight Marcos shell.

The ace up Marcos's sleeve was the GT's body. It might sound bizarre but the frame was made of marine ply more commonly found at a boatyard. It was a result of Costin's fascination with 'God's metal', wood. There was certainly a scepticism amongst rival car-builders, many of whom suggested that the Marcos needed a steel body. The company proved them wrong. The relatively lightweight two-seater arrowed along.

After 50 cars had been built, Marcos swapped the rather complicated De Dion rear axle with a more conventional beam axle. In 1966 a 1.5-litre Ford engine which had also seen service in the excellent Cortina GT, was fitted in place of the Swedish unit.

As with many specialist companies producing few cars, Marcos wisely decided to broaden the range to attract more buyers and the end result was the Mini-Marcos, which was launched in 1965. This had a fibreglass body and chassis unit and used mainly BMC Mini parts.

It proved to be quite successful. If enthusiasts bought one finished from the factory it was relatively expensive, though it was possible to buy in kit-form and make it at home. The lightweight body and use of proven mechanical bits and pieces meant this car was both sporty and economical, though not everyone liked the look of it.

Maserati *The spark plug maker turned supercar maker, and with considerable success*

Marcos

Founded by two British enthusiasts, a low-volume specialist that survived the recession-hit 1970s

Top of the Marcos range during the 1970s was the original Mantis V6 four-seat GT with a square-tube chassis frame. This proved very successful for Marcos, though escalating price tags put many a potential buyer off.

After a shaky period in the 1970s, Marcos is still in production today. The company produces the Mantara in coupe and convertible Spider form, and the LM, similarly in hard and soft-top. It suffers the same old problem though, high prices mean customers have to choose between these specialist cars and some very impressive machinery from more orthodox mass-producing car companies, but Marcos is hard to beat for interesting cars with character.

MASERATI

EVER HEARD OF Maserati spark plugs? Well, Italian car-owners before 1926 would have found plenty of them because that was all this company made.

It was not until 1926 that the Maserati brothers started to make cars, using Neptune's Trident – the traditional symbol of Bologna – as their emblem. In fact, it was not until the late 1950s that the Maseratis made a car for the road, up until then they had concentrated on their first love – racing.

In 1957 the 3500 series, with double overhead-cam, six-cylinder engines were launched. Buyers who waited a year or two had a choice of two power units, a 3485cc producing 260 bhp and a bigger unit, the 270 bhp 3692cc.

Both used the best of European hardware with Lucas fuel-injection as standard and five-speed gearboxes, or the option of a Borg-

Matra

Better at missiles than sportscars, but now produce the Espace people carrier

Warner automatic transmission.

The Quattroporte was launched in 1964 in four-door saloon format, powered by a double overhead-cam, 4136cc V8 engine with four dual-choke Weber carburettors.

As with most saloon cars made by sportscar companies the Quattroporte never really captured the public's attention. It wasn't until the Sebring, Mistrale and Ghibli appeared on the scene that heart rates began racing again.

The six-cylinder Sebring and Mistrale used 4.0-litre engines, though a new 4.7-litre V8 unit was found on the Mexico two-door saloon and the Ghibli coupe – the latter had four retractable headlamps. It could manage an impressive 175 mph.

As with most other Italian sportscar manufacturers, Maserati went for a mid-engine layout for the launch of the Bora in 1972. This compact car had all independent suspension and a five-speed gearbox and was powered by the well-known 4.7-litre V8 engine

block. The smaller but similar Merak used a 3.0-litre Citroen V6 engine – also seen in the Citroen SM – in 190 bhp carburettor form.

Two years later Maserati launched the front-engined Khamsin 2+2 coupe. This used a bigger 4.9-litre, four cam, V8 engine and came with power steering and either an automatic or five-speed manual gearbox. A year later, in 1975, yet another Maserati appeared, the Kyalami. It might not have appeared at all were it not for De Tomaso galloping to the rescue with a take-over plan and much needed investment. De Tomaso's plan was to continue with the Bora, Merak, Khamsin and Kyalami.

To many today it appears as if Maserati's glory days are over. Gone are the out-and-out racing machines which made their name, and in have come more refined machines, like the Spyder, Shamal and next generation Quattroporte.

For the enthusiasts, however, the Ghibli is still very much here.

MATRA

MATRA (Mecanique-Aviation-Traction) is best known for its aerospace and missile connections plus its successes in Formula One

racing – but this Renault-owned concern still plays a significant role in automotive designs.

Matra entered the fast car arena in 1965 when it took control of Rene Bonnet's sporting models before becoming involved in Grand Prix and endurance racing. Matra was very successful, scoring a world championship with Jackie Stewart and a clutch of Le Mans victories. However, its initial foray in road cars could not match its track achievements. The company's first in-house design, the Matra 530, used Ford's newly-launched V4 engine and failed to sell in large numbers.

Simca took over production in 1970 with much better luck. Simca, which in turn is owned by Chrysler, produced a novel three-abreast-seater called the Bagheera. This was spaceframe constructed, with a mid-engined design and found favour with enthusiasts. Production spanned from 1973 to 1980 before being replaced by the similar but improved Murena, although the car lasted in production for just three years.

Around the same time, French giant Renault acquired Matra and used its specialist expertise to manufacture the best-selling Espace people carrier.

MAZDA

MAZDA IS THE only mainstream Japanese car-maker with serious foreign investment in its operation – in this case America's Ford Motor Company has a 25 percent stake in the Japanese group.

This cross-fertilisation can be seen most clearly in the shape of 1996 European Ford Fiesta and the latest Mazda 121. They are the same car with slightly different trim and equipment levels.

Mazda has certainly produced some good, technologically appealing cars in its own right since its inception in 1960. The Toyo Kogyo Cork concern was actually founded 40 years earlier building specialised vehicles.

This was a formula Mazda thrived on. In 1967 it started to introduce a family of the then revolutionary Wankel rotary-powered car, the best-known being the RX-7. This power plant gave unprecedented smoothness, so much so that a buzzer used to be fitted to the rev counter to warn the driver of getting too near the red-line. When fitted with a turbo unit this car accelerated almost as quickly as a motorbike.

Mazda's problem, and others

Mazda

Though superb, the MX5 has failed to secure Mazda's long-term future

bold enough to try Wankel, was that development of the engine nearly bankrupted them. It was many years before such heavy investment began to pay off.

The other problem was the Wankel was never as efficient, at least in terms of fuel consumption, as had been intended. This meant it never became a popular alternative to the more common four, six and eight-cylinder petrol engines offered by rivals. Today, the rotary engine is not offered in any new Mazda, but it has by no means given up on the idea.

The real star in the current Mazda range is the delightful little MX-5 convertible which Mazda launched to fill the gap left long ago by the likes of the MG.

A dedicated luxury marque called Xedos has also proved popular, but Mazda is still going through hard times.

McLAREN

THE F1 SUPERCAR isn't this Formula One team's first foray into making a road car. Back in 1969, team founder Bruce McLaren wanted to build a sportscar to promote his racing company. His M6GT used a 5-litre Chevrolet engine which was a popular power unit in Transatlantic Formula F5000 and Can-Am racers at this time.

With a radical body design, the McLaren showed great promise and after an initial batch of three were built, plans for a limited run for wealthy enthusiasts was on the cards. However, the untimely death of Bruce McLaren in June 1970 while testing one his racers saw the project shelved for 20 years. The wait has been worth it, for the fabulous Gordon Murray-

MERCEDES-
BENZ

MERCEDES-BENZ may now be a mighty German vehicle manufacturer – but it was there at the birth of motoring too. The two pioneering strands of Mercedes and Benz amalgamated in 1926.

The name Mercedes came from Director Herr Jellinek's daughter, Mercedes which was deemed a better name than Daimler.

The Benz 16/50PS and the Mercedes cars with supercharged engines were continued, but the really interesting development was the launch in 1926 of the first true Mercedes-Benz cars. These were the six-cylinder, 2.0-litre Stuttgart and the 3.1-litre Mannheim. They were both heavy single-valve machines with coil ignition, three-speed gearboxes and wooden wheels. They later became the 2.6-litre Stuttgart 260 and the 3.5-litre Mannheim 350.

The Nurburg 460 was launched in 1928 with a eight-cylinder, 4.6-litre engine, later growing into the vast Nurburg 500. These were the forerunners of the massive Grosser Mercedes, favourites of Adolf Hitler and leaders of the German Nazi party.

One of the greatest cars of all time was the Mercedes K Sports with supercharged 6.2-litre engine. It was the fastest touring car on the world market at the time. From this original model a very successful range was developed; the 6.8-litre S, the 7.1-litre SS, and the 7.1-litre SSK and SSKL.

Following in the spiritual footsteps of the SK came the SL, one of Mercedes-Benz's most popular sportscars. The first SL was powered by a six-cylinder, 3.0-litre, 215 bhp unit with fuel injection. The original car was a hard-top with 'gull-wing' doors but was later also sold as an open-topped roadster. This version was available until 1963.

In 1968 the saloon range was heavily revised with new bodies

Mercedes-Benz

The founders of the motor car have stayed at the cutting edge ever since

and new independent rear suspension for the 200, 230 and 250. A 280 engine was introduced and this was used in the bodies of the former 300 saloons and the 250SL sportscar. Bridging the gap between the 300 and 600 was the 300SEL, a 300 saloon using the big 6.3-litre V8 engine. The first S-Series range of saloons and coupes came out in the 1970s and included the 300SEL 3.5-litre saloon and a 280SE 3.5-litre coupe, both powered by 3.5-litre double overhead-cam, fuel-injected V8 units. In 1971 the same engine was fitted in the 350SL sports coupe, and there was also a cabriolet version.

Several new and revised engines were unveiled for the new range of 123 models which were sold from 1976, including petrol and diesels from 2.0-litres upwards and including a single cam 2.5-litre six-cylinder with carburettors. Just to complicate matters, the new S-Series appeared in 1979 and offered a choice of engines, either a 2.8-litre six-cylinder, or the 3.8-litre and 5.0-litre V8s.

During the 1980s Mercedes-Benz launched the compact 190 saloon and this was followed by yet another S-Class, even bigger than before, and the latest generation SL roadsters, so beloved of international footballers, and recently the new E-Series.

Today Mercedes has one of the most revered model ranges in the world and is still at the forefront of automotive technology. A development with watchmaker Swatch, has resulted in radical mini car, while Mercedes has also released a small car for the Chinese market. A major development is the fabulous 'budget' priced SLK Roadster, demand for which already outstrips supply.

MERCURY

THE NAME MERCURY has been used by numerous car-makers throughout the decades, the first being recorded in the UK in 1914. No less than three manufacturers used the title afterwards, the most notable being Ford, which was looking for a new division to plug the gap between the mainstream Ford models and the luxury Lincoln label.

Originally, when introduced in 1938, the company's full title was Ford-Mercury. The Ford tag was dropped two years later. Arguably the decades just after the war saw Mercury at its best, with stylish,

individual and upmarket cars. A transparent hard-top was one of the company's hallmarks during the 1950s. Mercury joined the muscle-car market in the mid 1960s with its V8 Comet compact and the Ford Mustang-derived Cougar coupe of 1967. Two years later a rehashed Lincoln Continental was introduced called the Marquis.

By 1972 measures to balance the company books saw Mercury cars lose much of their individuality. Re-badged Ford designs were used to cut costs. This even extended to European-built Ford Capris and Granadas making an appearance in the US as part of the Mercury line-up.

Re-bodied Ford models have been a standard Mercury feature ever since. In 1992 the new Grand Marquis, a re-badged Ford Crown Victoria, was described as "for many Americans the only kind of car they've known; full-size six seater roominess, big boot, V8 power and a boulevard ride". That's just what Ford had in mind when it launched Mercury over half a century earlier.

MESSERSCHMITT

THIS GIANT German company was best known for building airplanes during the Second World War. In 1953 Messerschmitt turned its attentions to the ground with the launch of a three-wheeled bubble-car originally designed by Fend. The first model this Regensburg-based company produced was the KR175, which used a two-stroke, single-cylinder, 175cc engine designed by Sachs. Performance was, not surprisingly, poor.

By 1953, Messerschmitt saw a whole range of European and American companies producing altogether more appealing cars.

Although Messerschmitt's first attempt to compete in this more sophisticated market actually sold quite well, even in a still-depressed Germany, they decided to update the car in 1955 with the addition of a more powerful 200cc engine.

Messerschmitt also produced a four-wheeled car, based on the design of their first three-wheeler. The FMR Tg500, known as the Tiger, was made from 1958 to 1960.

Unfortunately, though the company's cars were interesting, at least as a novelty, they just could not compete with the increasingly sophisticated cars coming out of rival German factories. In 1962 Messerschmitt folded.

Like that other rather archaic German offering, the East German Trabant, the Messerschmitt has acquired something of a cult following today among those who want something very different from their motoring.

Mercury *The Moutaineer 4x4: one of the Ford-owned marques range designed as a bridge to their luxury Lincoln brand*

Legendary Marque

MG

WHEN BRITISH LEYLAND shut down the famous Abingdon works, home of MG, in 1980, it didn't reckon on the backlash it was to subsequently receive from enthusiasts and ordinary motorists alike. For many, to witness this once great name run down and reduced to being simply a badge worn on just any old BL car was the final straw. MG was a tradition that shouldn't be allowed to be thrown on the scrap heap. Ironically, it was through 'badge engineering' that the company first became known to car buyers, selling 'souped up' Morris cars from 1922 onwards. The initials 'MG' stood for 'Morris Garages', where the cars were developed near the original factory but perhaps 'CK' would have been more apt. Cecil Kimber was MG. As manager of the garage, first at the Oxford site and then Abingdon after 1930, he personalised Morris sportscars for road and track use. Such was the immediate success of MG with its little Midget that Sir William Morris (Lord Nuffield) approved a racing programme which soon put this tiny car company on the road to success. However, in 1935 Nuffield took more control of MG and immediately halted its participation in motorsport.

Kimber was forced out in a power struggle in 1941 and four years later was killed in a freak accident at London's Kings Cross railway station. Thus, he would never see his beloved MG achieve real greatness in the 1950s through models like the classic T-series sportscars and Y-Type saloons.

Both were huge hits at home and abroad, with drivers in the US, particularly, taking a shine to the badge. One satisfied customer was a certain Edsel Ford, who ran one for several years before placing it in his company's museum.

With the competition programme restarted, MGs enjoyed considerable success at both Le Mans and in land speed records with the EX-179, driven by Stirling Moss. The T-series gave way to the delightful MGA in 1955, which also gave rise to a road-going engine based on the racing unit – the fast, but unreliable, Twin Cam. The less adventurous MGB that replaced it in 1962 was just part of the ever-widening MG range which also relied on re-badged Austin and Morris cars ranging in size from the little 1100 to the antiquated Morris Oxford based-Magnette. There was even an MG Mini on the drawing board but the success of the Cooper killed it.

The 2+2 MGB GT launched in 1965 was billed at the time as a poor man's Aston Martin. It proved to be a great success, unlike the MGC of two years later or the MGB GT V8 of 1973. The former was an attempt to take over from the Austin-Healey 3000 but this heavy, lumbering car with its truck engine missed by a mile. Ironically,

independent MG tuner, Ken Costello, had been churning out some wonderful Rover V8-powered MGBs years before but BL were slow to catch on. When they eventually did get around to

producing an official model, the 1973 Yom Kippur War (and the subsequent oil crisis) killed the GTV8 off only months after it had been launched. Due to their paucity in numbers, both the MGC and

MG

The inexpensive Midget was always popular, even the rubber-bumpered models, largely aimed at the US

MG

Above *The MGA is an all time classic, while the MGF (previous page) carries on the great tradition.*

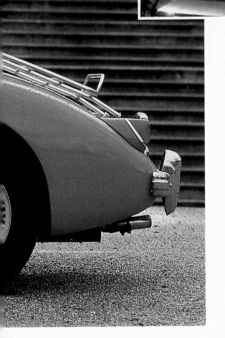

GTV8 are now rightly considered as classics by collectors.

By the mid-1970s – half a century since the octagon badge first appeared – MG had been reduced to something of a joke. The Midget (a re-badged Austin-Healey Sprite) and MGB were ridiculously out of date, having been starved of development to the point where many ordinary family cars could now out perform them. BL only made matters worse when, in order to comply with American federal rules, they fitted grotesque rubber bumpers and raised the suspension ride heights.

Finally, in the late autumn of 1980, BL closed Abingdon. Aston Martin tried to buy MG, as did several other enthusiasts' groups, but their offers were all refused. Instead, the MG octagon reappeared on the Metro in 1982. As a modern day Mini Cooper it showed promise, especially in turbocharged form – unlike the Maestro and Montego interpretations released a year later.

However, what was needed was an all-new sportscar that was worthy of the famous name. Finally, in 1995 (and now under BMW ownership), Rover launched what MG fans had been crying out for for nearly 20 years – the MGF. At last there is hope that Cecil Kimber's creation will be great once again.

MG

The MGB was more orthodox than the MGA but was very popular. However, lack of development reduced the sportscars' abilities considerably. **Left** *The famous octagon badge looks safe in the hands of BMW*

MITSUBISHI

ONE OF JAPAN'S biggest companies, Mitsubishi has been in both Europe and North America for many years now. It has earned a deserved reputation for producing high quality cars, as well as increasingly predicting both European and North American tastes correctly.

It wasn't always like this. As with Datsun, Mitsubishi's first foray into Europe introduced buyers to cars which were certainly well

Mitsubishi

Innovative and daring, Mitsubishi regularly dares to be different with its road cars

equipped but which lacked the style and ruggedness of European competitors. It soon rectified this. During the 1980s in particular, Mitsubishi produced some very interesting cars, not least the aggressive-looking Starion which was a two-plus-two coupe with a really gutsy turbocharged engine.

The first Mitsubishis, in 1917, were Fiat-based cars. It took more than 40 years before Mitsubishi became involved in making cars

again when the twin-cylinder 500 was produced. Always in the range since 1962 has been the Colt which is Mitsubishi's staple small hatchback. This has been successful from day one and won many admirers for its blend of good performance, good build quality and first-class fuel economy. It was Dodge who in 1965 introduced Mitsubishis to the US market.

The Galant, another long-running name since 1970, is now one of the best-equipped cars on the roads and provided the springboard for successive designs, including the latest Carisma – a joint venture with Volvo. Perhaps the best-known car is the Shogun which has been steadily and progressively improved, so much so that it is now a regular alternative to the cult Range Rover. Though not as elegant as the British vehicle, the Shogun nevertheless offers a very comprehensive specification at a competitive price.

For the best part of a decade, Mitsubishi has made a name for itself in designing radical concept cars which actually do make it into production. Four-wheel drive and four-wheel steering are used on

certain Mitsubishi models, and it has recently pioneered a new type of fuel-injected engine.

MONTEVERDI

SWITZERLAND is hardly the place anyone would imagine to find a supercar manufacturer but one-time BMW dealer Peter Monteverdi put the country on the automotive map with his elegant, fast and luxurious cars.

Introduced to the world in 1967, this car-maker lasted barely more than a decade. The appeal of his Chrysler V8-powered, Italian-coachbuilt delights live on, however. And they are still revered by enthusiasts to this day.

Regarded as a sort of 'Swiss Jensen', Peter Monteverdi went one better by making a varied line-up consisting of coupes, convertibles and even a five-seater limousine which surpassed many established rivals for performance and comfort.

In 1970 Monteverdi got a jump start on Ferrari by producing a genuine mid-engined supercar, called the HAI. Of unusual looks it was actually was sculptured by the founder himself and a top

speed of 180 mph was claimed. Like all Monteverdis few were produced and so they are all very collectible today.

MORGAN

IF A CAR-BUYER wants a Morgan today they must join the queue. At the last reckoning there was a 10-year wait for one of these most traditional of hand-built English sportscars. Some people even sell their place in the queue, so it's not impossible to get a Morgan sooner... but that's another story.

Morgan's first chapter opened in the 1920s when it built the very best three-wheelers, a curiously English obsession. From 1935 it was decided to follow the four-wheel route mainly because MG was proving so successful. The result of this change in direction was the Morgan 4/43, a two-seater sports machine which used a 1122cc four-cylinder Coventry-Climax engine, developing 34 bhp. It began a trend which Morgan continues to this day – an efficient, high-performing engine in a light body. Not surprisingly, top speed was a creditable 75 mph.

In 1938 a 1267cc Standard 10 bhp engine with overhead valves was offered as the 4/43's replacement, the 4/4. This engine continued until 1950, then Morgan fitted a tuned Standard Vanguard unit giving 70 bhp. At the same time the

car was re-named the Morgan Plus Four. Performance was increased yet again when the 90 bhp Triumph TR2 engine was offered to buyers in 1954. This unit gave a maximum speed of 100mph. However, the Plus Four was quite a large car by Morgan's usual standards, and the company felt the need for another smaller car.

In 1955 Morgan came up with the answer in the shape of the Series Two 4/4. This used the hard-wearing 1172cc Ford Ten engine and was the beginning of a relationship with Ford which continues to this day. The result was a cheap, pleasant and reliable sportscar. Eventually, the overhead-valve Ford 105E engine was used. Later versions used a 1599c, 98 bhp Ford unit mated with a four-speed gearbox, rear disc brakes and Morgan's own suspension. The Plus Four continued to use Triumph engines, and eventually used the 2138cc 105 bhp TR4 engine. When Triumph changed to a six-cylinder unit in 1968, the Morgan Plus Four became the Plus Eight, powered by Rover's potent 3.5-litre, 160 bhp V8. By this time top speed had risen to a heady 125 mph.

Today Morgan remains faithful to the original hand-built concept, still beating the body panels manually, still placing the metal over an ash wood frame and making each car to individual order the old fashioned way. In fact, it's because they buck the modern trend that Morgans are as popular as ever.

MORRIS

IT'S AMAZING how many British motor car-makers began life making bicycles. That is exactly how W.R. Morris, later Lord Nuffield, began his business. By 1913 the future Lord was busy launching his Morris Oxford light car. In truth this was less a Morris, more a collection of bits and pieces from a variety of manufacturers. The engine was a 1.0-litre four-cylinder unit made by White and Poppe. The price was right though and at less than £200, it proved popular. Within a year 1,000 had been sold.

Once Morris realised he was onto a good thing he launched the Cowley, one of the most famous of Morris's cars. It was based on the smaller Morris Oxford but also

began a long association with American companies. The engine was built by Continental and shipped to the UK.

The Cowley and Oxford models appeared after World War I and were nicknamed the Bullnose Morrises. They used English designed and built engines, this time made by Coventry-based Hotchkiss. It was a highly competitive market at this time and inflation was high but Morris took an inspired gamble. He slashed prices on his cars and at the same time bought out his main suppliers, Hotchkiss (engines), Wrigley (transmissions) and Hollick and Pratt (bodies).

The 1935 Ten-Eight proved to be the best-seller which Morris had been hoping for. Fitted with a 918cc single-valve engine, this was a very well equipped saloon and it helped Morris to produce their first million cars by 1939.

From 1939, and continuing after World War II, the real success story was the four-speed, overhead-valve, 1140cc, Series Ten. This was the first Morris to be produced using unitary construction.

The Minor came along ten years later and proved to be the most successful Morris ever made. Designed by Alec Issigonis (later to design the Mini) the first Minor, the MM Series, used the old single-valve Morris engine. It had a number of modern features, including rack-and-pinion steering and torsion-bar independent front suspension. This car set new standards in ride and handling and a million were sold by 1961.

Nuffield and Austin joined forces in 1952 and formed the British Motor Corporation. Like many such fusions in the British motor industry during this period, there was plenty of confusion. The Minor took Austin's 803cc overhead-valve A30 engine in 1953. The 1954 Series II Oxford and its less powerful brother, the Cowley, retained Morris bodies but their engines became overhead-valve Austin units. In 1955 the range was joined by the new Isis model which used the 2.6-litre six-cylinder BMC engine, though this was discontinued in 1958.

Morris eventually became part of British Leyland. Although various Morris-badged versions were launched during the 1960s, the name ceased to mean anything, merely becoming a name used by BL. The much criticised Morris Marina seemed to spell the end of the marque.

NASH

THE AMERICAN auto company Nash Motors Co. was started by an ex-General Motors man Charles W. Nash. He left 'the General' in 1916 to initially take over the Thomas B. Jeffrey company which he soon changed to the company bearing his name. Ironically, it was with trucks that Nash first made its mark, thanks to a US Army contract to supply nearly 12,000 four-wheel-drive Quads. It made Nash the world's biggest truck-producer at a stroke. By the mid to late 1920s Nash production was in top gear. In 1928 the company produced a record 138,000 vehicles, while its workers owned $20 million worth of stock in the growing company.

Some great Nash cars emerged during this era, including the 1928 two-door Sedan and the Advanced Six, a six-cylinder-engined machine which could be bought with a short chassis coupe body, or longer chassis saloon form.

By 1932 Nash was offering what it called Syncro-Safety Shift which was an early form of an all-synchromesh gearbox.

In the same year there were no less than seven different engines and as many wheelbases on offer to Nash customers – one of the widest ranges seen in the US at the time. Come the end of the 1930s, Nash was selling more cars than most of its rivals and exports were also going well, including strong sales in the UK. In 1950 the NXI convertible was unveiled by Nash and was later built, in modified form, as the Metropolitan by Austin Cars in England. In spite of all this, Nash could not survive. In the US during the 1950s big was beautiful, and Nash's cars were comparatively small. The company made its last cars in 1958.

NSU

NOT TOO SURPRISINGLY, NSU, like so many other fledgling car-makers, was first and foremost a maker of bicycles and motorbikes in Germany before embarking on large-scale car production in 1905. In fact, the first cars were a make called the Pipes which NSU built under licence. It wasn't until a year later that it launched a dedicated design of four-cylinder models, imaginatively named the 6/10PS and 15/24PS.

NSU continued to make small cars during the early part of the 1900s but also branched out into producing bigger cars with the launch of 2.5 and 3.0-litre engines. By 1930 NSU decided to rationalise its production facilities – at the time the company had three different factories – and decided, somewhat curiously, to concentrate again on motorbikes rather than produce cars. NSU sold one factory to Fiat and did not make another car until 1958.

The Prinz was the first of the company's many rear-engined, air-cooled cars and was available in small saloon form as well as in GT coupe guise. The cars got larger and larger as the engines increased. By 1967 the major model in their line-up was the TTS which could reach a respectable 75 mph.

NSU is perhaps best known for its pioneering work with the Wankel rotary engine – later developed further by Mazda in Japan. The first Wankel-powered NSU was the Spider, a convertible version of the Prinz Sport.

A rather messy legal wrangle between NSU and NSU-Fiat then surfaced. The Italian-owned company were worried that the new Wankel could eclipse their car sales and claimed legal use of the NSU badge. NSU won its case and Fiat had to drop the NSU part of its badge, instead taking on the Necker badge.

In 1967 NSU launched the revolutionary Ro80 Wankel-engined saloon with a capacity equivalent to 2.0-litres of a conventional engine. There were problems with this car, not least its tendency to foul up its spark plugs and to use copious amounts of fuel. Owners eventually learnt that the plugs needed to be regularly taken out and cleaned to ensure smooth running. But otherwise the

NSU *Pioneering work with the Wankel engine broke this company, later rescued by Audi*

car was a marvel, thanks to its very modern looks and creamy smooth performance.

However, the financial drain of the problematic Ro80 saw the company flounder. NSU was merged with Audi in 1969, coming under the overall control of Volkswagen. The Ro80 continued until 1977 when sadly, the NSU name finally disappeared.

OLDSMOBILE

AFFECTIONATELY called the 'Olds', Oldsmobile is one of America's most famed car names. It all began in 1896 when Ransom

E. Olds drove into the history books at the wheel of a one-cylinder, six-horsepower, petrol-driven car in Michigan. A year later, on August 21, the Olds Motor Vehicle Company was formed in Lansing, Michigan – the first car-maker to set up in what would become the heart of American car production. The first production Oldsmobiles had single-bore engines and tiller steering – no steering wheel as yet. They were to become known as the Curved Dash, a very famous and practical design.

Not long after these first cars were launched, Oldsmobile became part of the fledgling General Motors. Oldsmobile cars have played an important part in the development of the world's largest company ever since.

Olds had also set up the Reo Car Company, making a range of cars which often competed directly against the Oldsmobile. By 1940 Oldsmobile was competing directly with all other American

manufacturers, this even included some of the other makes within General Motors. That same year Oldsmobile launched its first convertible saloon version. It wasn't a great success, only 50 were built and sold.

This, though, was not dwelt on for long and in 1941 Oldsmobile added fastback saloons, and managed to reach sixth place in the industry league table. Buyers liked the solidity and reliability of the Oldsmobile and also found its value for money appealing.

After World War II Oldsmobile shrugged off any dowdy image it might have had and became one of the new breed of super-smooth, aerodynamic General Motor's cars. Most of these were penned by automotive artist Harley Earl, who took many of his design ideas from the flowing lines of aircraft. By 1949 Oldsmobile were just one of the American car-makers to opt for high-compression, overhead-valve, V8 engines. In Old's case this

manifested itself in the Rocket, a truly appropriate name for a 135 bhp output machine.

Olds went one further later that same year by putting this engine into a lightweight Olds 88 body, giving the car an impressive 0-60mph time of 12 seconds.

Today, Oldsmobile produces some good cars... and some less-than-exciting cars. The Trofeo, which came out in the early 1990s, may well be an excellent car in some peoples eyes but to most Europeans the gold Trofeo nameplate on a vinyl roof did not look particularly tasteful. The Bravada 4x4, on the other hand, was much better suited to European ideas of style.

Oldsmobile

Perhaps America's most famous car makers, Oldsmobile still plays an important role in the GM empire

---

OPEL

Opel

German arm of General Motors which also provided salvation for the British Vauxhall Motors

THE FIVE Opel brothers originally started by making bicycles and sewing machines. Before long the brothers decided to attempt a motorised cart-making operation.

They began by buying the rights to the Lutzmann engine. The first Opel-Lutzmann car appeared in 1898 with a rear-mounted, single-cylinder engine – this was soon replaced with a twin-cylinder unit. Neither were successful so the Opel brothers decided to head in a different direction.

They signed a deal with French car-maker Darracq to build their cars under licence. The Opels learnt much from this and in 1902 they were ready to launch their own design, a rather crude 10/12 hp car with an orthodox two-cylinder 1884cc engine.

Opel's first four-cylinder car was the 35/40hp. This came out in 1903 and showed that by then the

brothers seemed to be mastering the art of car-making. This was swiftly followed by the two-cylinder 8/14PS, commonly known as the 'doctor's car' thanks to its amazing reliability.

In 1924 Opel launched the Laubfrosch, or 'tree frog', as it became known because of its standard green paint. This was the first Opel to be built on a Henry Ford-style assembly line. This system kept costs down and the car was inexpensive to buy. Not surprisingly it was a success, 39,000 had been sold by 1927.

The Kadett, Regent and Olympia were Opel's 1930s cars. The engines began with a four-cylinder, 20 PS unit. This was later developed into the 1.0-litre produced from 1931 to 1933, the 1.2-litre from 1933 to 1935, the P4 from 1936 to 1938 and the Kadett from 1937 to 1939, the latter having an engine capacity of 1074cc.

The Regent 1.2-litre produced from 1932 to 1933, grew into the Regent 1.3-litre from 1934 to 1935 and the 1.3-litre Olympia produced from 1935 to 1937. The 1938 Olympia had an increased engine capacity of 1488cc and an output of 37 bhp. Development of other Opels continued during the 1930s with the Super, Kapitan and Admiral which were basically the 1920s six-cylinder models up-rated and up-dated.

Opel's frantic model development came to a grinding halt with the start of World War II and the end of hostilities brought the enforced dismantling of the Kadett production lines, which were transferred to Russia. At the Opel works car-making started again in 1947 with the Olympia, followed in 1948 by the Kapitan.

It wasn't until 1968 that Opel showed any real flair again with the launch of the Opel GT. This two-seater sportscar was not very quick but it did look attractive. Although only sold on mainland Europe, several thousand were bought.

Successive designs such as the Manta, Ascona, Rekord, Commodore and the beautiful Monza put the company firmly on the map as a quality car maker.

General Motors had bought Opel before World War II but it wasn't until the 1970s and 1980s that the American giant took full charge of Opel's operations.

GM integrated Opel into its European operation so that all models produced in Germany mirrored those built in other European countries. Today Opel is a major seller in Germany. Opel has also become a sister company to the UK's Vauxhall, which since the mid 1970s used re-badged Opel models in its product portfolio to good effect.

PACKARD

THIS IS ONE American car-maker who was really in at the dawn of motoring. James Ward Packard made his first automobile in 1899, about the same time as Europe's pioneers were getting on-board. Packard took his baby out on November 6, 1899 in Warren, Ohio, and was so impressed with its performance that he decided car-making was the life for him.

He went back home and started making more cars, all of them until 1903, simple single-valve machines. In fact, until 1902 the cars were not known as Packard, the company was instead referred to as the Ohio Automobile Company.

From 1911 onwards the engineering expertise in the US fledgling auto industry was gathering pace. Packard announced that single-valve machines would be replaced by the more efficient four-cylinder engines. Such was the success of Packard's move that it posted $1 million dollar profits in 1907, a year in which the general economy was certainly not very robust.

In 1912, while Packard was introducing its first six-cylinder engine, a loaded Packard truck was the first vehicle to make a westbound crossing of the USA in 46 days. By this time Packard was at the cutting edge of automotive technology, being the first US company to launch a V12 engine in its Twin-Six car and the first to use aluminium pistons. By the 1930s Packard was producing a wide range of cars, though often the bodies were still built by specialists. This caused a hike in costs across

the range, to counter this high pricing problem, Packard brought out the Model 1101 Coupe-Roadster. At $2,500 this combined competitive pricing with first-class build quality.

Despite its overall success, Packard was tending to concentrate too much on the top end of the market. This strategy may not always be sufficient to keep a company afloat, unless the products really do not have significant rivals.

The demise of Packard is interesting. It eventually became part of the American Motors Corporation which had been formed by the amalgamation of Nash and Hudson in 1954. The architect of this, Nash President George Mason, wanted to include Studebaker and Packard too, but he suddenly died in October 1954 before the arrangements could be finalised. Instead, later that year Packard bought out Studebaker. Unfortunately, the new Packard found it could not survive, profits were not sufficient and a few years afterwards, Packard sank. It was a sad end to a motoring legend.

PANHARD

PANHARD AND LEVASSOR, to give the company its full name, was born in France right at the dawn of motoring. The company successfully continued making some very interesting cars right into the late 1960s. Like many pioneers of the motoring world, Panhard began with a car which was not wholly its own, in this case a Daimler V-twin engine which the duo placed in a simple body in 1891. They didn't sell many and after some tests with rear engines, Panhard settled into the traditional arrangement.

By 1900 Panhard was selling the Tourer which had an armoured wood frame. So successful was the Tourer's design that companies across Europe began copying the

details. Panhard was really making a name for itself. In 1922 Panhard was using modern sleeve-valve engines and the range was extended at both ends by a rather slow 1.2-litre Model 10 with central gearchange, left-hand drive, thermo-syphon cooling and a cone clutch instead of the usual wet-plate. The top-of-the-range model of this period was the big 6.3-litre Straight Eight with front-wheel brakes, twin magnetos, and twin carburettors. This latter model was made until 1930.

Introduced in 1927, the 16, 10 and 13 were the first Panhards with six-cylinder, sleeve-valve engines. The 16CV was first and used a 3.4-litre unit, this was soon followed by the 1.8-litre 10CV and the 2.3-litre twin-carburettor 13CV.

Ten years later the Dynamic was launched, powered by a six-cylinder engine which came in 2.5, 2.7 and 3.8-litre forms. It was a rather strange looking car, not because of its modern backbone chassis, hydraulic brakes, worm drive or all-round torsion bar independent suspension, but rather because of its faired-in headlights, wheel spats and a central driving position! This feature did not last too long though, 1939 saw a change to left-hand drive.

After World War II the new austerity across Europe affected Panhard too and out went the elaborate designs, in came the simple but popular Dyna with its air-cooled, flat-twin engine of 610cc. The light alloy body was made by Facel-Metallon, and front suspension was independent with the rear system by torsion bars and a live axle. The four-speed gearbox had overdrive and a dashboard change.

Packhard

The first American car maker to utilize a V12, but Packhard had floundered by the mid-1950s

---

In 1953 Panhard launched the Junior, with 38 bhp, and a year later a supercharged 62 bhp model.

The Tigre was available from 1961 and was a variation on the Dyna theme and it too proved very popular. Over 100 mph was possible in the hotter 24CT and CD sports coupes introduced for 1964. 1967 was Panhard's last year after being taken over by Citroen.

PANTHER

PANTHER IS as interesting a company as some of its cars. The story begins in 1972 in Byfleet, England with the launch of the J72, which was basically a replica car based on the pre-war SS100 (a forerunner to the famous Jaguar sportscars). This Panther used a 3.8-litre double overhead-cam, six-cylinder Jaguar engine. If that wasn't enough, a V12, again a Jaguar unit, was offered from 1974. This was followed in 1975 by the De Ville, a four-door sports saloon loosely based on the Type 46 Bugatti of the 1930s, again using Jaguar V12 power. It was a lavishly equipped car with a cocktail cabinet included in its specification. The price was staggeringly high for the time. Not surprisingly few De Villes were sold, though it continued in production until 1980.

Other small-scale production models appeared throughout the late 1970s and early 1980s, including the curious Rio which was a Triumph Dolomite saloon with a Rolls-Royce style front grille. Perhaps the most bizarre offering was the Super Six, a six-wheeled convertible sportscar. It was extremely powerful thanks to a massive 8.2-litre Cadillac V8 engine which was mid-mounted and developed no less than 600 bhp courtesy of its twin turbochargers. The next model was the Lima, which was more accessible to the public and similar in looks to the Morgan. This later grew into the Kallista, a car which proved very popular indeed. Financial problems occurred though, and Panther only survived with the injection of capital provided by the company's new South Korean owner. Kim Ill Sung ploughed money into the development of the Solo, a very promising modern sports two-seater but this only existed in prototype form.

PEUGEOT

TODAY PEUGEOT FAMILY members still sit on the board of the company that they started more than a century ago. In fact, when they first began making cars in 1876 there were two Peugeot family companies competing with each other, making different cars. It took a few years of this rivalry before the two joined forces. The united Peugeot company went from strength to strength. The 1912 Bebe was the first product of the joint team and was in fact an Ettore Bugatti design which proved very popular. In 1914, just months before the outbreak of World War I, Peugeot launched the 2.6-litre Type 153. This 12 bhp, V4-engined car was made until the outbreak of war when production ceased. It was resurrected in 1918 and was the basis for a series of 3.0-litre, four-cylinder, single-valve cars.

At the same time the Quadrilette was launched, a successor to the Bebe. A rear track of only 2ft 6ins meant it had to have staggered, tandem seating, the lighting was by acetylene... and worst still, in its original, cheapest form, it had no starter system!

In 1936 the thoroughly modern 401 appeared. It was the shape of things to come with its dashboard gearchange and a smooth, flowing body in which not only the headlights, but also the battery were housed between the grille and the radiator.

By 1955 it must have seemed as if everything Peugeot touched turned to gold. The Type 403 was incredibly successful and by 1958 automatic gearboxes were being

Panther *Off-the-wall designs from this small British company resulted in cars like the Super Six (above), with six wheels and an amazing 600 bhp!*

Peugeot

Continues to produce fine cars, from superminis to luxury saloons

offered, plus the option of a diesel engine by 1959. This led on to the 404 in 1960, the first Peugeot to be styled by Pininfarina. Buyers could have a 404 in coupe, convertible or saloon form. Another trend-setter

was the late 1960s 504, also available in coupe, convertible and saloon form. V6 versions didn't appear until 1974, the same year it acquired Citroen, but they were worth waiting for.

The V6 engine is still used by Peugeot today in a number of its cars, though it has been developed considerably since the demise of the Cabriolet for the 605 executive saloon. Peugeot has also seen success with the 205 hatchback

during both the 1980s (by which time it had taken over the ailing Rootes group from Chrysler), and 1990s. The 405 saloon and the 406 are also acclaimed designs. There hasn't been a time when this French company was producing bad cars.

PLYMOUTH

PLYMOUTH MAY be just a part of the giant Chrysler Corporation but

it has produced some very interesting cars for the enthusiast over the years. Plymouths have also proved very popular with ordinary American buyers.

The first automotive offering from this company appeared in 1928 and proved an able rival to inexpensive Fords and Chevrolets. It used a four-cylinder engine producing a fairly meagre 21 bhp, though for the time this was par for the course. By 1933 Plymouth was changing many of its models over to the bigger six-cylinder arrangement which most American companies were adopting. After World War II Plymouth lost ground to its rivals – slipping from its regular third place slot in the US best-selling cars table – simply because, in common with other Chrysler products, old fashioned and rather staid styling had become the company's norm. It wasn't until the late 1950s that Plymouth were in the ascendant again, when it launched the Valiant, mechanically an innovative car.

The biggest breakthrough came in 1965 when the GT Barracuda was launched, based on the floorpan of the Valiant but with a 4.5-litre V8 under the bonnet. Other successful Plymouths of this period were the Belvedere, Fury and VIP.

By the late 1980s and early 1990s, Plymouth, in common with Chrysler, was producing cars which had their roots in the US and Japan. The Laser was a prime example – it was a re-clothed Mitsubishi Eclipse. The Plymouth Acclaim saloon, however, was still pure Chrysler. One of today's best selling Plymouths is the people-carrier Voyager, one of the first and most popular versions of this type of vehicle.

Pontiac *The 1991 Trans Am is one of the company's best recent efforts*

PONTIAC

THE FIRST PONTIAC rolled off the production line in 1926. The marque was basically a sister make to the Oakland, a car which had been around since 1907. This had been born when buggymaker Edward M. Murphy opened the Oakland Motor Car Company and produced a simple twin-cylinder car. The Pontiac was intended to be the lower priced alternative to the Oakland and thereby open up another market at a time when the US economy was approaching serious depression and money was becoming tight. Unfortunately, there was not a lot of difference between the Pontiac and the Oakland. Buyers became confused by the model choices.

However, by 1947, after a number of years struggling along, Pontiac suddenly found that its more costly eight-cylinder cars were beginning to outsell the smaller, less expensive sixes – the first time this had ever happened. It proved to them that buyers were willing to spend more money to get more power and more features.

The next big development did not occur until 1952, but what a development it was – the fitting of the Dual-Range Hydra-Matic transmission. This system allowed for much smoother progress and was well matched to Pontiac's engines. They were not the only US company to take Hydra-Matic gearboxes, Oldsmobile and Cadillac took them too.

In something of a departure from normal custom, Pontiac decided to launch what they called a sedan delivery – today we would call it a car-based van. Today this machine looks simply superb, especially the Silver Streak versions, so named because of the slither of chrome along the side. Buyers in 1952 were not as impressed and only just under 1,000 were sold.

Today Pontiac is no longer an individual company, being part of the large General Motors listing. It still produces good cars on occasion, however. The beautiful cars of the 1950s may not be repeated but today's buyers know that a Pontiac is a well built car with a good range of engines and some high equipment levels.

PORSCHE

FERDINAND PORSCHE'S employment history looks very impressive. He had worked for Lohner, Austro-Daimler, Steyr, Mercedes and Volkswagen, as well as helping build racing cars for the successful Auto-Union team. Then in 1948 he decided to set up his own car-making company.

Today there can be few corners of the globe where the word Porsche is not recognised for its symbol of supreme auto engineering.

Yet production of these most desirable sportscars began in Weissach in Germany in 1950 only after Porsche had finished his design of a very important car for another company – the Volkswagen Beetle.

The 356 was the first real Porsche, even though its rear-mounted engine was a VW-based air-cooled, four-cylinder unit of 1086cc and it was more the work of the founder's son. Power was not that impressive but the sleek shape of the 356 pointed the way forwards – it was the forerunner of the classic 911. Except for minor alterations the 356's shape remained unaltered until the last model, the 2000GS of 1964, which developed no less than 130 bhp from its 1966cc engine. Replacing the 356 was the best known Porsche of all, the 911. This rear-engined car still survives today and offers mind-bending performance in its latest guises.

Porsche also built another fine sportscar during this period, the 928, which came about when Herr Porsche was given a simple smoothed piece of wood for his birthday by the Design Department at Porsche. He looked at the curved lump and said, why don't we build this? The 928 was born, its bumpers built into the body of the car to give a smooth, flowing shape. It proved to be one of the world's best Grand Tourers.

While the 911 was being continually improved Porsche tried its hand at more conventional sportscars, the first of these being the 924 which was originally a design for Volkswagen. They decided they didn't want it – because VW was about to launch the Scirocco – so Porsche decided to go ahead anyway. With the engine at the front and the hefty transaxle at the rear, the 924 had an almost perfect 50-50 weight distribution. This gave it a cornering ability which few rivals

Porsche

The father of the VW Beetle laid the foundations for one of the greatest cars ever made – the 911 – and one of the greatest names in car making

of the time could match. Original versions produced 125 bhp and drive to the rear wheels through a four-speed gearbox, a five speed 'box arrived in 1977 and the Turbo with 177 bhp, came along in 1979.

The 944 was like a larger 924 and shared some of that car's engineering and components, not least an up-rated version of the 2.5-litre engine. The first 944 appeared in 1981, followed by a 220 bhp Turbo in 1985, the 16-valve 944S in 1986, a 2.7-litre model in 1988 and 3.0-litre Series Two versions in 1990. The following year the Cabriolet was launched, followed in 1992 by the similar looking 968.

Today Porsche is almost the watchword in supercars and concentrates on the 911 design it has continued to improve since its launch more than 30 years ago. Truly it is one of the world's best supercars and one of the least temperamental. And that's not the end of the Porsche story, the new cut-price Boxster roadster appears to have all the ingredients of a future classic, too.

PROTON

MALAYSIAN PROTON has come along way in just over a decade. From it's humble beginnings as a Government-controlled car maker, producing discontinued Mitsubishis – the National Car – Proton's growth in the Asian market has been startling.

Britain became the first country to import cars from this one-time colony in 1989 and is still Proton's largest export market, although left-hand drive cars have been made since the early 1990s for European sales.

As Proton took more control of its destiny and car designs, the Malaysian Government's stake-`hold shrunk as private enterprise took control. Proton's crowning glory came in 1996 when it bought an 80 per cent share of Lotus.

With an aim to break the half million production mark by the year 2000, Proton's future definitely looks bright.

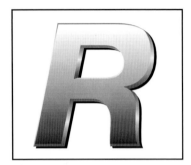

RELIANT

RELIANT IS ONE of those small companies which seems to lurch from one financial crisis to another but at the end of the day always return from the abyss. That's not too surprising because this company has made some very good cars. Unfortunately, it's made some rather unattractive ones too.

Let's start with the bad news. The Reliant Robin. Reliant will say that this three-wheeler – one at the front and two at the rear – has a loyal following, and it is true it has been on sale for decades now and there are those who swear by them.

There are also those who swear at them, chiefly because of their handling characteristics. In fact, strange though it may seem, Reliant strengthened the two front edges so that if this car dipped down on to the road, which it could do if drivers jerked the steering wheel hard, then it could continue to travel (for short distances, it must be said) without serious damage to the bodywork! This, incidentally, is made of glass-reinforced-plastic.

Reliant was founded back in 1935, originally just making three-wheelers. The Rebel and Supervan ranges of the 1960 a gave way to the Robin in the early 1970s which even saw a more conventional derivative, the Kitten in 1975. Fellow three-wheeler manufacturer Bond was bought out in 1969.

A far more serious proposition

were the high performance Sabre and Scimitar models. The Scimitar, in GTE form, was the world's first sporting estate and since it ran on Ford engines and gearboxes it was reliable and popular. It looked good too, and performance from the 3.0-litre V6 was always impressive. Built between 1968 and 1975 in Tamworth, Staffordshire, the GTE was capable of over 120 mph, and gained Royal approval when Princess Anne became a firm fan of the car.

The GTE was joined by the SE6 in the late 1970s, a car which was wider, longer and heavier than its brother. It was not as popular as the GTE, but a convertible option increased its appeal.

Reliant then brought out the SS1 during the 1980s. This was a two-seater convertible available

Reliant

Best known for three-wheelers but noted for sportscars like the Scimitar

with either a normally-aspirated engine or the Nissan turbo unit. Fine performers though these were, especially the turbo, their glass-fibre bodies were hardly the last word in pleasing design and build quality, and not many were sold. Today, Reliant, having been owned by a succession of enthusiastic companies, is producing the evergreen three-wheeled Rialto in small quantities.

RENAULT

LOUIS RENAULT, and his brothers, Marcel and Fernand, unveiled their first car, a simple 1.75-litre, air-cooled De Dion engine sitting on a tubular chassis with shaft drive and a differential rear axle in 1898.

In these early years the Renaults were more concerned with having fun, so they raced a number of their fledgling cars. In 1902 Louis took part in the Paris-Vienna race and finished second. The vehicle he used had a 3.8-litre Viet-

designed and Renault-built four-cylinder engine. The following year it was a 6.3-litre light racer entered in the Paris-Madrid race and by 1904, at long last, the experience that had been gained in these races was introduced to the public.

The AX and AG models launched in 1905 were the first of a range of 1100cc, two-cylinder cars which were Renault's pre-1914 best-sellers and the ancestors of the renowned Taxis de la Marne. The short chassis AX two-seater was a real bargain in 1908 and Royal favour for these excellent French cars was granted when King Edward VII decided not to buy British and instead plumped for a 3.0-litre, four-cylinder model in 1906.

By 1908 Renault was making six-cylinder cars, the first being a 8.5-litre, and by 1914 the range included no less than two wheelbase lengths, four-cylinder cars of 2.1, 2.6, 3.6, 5.1 and 8.5-litres, as well as two sixes with 5.1 and 7.5-litre engines.

Renault's Light Six was launched in 1927. This had a new 3.2-litre engine and also benefited from the then modern addition of coil ignition. The following year a 1.5-litre Light Six appeared.

The Reinastella which was launched in 1929 was something of a change in direction for Renault. This 7.1-litre car was Renault's first straight-eight engine and carried modern features such as a front-

mounted radiator, pump-cooling and servo brakes. These features were not common on other cars until at least three years later.

After all this development, imagination and innovation it was hardly fitting that Louis Renault should die in prison. But in 1944, he did after being accused of collaborating with the Nazis. The company was nationalised and under Government control, two private cars, the revised four-door 1.0-litre Juvaquatre and the 760cc 4CV, developed secretly during the war years, were produced.

The rear-engined format seen in the 4CV formed the backbone of Renault's engine development until the early 1960s, but in 1951 they came out with the Fregate. This car had a short-

stroke, 2.0-litre, four-cylinder engine, all-round independent suspension and a four-speed gearbox.

Other great Renaults were the rear-engined Dauphine, the front-wheel-drive 16 (arguably the first true family hatchback which was first produced in 1965), the famed 5 which was one of the first superminis, and the Espace, the first of the 'people carriers'.

Today Renault makes the Safrane and Laguna, the Espace and the Clio, all worthy vehicles, but a good number of its current models seem to lack the individual style which was so often a Renault strength in days gone by. The new Renault Mégane and in particular its novel 'mini MPV' Scenic, however, was voted European Car of the Year for 1997 and seems to signal a new exciting direction for the French car-maker.

The new Mégane range signals Renault's return to individuality and interesting styling

RILEY

ONCE A PROUD British company, Riley is now all too often only remembered in the history books. This is to forget what this great car-maker achieved during its many years of car production.

The Torpedo Tourer was launched in 1909 and right from the start proved to be very popular with buyers. It was one of the first Rileys to feature round radiators, pressure lubrication, shaft drive, three-speed gearboxes and Riley's own patent detachable wheels, the demand for which almost brought car production to a standstill by the end of 1910.

The Tourer was a development

Riley *This once famous badge may be revived by BMW*

The Nine was one of the most successful cars produced by the Riley concern, and was one of the most advanced. Powered by a 1087cc, 32 bhp, four-cylinder engine with twin camshafts, this unit became the backbone of Riley development for three decades, and in one form or another continued running until 1957.

Along the way the Nine gave birth to the attractive Monaco fabric-bodied sports saloon in 1928, and the highly-tuned Brooklands sports. The Brooklands had a low weight, a twin carburettor 50 bhp engine and was capable of 80 mph, all at a very competitive price.

Over the following years both the Nine and the later Fourteen were steadily improved. This meant a lowered chassis and semi-panelled bodywork in 1932, and an optional (later standard) pre-selector gearbox in 1934. A Super Sports six-cylinder, 1.5-litre appeared in 1932, followed in 1933 by the touring Mentone.

By 1933 Riley was in its element, making the fastback Kestrel saloon and the Falcon which had stylish doors opening into the roof. In 1935 Riley's newcomer was the classic 1.5-litre Four with a Wilson gearbox. This car soon outsold all rivals, thanks to offering the choice of two superb engines, an economic single carburettor or sporty twin carburettor. The 1.5 was the inspiration for the Sprite two-seater, the Kestrel-Sprite, and the Lynx-Sprite saloon and convertible, which offered more room but the same highly-tuned engines, again at a very competitive price. However, despite sporting successes during the decade, financial troubles hastened William Morris to buy the company in 1938.

By the swinging 1960s the Riley range simply consisted of more luxurious and upmarket Morris cars as BMC increased control.

The final cars were the Mini-based Elf (an upmarket, leather upholstered Mini, with a boot), the Kestrel (based on a Morris 1100 or 1300) and the Morris Oxford based 4/72 saloon.

It was all over before 1970 as a result of range rationalisation. Now, nearly 30 years later, it is whispered that there are plans to resurrect the Riley name, just one of a drawer full of evocative British badges bought by BMW when it acquired the Rover Group, back in 1994.

of the Torpedo and preceded the Lynx which appeared in 1915. This was a 1.5-litre sports convertible and it was the basis for the first post-World War I Rileys.

The Eleven boasted alloy pistons and the good-looking 1923 Redwinger had wire wheels and polished aluminium coachwork. Following on from the Eleven was the Twelve, one of which amply proved its hardiness when it was successfully used to map out Kenya's road system in 1926.

ROLLS-ROYCE

SOCIALITE Charles Stewart Rolls and electric crane-maker Frederick Henry Royce were two of the most unlikely associates in the history of the motor car, yet together they created a company that has consistently produced the best cars in the world for almost 90 years.

Rolls-Royce was founded in 1904 after a meeting of the two in a Manchester Hotel. Rolls had previously been selling Panhard cars but was becoming increasingly disenchanted, wanting to sell something of superior quality.

Royce was an engineer of the highest quality, and after setting up his own electrical business, set about designing and making quality cars that far exceeded contemporary standards. It was Charles Rolls' business manager, Henry Edmunds, who instigated the meeting. It was decided that Royce would design and make the cars while Rolls looked after the sales and public relations side of the business. The former's early attempts at building his own car gave little indication of such future greatness, but Rolls was impressed enough with both the man, and his products, to forge the partnership.

In 1907 they created the now-legendary Silver Ghost, and although its design failed to set any new technological standards, the real breakthrough came in the quality of workmanship embodied in the finished product. Beautifully sculptured, the Silver Ghost ran like a Swiss watch and was just as reliable. Its successful completion of a 15,000-mile endurance trail in 1907 under the watchful eye of the Royal Automobile Club (RAC) became folklore, as did the car's price. Costing £995 for the chassis unit alone, this Rolls-Royce was never destined for the masses and it established a tradition that the company has firmly adhered to into the 1990s.

The Silver Ghost survived in production until 1926, being the only model produced throughout this period. However, such was its popularity with the elite that it enabled the company to move from Manchester to a larger site in Derby. The fruitful partnership between Rolls and Royce had already been broken in 1910 when the former had become the first passenger killed in a flying accident in Britain. Prior to his untimely death, Charles Rolls had become the first man to fly the English Channel both ways.

Just prior to Rolls' demise the famous Spirit of Ecstasy mascot had been created. Inspired by Eleanor Thornton, Rolls-Royce wanted a standard bearer that would give the marque style and dignity at a time when all sorts of novelties were being stuck on the front of cars. Thornton was the model for artist Charles Sykes, who had been commissioned by the company to design the mascot.

In 1920 Rolls-Royce of America was founded at Springfield, Massachusetts, but the depression of the next decade caused its premature closure in 1931 – the same year Rolls-Royce took control of Bentley. Only two years later, after establishing Rolls-Royce as both a car and aero-engine manufacturer of the highest calibre, Royce died at the age of 70. Although he had been ill for some time, Royce had continued to design and oversee the building of cars like the Wraith and the Phantom right up until his death. His passing sparked off one of the great myths of the marque – the changing of the Rolls-Royce badge from red to black. Many still believe that it was done as a mark of respect for the great founders but company records show that Royce had approved the move years before he died.

After the war, Rolls-Royce moved to Crewe and restarted production with the Silver Wraith and the Silver Dawn. The latter was a first for the company as it featured fully standardised bodywork – this aspect of the Rolls-Royce's construction had previously been left to a select band of coachmakers like Park Ward and James Young. The introduction of a new V8 was to provide the power train for a succession of Rolls-Royce models over the next four decades. Indeed, it is still used in a radically updated form today, having steadily grown in size from 6.2 to 6.7-litres. A version is also available fitted with a turbocharger.

The release of the Silver Shadow in 1965 marked a real change for Rolls-Royce. Now with fully-integrated body construction and all-round independent suspension, the car moved the company towards younger buyers and formed the basis of the Corniche and Camargue models. The ungainly slab-sided Camargue lasted in production for less than 10 years (a short run for the company) but the Corniche soldiered on until 1994, having enjoyed a lifespan of some 23 years. A special long-wheelbase Silver Shadow originally developed for the US market was also finally released to a global audience as the Wraith in the 1980s.

Although continual developments kept the Shadow up to date with contemporaries, the great debate as to whether the company still produced the best cars in the world raged for a long time until replacement models were announced in 1980. The Silver Spur, Silver Spirit and Flying Spur helped drag the company into modern times but it was widely believed that other more humble makes of prestige cars could match, and even better, these vehicles. Bentley, however, was fast gaining increased respect with its more youthful sporting derivatives of standard Rolls-Royce models.

Even the company's enviable reputation couldn't save it from experiencing some hard times during its recent history and many a lesser company would have crumbled years before. Rolls-Royce finally went bankrupt in 1971 as a result of the disastrous RB211 jet engine project, and for two years it was in the hands of the receiver. It was while the company was in this state of flux that the new Corniche was allowed to be launched – a bold move that fortunately paid off.

Rolls-Royce was bought in 1980 by Vickers, who cautiously charted the company back into calmer seas, before entering into a multi-million pound joint co-operation deal with BMW in 1995 that will see the firm producing a new range of high-tech engines well into the next century.

As expected, there was considerable hue and cry over a foreign concern buying into this great institution, but the more level-headed saw the move as a life-saver for Britain's premier automotive marque. Now the technical excellence of BMW and the craftsmanship of Rolls-Royce will hopefully work together to produce the best cars in the world.

Rolls-Royce

The Silver Dawn, the first Rolls-Royce to feature its own bodywork

Rolls-Royce

Above *The Silver Wraith model was one of Royce's last designs, with bodywork by Hooper* **Right** *What Rolls-Royce motoring is all about; armchair comfort, luxurious interiors, outstanding build quality and lastly, that famous Spirit of Ecstacy grille mascot* **Overleaf** *The 1965 Silver Shadow, aimed at a younger market*

ROVER

ROVER DROVE into a real quagmire in the 1970s when it became part of the ill-fated British Leyland. During this period the company produced some poor cars, although the Rover 3500 was voted European Car of the Year in 1977. Today, Rover is a success story. The company has been bought by BMW and now produces some fine cars, using British engineering and design expertise to make products up to the quality demanded by BMW.

Built in Solihull, Rover started life in the hands of J.K. Starley and W. Sutton in 1904 with a neat little 8 hp model. Before this, Rover specialised in bicycles and even a motorised bath chair!

By the 1920s Rover had established itself as a maker of upmarket quality cars and one of the finest of its type was the P4. Some 131,000 were built with a variety of engine choices. The first P4 went on sale in 1949, initially as the six-cylinder 75 model. There were no major body changes in 14 years, though the catalogue of engines used is long. The 110, the ultimate P4, was built between 1963 and 1964.

During this time, Rover created automotive history when it became the first car-maker to produce a gas turbine car which also spawned a Le Mans racer during the 60s. In 1956 a more dedicated design saw the turbine coupled to four-wheel

Rover

From motorised bath chairs to world renowned off-roaders

drive. The T4 derivative of 1961 gave strong indications of an equally radical car which appeared two years later: the Rover 2000, which was also voted European Car of the Year. With its skeleton superstructure, bolt-on panels (including the roof), sophisticated rear suspension and the most modern of styles from this once straight-laced car-maker, the 2000 was one of the cars of the 1960s. A Buick V8-powered version, the 3500 became the ultimate police pursuit car in the UK.

When the car was replaced in 1976 by the Ferrari Daytona-inspired SD1, quality standards were slipping (Rover had been owned by British Leyland for many years). It was only during the 1980s with the help of Honda, that Rover together with the Austin brand, emerged from the British Leyland shambles as an independent

company, with new cars and a new image to save its skin. So successful was the turnaround that BMW decided to buy the company from British Aerospace.

After the Second World War a commercial offshoot called Land Rover was established. Initially just seen as a British alternative to the Jeep, Land Rover became a successful company in its own right. The evergreen 'Landie' became an institution, as did the more luxurious Range Rover of 1970. So successful was the design that it wasn't until the late 1980s that a new model came along to appeal to new markets – the Discovery. The original Range Rover lasted more than 25 years before making way for the new model. Some suggested that the only reason BMW bought Rover was for the Land Rover company – the jewel in Rover's crown.

SAAB

DURING WORLD WAR II Sweden was neutral, which was ideal for Saab because it was able to get on with testing its first car in relative peace. However, it wasn't until five years after the end of hostilities in Europe, 1950 in fact, that Saab actually unveiled their offering.

Saab stands for Svenska Aeroplan AB; as the name suggests, it was initially an aircraft maker, and much of this expertise was carried over to its car division.

Saab's first car was the Model 92 which used a 764cc, two-cylinder, two-stroke engine developing 25 bhp and driving the front wheels. Suspension was torsion bars all around and the aerodynamic saloon body was not all that different from the Saabs we are perhaps more familiar with today. Very sure-footed roadholding, flexible power and the compact shape made it a popular car for rallies, where it soon achieved notable successes.

Such was the confidence at Saab that in 1955 more power was added and the Model 93 was launched.

SAAB

The Swedish aircraft manufacturer turned car maker after WW II, are now part of General Motors

This used a three-cylinder engine of 748cc producing 38 bhp. Again performance was very impressive. The tuned GT model could reach 100 mph. Like all Saabs, then and now, these early models gained a deserved reputation for reliability and ruggedness.

The 96 was a direct development of the 93. It was first seen in 1966 powered by a 841cc, 46 bhp engine, or buyers could choose a tuned Monte Carlo 850cc engine which produced no less than 60 bhp. In 1967 a Ford V4 engine was fitted. The 96 was excellent publicity for Saab because it won so many international rallies during the 1960s. The company also enjoyed some success with its Sonnet two-seater sports coupe –particularly in the States – until it was discontinued in 1974.

Saab launched the new 99 two and four-door saloons in 1969. Again, they were a straight development of the earlier models, but with the advantage of a new 1709cc four-cylinder, overhead cam, in-line engine which Saab developed from a British Triumph unit. A year after the launch fuel-injection became available and in 1971 the engine was up-rated to

1854cc with a further increase to 1985cc a year later. In 1978 Saab launched its first turbocharged car, a 99 producing 145 bhp. Following this they launched one of their most successful cars, the 900 which is still being sold today. The Turbo models were terrific performers and this hatchback offered no less than six feet of luggage space with the seats folded flat.

By the late 1980s Saab, one of the smallest of Europe's car-makers, realised it could not expand without a bigger partner. Originally a deal was struck with Renault to co-produce new cars and engines. However, the deal came unstuck and Saab later teamed-up with General Motors.

SEAT

SEAT, THE SPANISH car-maker, began life as a Fiat subsidiary as far back as 1919 but didn't become state-owned until the late 1940s, still producing Fiats. In 1979 Fiat took full control with Seat using

cast-off designs. By the early 1980s Seat started to become more independent and although many of its wares were still the previous versions of Fiats. It began to shake off its cheap and cheerful image and became better known across Europe. The pretty Seat Ibiza hatchback of this era used a special engine developed by the prestigious Porsche Systems.

During the 1980s Seat started to interest numerous car-makers. Volkswagen won the race to take over the Spanish manufacturer and it quickly came up with some good new models, including the new-shaped Ibiza and the Toledo. Today, Seat's cars are all based on Volkswagen floorpans. Much of their interior equipment and engines come from the massive VW parts-bins. They are still competitively priced, offer good

Seat
Few manufacturers have enjoyed such a change in fortune as Seat

equipment levels and now perform very well indeed. In fact Seat has been the pioneer of several fruitful designs in the Volkswagen stable – the new Ibiza came before the VW Polo. The saloon version, the Cordoba, beat the Polo version on the market by more than 18 months. VW has invested heavily in this potentially promising car-maker and the future looks bright.

SIMCA

THE FRENCH company Simca was formed to manufacture Fiat cars under licence back in 1935. It did not start to make its own cars until 1949, relatively late when compared with most European car-makers. The first car was the 50 bhp sports Simca 8CV with beautiful coupe bodywork by Facel Metallon. This car won the 1950 Alpine Rally while the standard Simca 8s scored impressively in their own classes in the Rally.

One of the most successful Simcas of all time, the Aronde, was completely new and appeared in 1951. Such was its success that it was continuously made until 1963, receiving regular up-dates on the way. The first Aronde used a 45 bhp version of the old Simca 8CV unit but the

Simca *An interesting maker of a diverse range of cars, but never able to match the popularity of rivals Citroën or Renault*

rest of the car was completely new. Technical specifications included unitary construction, coil spring and wishbone independent front suspension and hypoid final drive. The Aronde was pitched into the market directly against Citroën. Simca attacked long distance records held for many years by their rivals, proving that Simcas were reliable and keeping them in the public spotlight.

Buyers loved the Aronde's economy, soft ride, easy driving manners and, above all, its unprecedented reliability. In 1953, in a bid to widen its appeal, Simca launched a sports version of the Aronde, with a more powerful 50 bhp engine. By 1954 it was also available to British buyers. There was a choice of several models, the Plein Ciel, Ocean, and Coupe. In 1956 Arondes received a 1.3-litre 48 bhp engine as standard, though 57 bhp units were found in the sports coupes and convertibles and the Montlhery saloon. Estates continued with the 45 bhp engine.

By 1958 Simca was looking to expand. It did so by buying the French Ford division and was soon producing its version of the Ford V8 2.3-litre, single-valve Vedette. The V8 sold well and in 1958 Simca gave the car a more powerful 84 bhp engine. Production ceased in France in 1961, though as late as 1967 the Chambord and Presidence versions of this car, by then with 112 bhp output and an overhead-valve engine, were still being made under licence in Brazil.

During the late 1960s some excellent saloons, estates and pretty coupes were produced but, like the British Roots Group, Simca was struggling.

Ultimately Simca was bought by Chrysler. A rather lack-lustre period followed until the American company pulled out of European operations and retreated to the USA. During this time some weird 'badge engineering' took place. During the early 1970s a Simca-powered, but UK designed car, was produced – the 180 range. The

Simca name died around the same time, replaced first by Chrysler Europe, then the Talbot name was used and finally Peugeot came along in 1978 to buy up the residue.

SINGER

SINGER WAS ALWAYS regarded as a frontrunner in British motoring tradition. Unfortunately, that didn't save it when, after 70 years of car-making, it was killed off.

Originally a motorcycle manufacturer, George Singer made not only sound reliable cars but also a noteworthy endurance racer during the 1930s. However, just 20 years later, Singer had fallen from being the third biggest car-maker in the UK to virtual insignificance. It ended up being dropped in 1970 by the then ailing Rootes Group.

The 1930s saw Singer at its peak: car sales were buoyant, beaten only by Austin and Rover, and success at the Le Mans 24-Hours race brought about a car of the same

name which is now a collectors item. Like the sporting MGs of that era, Singer was not afraid to use advanced designs and draw upon competition experience.

What went wrong is unclear, certainly the company was never the same when production resumed after 1945. Despite making some promising contemporary cars, Singer fell on hard times and required the expanding Rootes Group to save it.

Singer then became the more upmarket arm of Hillman with better trimmed and equipped re-badged alternatives. Badge marketing took its toll during the 1960s where Hillman cars were also marketed as Singers, including the Imp (known as the Chamois).

As Rootes fell on tough times, its American parent Chrysler decided to rationalise the lines. The Singer name was deemed too old fashioned, and was discontinued. With that a great chunk of English motoring heritage was lost.

SKODA

HARD THOUGH it may be to believe, Skoda, sometimes today the butt of so many motoring jokes, was once one of the most powerful industrial concerns in Europe. The Skoda story began back in the days of the Austro-Hungarian Empire, the biggest collection of nation states Europe had seen since the Romans. With the fall of the Empire and the separation of states, Skoda became marginalised and declined to a far smaller company. During its time, though, this interesting company has produced some very desirable cars. That trend is now returning following Volkswagen's take-over of the company.

After World War One, Skoda's mighty factories became part of the spoils of war, its main production facilities finding themselves in the new Czechoslovakian republic. Such up-heaval had a profound effect on this

once-proud company. It was not until the late 1920s that Skoda was really fashioning anything worth serious consideration.

The 420 used an advanced 995cc unit developing 20 bhp. The chassis was a centre tubular layout with rear-swing half-axles. The 420 was a great success and was first of a range of 1930s cars which made Skoda famous. The 420 was developed into the Popular and the same technical features were to be found in the four-cylinder Rapid (1380cc and 22 bhp) and the six-cylinder Superb (2480cc and 50 bhp). The Popular also appeared with a streamlined coupe body. All models were progressively improved and had their power and output increased. Meanwhile the engines changed from side to overhead-valve designs. The range also saw the

introduction of the 1.8-litre Favorit and the Monte Carlo which was home to a Popular chassis and Rapid engine.

After World War II the Skoda 1100 OHV and 1200 OHV – based on the pre-war designs – appeared and were developed into the well known 40 or 50 bhp Octavia with a capacity of 1089cc. The Octavia Super had a 1221cc engine producing 45 bhp and the Felicia was a two-seater Octavia with a 50 bhp engine. The Octavia/Felicia range was discontinued, with the exception of the estate cars, after the launch of the 1000MB in 1964

The 1100 Estelle models appeared in the 1970s and once again were rear-engined. They proved themselves hardy and reliable, and won their class many times in international rallies.

Following the end of communism in the old republic of Czechoslovakia and the splitting of the country into two, Volkswagen went in and bought the company. Today Skoda's cars are improving dramatically and are fast becoming a match for many mainstream European rivals.

SS

SWALLOW SIDECARS began production of cars in Britain in 1931. The company later changed

---

Skoda

Slowly returning to quality car making thanks to VWs support

its name to Jaguar as the name coincided with the fearful German regime of the time. However, before this, in the early 1930s , William (later Sir) Lyons and William Walmsley started to build SS cars based on the chassis of Austins, Morrises, Fiats and Swifts. The first real SS was the uniquely titled 'One' of 1931 which borrowed its mechanicals from the Standard Cars parts bin. The engine was a six-cylinder unit of 2.0-litre capacity and was coupled with a handsome Swallow-built body. So good-looking was this car that buyers expected to pay a good-looking sum for it but in fact it came to the market at under half the price most people expected. This strategy ensured the One's popularity. By 1933 the body had an even more flowing look to it, the quality of build was markedly improved, and was still good value.

The Jaguar name first appeared in 1936, by which time the SS badge was becoming something of an embarrassment. This first Jag used a 2.7-litre engine, while the SS1 and SS2 models continued alongside. These cars were still being built in 1940, then the war really erupted and production ceased. Come the end of the war the company's name was changed to Jaguar and SS was no more.

SSANGYONG

A NEW NAME to many but one tipped to expand rapidly, SsangYong is Korean and has been producing vehicles since 1954. Translated, the name means 'twin dragons' and relates to the legend of these two sacred creatures which lived in the mountains of Kangwon province. Presented with a cintamini or 'wish-fulfilling gem', they spent 1,000 years hoping for the chance to fly to heaven. The legend states that only one dragon could go so they waited until the king of heaven sent down another cintamini. Then both could make

SsangYong

An odd name but one to watch with the emergence of this Korean company, partly owned by Mercedes-Benz

the journey.

Originally SsangYong was founded in 1939 with interests in the oil-refining and cement industries. Vehicle production started with the launch of the Ha Dong Hwan Motor Company making tough 4x4s, trucks and specialist vehicles.

In 1986 SsangYong acquired both this company and the sporting Essex-based Panther Car Company. A close alliance with Mercedes-Benz was formed in 1991 with Daimler-Benz holding a small but significant stake in the company. It would help Mercedes expand in the lucrative Asian Pacific markets. SsangYong's first venture into the mainstream car market occurred in 1995 with the launch of its Range Rover rival, the Mercedes-powered Musso. A development of Mercedes-Benz's old E-Class is expected to be badged as the next SsangYong and will prove an interesting newcomer in the luxury car market.

STANDARD

THE STANDARD MOTOR Company can be credited with helping put Britain's motorists on the road, thanks to its cars' blend of engineering excellence and sheer value for money. From 1923 Standards all carried the emblem of the Roman Ninth Legion on their bonnets.

The Vintage SLS and Vintage SLO models of the early 1920s became the backbone of the Standard range, with the SLO using an overhead-valve engine with exposed valves. The most successful model was the Pall Mall. Sadly, but not too surprisingly, Standard was another of those companies faced with regular financial difficulties.

Ironically those dire straits forced Standard into making one of their best cars of all time. It was called the Nine and it was a huge success. The Nine was offered in a variety of forms, the best of which was the Teignmouth saloon, with a 1155cc worm-drive, single-valve engine and fabric bodywork.

By 1929 there were also supercharged sports two-seaters and the Avon Standard Specials, a two-seater sportscar penned by the renowned Jensen brothers.

The all-new Standard Eight was launched in 1953 and was offered in four-door body form with an 803cc engine.

The company was now known

Standard

Saved Triumph in 1945 but couldn't survive British Leyland

as Standard Triumph, after taking over that ailing company at the end of the war.

The 948cc Ten arrived a year later with an opening boot lid and better trim. The Ten Companion, the estate version, came along in 1955. Two years later overdrive became an option.

The Flying Standard was unveiled in 1936 and by 1937 buyers had the choice of four four-cylinder and two six-cylinder engines from the Nine to the Twenty, as well as a very quick V8 2.7-litre in a Twelve chassis.

The Vanguard was Standard's first new post-war design, using a 2.1-litre, overhead-valve, four-cylinder unit. This car survived until the close of the Coventry factory in 1961, after Leylands takeover and the dropping of this once renowned name.

STEYR

AUSTRIAN COMPANY Steyr were originally a leading arms manufacturer but at the end of World War I, with Austria on the losing side, the company had to look for something else to produce. Steyr had been considering auto production just before the War, so plans were already laid – they just

needed to be put into effect.

The company's first car was called Waffenauto and was designed by one Hans Ledwinka who carved something of a name for himself in automotive design during the immediate post-war years. The Waffenauto appeared in 1920 and used a six-cylinder, 3.3-litre engine. This car proved very popular with new car buyers and was soon followed by other Steyrs, like the Type Four with a four-cylinder engine and the Type Six Sport which used a six-cylinder unit and was available in both touring and sportscar versions.

By 1929 Steyr attracted Ferdinand Porsche to their works. This legendary engineer, who would of course later start his own company, came on board as Chief Engineer. Under Porsche's guidance the company launched the Type 30 with a six-cylinder, 2.0-litre engine. Porsche actually only worked at Steyr for a year but he also produced the Austria for them, an eight-cylinder-engined beast. In 1929 Steyr joined with Austro-Daimler and a full merger came in 1935. The joint company produced some very interesting cars until the outbreak of World War II.

Steyr did not reappear after the war, though they continued to build engines, many of which appeared in Fiats assembled for the Austrian market, more recently known as Steyr Puch, a four-wheel-drive specialist.

STUDEBAKER

THE STUDEBAKER BROTHERS lived at South Bend, Indiana, USA, which didn't seem to have too much of a chance of becoming the launch-pad for a major new make of car back in 1852. Perhaps the brothers knew something the rest of the world didn't. Whatever, a high proportion of the early car-making companies do seem to have been started by brothers working together.

The Studebaker boys started off building ordinary horse-drawn wagons in 1852. Then they progressed to making bodies for electric vehicles. It wasn't until 1902 that the Studebakers brought out their first electric car, which was one of the first horseless carriages in America. Two years later they decided to turn away from electricity and start making petrol-powered cars. This wise move was followed a year later, in 1905, by the first four-cylinder Studebaker. It wasn't until 1911 though that the

Studebaker Corporation was formed and the new company finally decided to completely do away with electric cars and to concentrate wholly on petrol-engined models.

By 1947 Studebaker was well established as one of America's premier car-making companies. That year saw the launch of the Champion and Commander models. These were especially interesting because the front and rear design was very similar and many joked that these cars looked

the same whether they were coming or going. No matter, these new Studebakers were well received by the public.

By the late 1950s and early 1960s, there was a different wind blowing through America. Gone were the days when auto-makers could

Stutz *One of the most popular early sportscar makers, all Stutzs are now blue-chip classics*

simply make cars and sell them, the public were becoming more discriminating and wanted more for their money. In 1960 this prompted Studebaker to offer a $100 rebate on their late 1960 models. Today buyers would simply accept the $100 off as a small discount. Back then, it was different. Car buyers loved the idea of 'getting something back' when they bought a new car. Studebaker sales rose once again.

Unfortunately though, like so many other American car-makers, Studebaker did not have the muscle to fight it out with the big three auto companies. It found itself getting into financial difficulties and was taken over by Packard. The joint company failed to perform as well as it hoped and together both makes sank. Studebaker production was transferred to Canada in 1964 before the inevitable happened two years later and another chapter of American motoring history closed.

STUTZ

HARRY C. STUTZ launched this US car company in 1911 as the Ideal Motor Car Company. Two years later it became known as the Stutz Motor Car Company. The following year, 1914, the most famous Stutz of them all was unveiled, the Bearcat sportscar. The engine was made by Wisconsin and was a four-cylinder design producing 60 bhp. The Bearcat was a rather rudimentary machine, with two bucket seats and a Stutz three-speed gearbox mounted in the rear axle. There was also a rare six-cylinder engine on offer, a massive 6.2-litre affair. Both this and the four-cylinder model, in spite of quite high prices, became the most popular sportscars of the day, thanks in no small way to their incredible successes in American and international races.

By 1928 Stutz was offering more luxury in the shape of the BB Series, which were fast tourers fitted with a variety of bodies with evocative European names – the Versailles and Biarritz, for example. At the same time the Blackhawk Speedster had the enviable cachet of being the US's fastest production car. By 1929 Stutz downsized to appeal to more buyers and the result was the Blackhawk compact range which were cheaper and less powerful than the earlier cars.

Other models made before production ceased in 1935 were the DV32, Series M and Monte Carlo. There was a brief revival of the company name in the late 1960s when the Stutz Car Company produced a Bearcat replica, though few were made.

SUBARU

THIS JAPANESE make became something of a cult car in the USA during the 1980s, thanks to its rugged no-nonsense style and the superb four-wheel-drive system. It also gained many friends in Britain and, to a lesser extent, in mainland Europe. Today Subaru thrives by virtue of its ability to offer cars which are different from the mass of look-alike boxes often offered by modern auto manufacturers.

Subaru began serious production in 1958 as part of Fuji Heavy Industries, one of Japan's most expansive industrial concerns involved in everything from photographic film to ship-building. Like many other Japanese manufacturers, when Subaru started out making cars they were most often supplied with two-stroke air-cooled engines which were really only noted by European motorists because of their somewhat odd mechanical formats.

What a difference a couple of decades can make. By the 1970s the range had expanded and been modernised. Subaru were beginning to concentrate on simple but effective mechanicals which normally ran on two-wheel drive but could easily be switched into four-wheel-drive mode. Today, there is a wide range available, with Subaru still ranking as experts in four-wheel-drive design. Success in international rallying with the Impreza (below), has boosted the company's profile considerably.

SUNBEAM

ANOTHER OF THE great names in British car manufacturing which died unceremoniously. Sunbeam has always been traditionally linked with sporting cars and was so right up to its demise in 1974. However, its chequered-flag past became sullied by its use as rebadging for hotted-up Hillmans. Yet in its heyday in the roaring 1920s, Sunbeam was the first British car maker to win a Grand Prix.

The company was founded by John Marston, but by 1935 had run into difficulties and was taken over by the growing Rootes Group. Amazingly, Sunbeam was mothballed from 1937 to 1953, when the famous Alpine and Rapiers started to appear, the most famous of the line being the terrific Tiger; a 1960s Alpine convertible with American Ford V8 power. This was as good as it got for Sunbeam, with Rootes' parent Chrysler losing interest in its UK arm in the recession-bitten 1970s, eventually killing the mark off.

Subaru

Leading maker of four-wheel-drives, Subaru has enjoyed considerable success in the US and motorsport

SUZUKI

BEST KNOWN FOR their top-selling motorbikes, Japanese company Suzuki is also a maker of small yet efficient cars which combine lively performance with

Suzuki

Famous for motorbikes, their Vitara 4x4 car range is also very popular

very good fuel economy.

The company opened its doors in 1961 and, apart from the motorbikes, it was soon producing the Suzulight front-wheel-drive two-door car. This was one of the first multi-purpose cars – it could be used to carry four people or the rear seats could be ditched in favour of a cargo carrying area. As with most Japanese cars of this era the engine was a two-cylinder air-cooled unit, in this case producing 20 bhp. By 1966 the small-car format was being left behind. Suzuki launched the Fronte 800, a larger saloon car with a two-stroke engine of three cylinders and with a four-speed gearbox. In 1971 the company launched into the four-wheel-drive market for which they would become famous. Their first offering was the Jimny which used a small 359cc engine. By 1979 Suzuki were also producing higher performance cars, the Cervo coupe being the most popular, with its four-stroke overhead-cam engine.

In the range today there are no overtly sporting machines but there are plenty of four-wheel-drive offerings, including the extensive Vitara range. This is a Jeep-like vehicle available with hard and soft tops. The Samurai is rather more basic but follows the same mechanical formula. For those who prefer staying on the road, there is a choice of the Swift, one of the company's longest running small hatchbacks, and the Baleno range.

SWALLOW

THE SWALLOW range of cars were made in England from 1922 onwards, and interestingly, marketed by the same firm who sold the rare Edmond and North

Star cars which proved incredibly popular with buyers of the day. It was this success that persuaded Swallow to launch its own breed of very desirable cars, one with a two-cylinder Blackburne engine, the other using a four-cylinder Dorman. Both cars had two-speed epicyclic gearboxes and worm-driven rear axles. The company moved up a gear in the early 1950s by launching the Doretti which was built at Swallow's factory at Walsall, Staffordshire.

Like many car-makers of the period, Swallow tried to keep costs down without compromising quality or performance. In the Doretti's case this meant using the excellent engine, gearbox and running gear of the hugely successful Triumph TR2 sportscar. Swallow married this collection to its own tubular steel frame and flush-sided body. The end result was a very quick, fine handling yet comfortable tourer, though it was not fast enough to compete with the best sportscars of the period. Swallow though did not want to compete but rather wanted to

create a unique niche for their cars, and it succeeded. Unfortunately, all this hand-built craftsmanship pushed up prices. Buyers had to pay several hundred pounds more for the Doretti than for a Triumph TR2 using the same power unit. This was a considerable sum of money in the 1950s, so Swallow did not sell a great number of cars. However, unlike the TR2 which

only came in one basic style, the Doretti offered either a convertible two-seater or a very high quality hard-topped coupe. The Doretti was a wonderful, hard wearing piece of machinery, a good performer – it could comfortably top 100 mph – and economical. The problem was the lack of models

available to the public and the relative high cost of the Doretti.

The company simply could not compete with MG and Triumph, who did the job equally well, yet were considerably cheaper. In 1960 only a trickle of cars were produced, and Swallow folded in 1961.

TALBOT

THOSE WHO can remember Talbot's cars of the 1970s and early 1980s might be inclined to yawn at this stage. Admittedly, with a couple of exceptions, the relatively modern Talbots – built and marketed by Peugeot – were not very impressive. The Chrysler Horizon was virtually identical to the Talbot Sunbeam and it was flattered by the European Car of the Year award in 1979. The Talbot Alpine range had

decent engines but was very susceptible to rust. The reason for these lacklustre cars was simple: the Talbot name was resurrected for just a short while, simply to bridge the gap between the outgoing Chrysler concern and the new French owners.

It hadn't always been like this. The original Talbots, or to give them their proper name, Talbot-Lago, were built in France and had their big sales days in the 1940s and 50s. They produced a competent, if largely unexciting, range of cars. The styling was good, the prices were right and the cars offered fine performance. The Talbot 80 and 90 models which both appeared in 1948 were sensible, if a little staid, French cars which rivalled Renault and Peugeot. The Record, built from 1947 to 1956, formed the backbone of the range of that period and was joined by the 2500 coupe, Grand Sport convertible and Grand Sport coupe in 1953. The only down side to these cars was a patchy build quality, sometimes they were good, sometimes they weren't.

Buyers were impressed by the

competitive prices and sales were healthy enough.

Talbot's less successful days began with the takeover of the company by the American Chrysler Corporation – who took over Rootes Group in the UK and Simca in France – and who presided over a period of mostly mediocre offerings. Eventually Peugeot bought Talbot and, as mentioned earlier, most of the Talbots offered during this period such as the hatchbacked Alpine and its Minx and Rapier variants, were not overly impressive. There was one car which was much in demand, however, the Talbot Sunbeam-Lotus. This, as it name suggests, was a Lotus-engined rear-wheel driven car and moved like a scalded cat. Even today this is one Talbot which is much in demand. Talbot also made its way onto a Formula One car in the early 1980s.

The Talbot name was eventually consigned to the history books. Peugeot found it was duplicating some of the models with Peugeot badges, in addition to which the French company was embarking on a period of change, introducing modern models using numbers, not names, like the hugely-successful 205.

TATRA

TO DESCRIBE Czech car-maker Tatra as a more upmarket Skoda is a simplification but not far from the truth. Both companies used a similar design base and both did surprisingly well in motorsport.

Tatra was founded back in 1923 and the first car laid down the ground rules which are still adhered to this day. These are chiefly – a large, roomy, rear-engined saloon with surprisingly good performance and style.

Originally, Tatras were all air-cooled but as engine sizes grew the company produced more conventional water-cooled engines. The engine sizes certainly grew! As far back as 1930, a luxury model was produced with a choice of a 3.8-litre six-cylinder engine or a mighty 6-litre V12. In 1934 an air-cooled V8 model, called the Tatra 77, was produced with particular attention being paid to its aerodynamics, an area many other

> **Talbot**
>
> *This 1970s Talbot Sunbeam-Lotus is a much sought classic*

car-makers barely understood. Tatra briefly flirted with a conventional engine location on more downmarket models but after the war returned to concentrate on luxury rear-engined V8s. From 1955 to date various versions of Tatra's 600 series have been produced, with most going to Eastern Bloc Governments.

The 603 and the later 613 featured twin-cam V8 engines and all-round disc brakes. Most recently a concentrated effort has been made by a specialist importer to introduce the Tatra name to western executives who yearn for something different to their usual BMWs and Audis.

common with other Japanese manufacturers, drove into Europe and America with a pretty basic range of cars which were low on style but very high on value-for-money and equipment. Sales were sky-high and along the way Toyota honed and perfected its operation so that it is now rivalling General Motors as the world's number one company. Rumour has it that Toyota makes so much money and has invested so wisely that it could afford to pay all of its workers until the end of time without ever making another car again!

marque. The ability and quality of the superbly built Lexus LS400 scooped the influential J.D. Power survey in the US. The more established prestige rivals have been worried ever since...

TRABANT

WITH THE decline of communism in Europe and the dramatic fall of the Berlin Wall, motorists in the West were at last able to see the East German Trabant in all its glory. This car was available not only in fibre-glass bodied form but also with a

the end of the Trabant, a car which simply had no means of competing with mainstream cars offered in the west. Today they have somewhat ironically become collectors' items but are not hard to find, simply because so many were produced.

TRIUMPH

THERE IS TALK of resurrecting the famous Triumph name, now that BMW has bought Rover Group and owns the rights to the badge. If it happens there will be much rejoicing in the British motor industry because when Triumph was in full-flight in the 1960s and 1970s it produced some of the very best cars around.

Founded in 1923,

Such resources have been put to good use. Toyota is expert at making cars and today's range is indicative of their foresight to move with the times. It introduced the sporty Celica coupe at exactly the right time in 1970 to cater for the growth of the coupe market, while significant successes in motorsport have kept Toyota in the public's eye. The brilliant mid-engined MR2 of the mid 1980s showed Toyota's commitment to all sales markets. The MR2 came at just the right time to take advantage of the new-found interest in sports two-seaters, while an expanding 4x4 model line-up has proved among the most popular in the world, particularly the Landcruiser off-roader and Hi-Lux pick-up.

As Toyota's image spiralled it saw the need to pitch the company in at the prestige end of the market, and so by the end of the 1980s introduced its high-brow Lexus

form of reinforced cardboard. This gave it a lightness unmatched by any other major car manufacturer, even though became something of a sorry state if left out in the rain for too long!

Trabant began production in 1959 based in Zwickau, East Germany. Its first car was called the 50. The engine was a 500cc, two-cylinder, two-stroke affair which produced very little performance but lots and lots of acrid black smoke, making life difficult for pedestrians. The driver didn't fare much better either, having to contend with raucous engine noise, poor gear changes and a very poor build quality. At the time of the collapse of the Berlin Wall cynics in the West suggested that the Wall had only been put up to stop Trabants coming to the West and spreading their pollution. Thankfully the collapse of communism in Germany also saw

Triumph was better known for its bicycles. Aimed at the more sporting buyer, some fine cars were produced in the pre-war years.

The finest was the supercharged Dolomite, which was seen as a British Alfa Romeo. Yet, in spite of Triumph's flourishing image, it fell on hard times. The company was put into the hands of a receiver just before the war and it wasn't until 1945 that Sir John Black's Standard Motor Company saved the day. Apart from cars like the Mayflower saloon, it was Triumph's brilliant TR sportscars which pulled the company back on its feet. By the late 1950s the novel

Toyota
One of the most forward-thinking car makers around also produced the world's best-seller

TOYOTA

TOYOTA HAS THE distinction of making the world's number-one selling car, the Corolla, versions of which have been on sale for three decades and which is produced in satellite factories all over the world.

The company first broke into cars when the then Toyota Loom Company produced a 45 hp offering in 1935. By 1965 the two millionth Toyota had rolled off the assembly lines. The immediate post-war years saw the Toyopet saloon and the Crown, with the Corona arriving in 1957. Toyota, in

Triumph
Rescued by Standard, Triumph became a name in sporting cars – and may do so again

Herald family car was launched. This spawned the pretty two-seater Spitfire and the Vitesse (pictured on previous page), a compact six-cylinder-engined 'super Herald'.

Out-and-out sportscars were Triumph's stock-in-trade. In 1966 it unveiled the GT6, based on the Spitfire, but only available with a hard-topped body. Thanks to its straight six-cylinder, 2.0-litre engine and lightweight body, the GT6 went like a rocket. More than 25,000 were made between 1966 and 1973. The early models did not handle terribly well but from 1968 Mark II owners found a much better package.

The TR range was going great guns with the fuel-injected TR5 and TR6, but in 1975 it all went wrong with the TR7. This quirkily-styled two-seater was criticised by TR enthusiasts. Now it has become something of a classic, especially the convertible model.

Earlier, Triumph tried its hand at something altogether more adventurous, the

pretty 2500 and 2.5PI. The original 2000, a four-door saloon with a 90 bhp six-cylinder engine, went on sale in 1964 and two years later an estate car was added. The 132 bhp fuel-injected (PI stood for Petrol Injection) 2500 went on sale in 1968. A year later this became the Mark II with a restyled nose and tail.

From 1974 a 99 bhp, 2498cc, twin-carburettor 2500TC model was added but a year later the PI and the 106 bhp 2498cc 2500S took its place. This Triumph was the first car to have good all-round independent suspension linked to coil springs.

The Dolomite range of the 1970s saw Triumph aim at a more youthful buyer, particularly with the 16-valve Sprint.

Sadly, Triumph declined as part of the ailing British Leyland empire. The last car to bear the famous badge was a sensible Honda saloon called the Triumph Acclaim. Hopefully BMW can rekindle something truly triumphant.

TVR

BASED in Blackpool, England, TVR sportscars are sought-after around the world and with good reason. Built by hand, these are some of the most exciting, most competitively priced supercars available today.

TVR, however, has led a chequered life. The company was first formed in the early 1950s by Trevor Wilkinson, TVR is based upon his Christian name. Since the early days it has gone through countless changes of ownership and shaky periods, but has emerged fitter, better and more respected than ever. Backbone of the early days was the Vixen, a two-seater made from 1967 to 1973 and the original Griffith. The Vixen

used a 1.6-litre Ford Cortina engine, driving through a four-speed manual gearbox to the rear wheels. The Series Two Vixen, launched in 1968, had a longer wheelbase and more spacious cabin. The Griffith, was much more powerful with a larger Ford V8 engine.

The economic downturn of the 1970s hit many smaller specialist car-makers and TVR was no exception. It survived with its 3000M and Taimar, Ford Capri V6-powered cars. A turbo model also figured on the latter and was good for 130 mph.

During the 1980s the company brought out the wedge-shaped Tasmin, again using Ford engines, though this time the 2.8-litre fuel-injection unit was from the Capri. Following this model was the 350i which used Rover's potent V8 engine. This car not only handled well – though the ride could shake the filings from the driver's teeth – but it also sounded terrific.

In the late 1980s TVR did away with the wedge shape and opted instead for altogether smoother machines. By this time quality control had improved tremendously. These cars were being taken seriously by buyers who started looking at TVR's in preference to cars like Porsche and Aston Martin.

Today the company produces three different cars, the Chimaera convertible with either 4.0 or 5.0-litre V8 engines, the Cerbera 4.0-litre which is basically a Chimaera with two additional seats in the back and a hard-top, and the Griffith with the 5.0-litre power plant. All these cars look mean and sporty, and they perform like missiles, even if they can be a handful on a damp road.

What makes TVR such a potent force these days is its enthusiastic owner, the colourful Peter Wheeler, who not only builds Blackpool's finest cars but also races them. The new AJ8 engine, developed specifically for TVR, is a work of art, the cars look and sound great, and offer performance levels unheard of for the price. Long may TVR continue.

UNIPOWER

SUCH WAS the driving brilliance of the Mini that sporty offshoot derivatives produced by independent car-makers became common during the 1960s. Few, however, showed as much promise or style as the 1966 Unipower GT.

Using a strong, low-slung, two-seater fibreglass bodyshell, the Mini's engine and transmission were rear-mounted and coupled to a specially developed chassis using coil spring suspension. Called the GT, most were Mini Cooper powered. Thanks to its light weight and superior aerodynamics over the standard brick-shaped car, that

---

TVR

The beasts of Blackpool have never looked or sounded better!

Unipower *A great little specialist car based on the Mini but rear-engined*

even in 55 bhp tune an impressive 120 mph was claimed.

Cooper S-powered versions were very quick indeed. The Unipower GT lasted for four years in production and quite a number were exported.

VANDEN PLAS

A WORTHY OLD traditional British company, Vanden Plas opened its doors for business in 1960 and survived in its own right until 1980. Its badge has since been seen on a number of highly equipped and trimmed British cars,

notably Jaguar, when sold in the USA, and Daimler when sold in the UK.

In fact, VDP was not British to start with, it was the off-shoot of a Belgian coach-building business. Prior to World War II its bodywork designs were seen on luxury cars such as the Bentley. However, after the war VDP was bought by Austin. There then followed a period of 'badge engineering' when the VDP emblem was added to a whole range of specially trimmed cars, rather than those with unique bodywork.

Badge engineering not-withstanding, in 1960 the Vanden Plas Princess was marketed as a specific model within the Austin range. It was quite clearly distinguished from other models in the line-up thanks to luxurious interior appointments and a traditional radiator design with the crown emblem placed on the bonnet.

By 1964, however, the VDP badge was becoming more common, and moved downmarket in the process, finding itself glued to the bonnet of the Issigonis-designed Austin 1100 saloon. The following year VDP did come to mean something once again when Austin launched the Princess R with a 3.9-litre six-cylinder engine which was actually made by Rolls-Royce, and with automatic as standard. Vanden Plas also fashioned the bodies for the 4.2-litre, six-cylinder Daimler.

By 1973 only the 1300 saloon carried the Vanden Plas name and that was replaced a year later by a VDP version of the unfortunate Austin Allegro.

By this time VDP had really dropped its luxury pretensions and many, quite correctly saw the badge being used in quite a cynical way. Industry bosses were inclined to badge a model as a Vanden Plas to make it sell, no matter whether

the car was good enough to deserve it. The problem with this approach is that the value of such badging soon becomes belittled. This is what happened to VDP. Production of Vanden Plas cars came to an end when British Leyland's Abingdon plant was closed in 1980, but Vanden Plas badges have since been placed on Jaguars and Daimlers, which are altogether more fitting recipients than the Austin Allegro.

VAUXHALL

BRITAIN'S VAUXHALL CAR company began life in the early 1900s as marine engineers, though it began making cars seriously from 1904. Today Vauxhall is one of the most successful operations within General Motors, the world's largest company. When Vauxhall packed its bags and moved from London to Luton in 1907 it immediately began to produce cars which just about everyone wanted. Thus began a glorious period of design and development which saw Vauxhall become one of the world's major automotive names.

The Prince Henry which appeared in 1910 was the first success and gave birth to several other Vauxhalls. The best version carried a 3.0-litre, four-cylinder engine though it soon received a more powerful 4.0-litre unit in 1913, producing 70 bhp and capable of a top speed of nearly 80 mph. The D and E type (not to be confused with Jaguar's later cars of the same name) were produced just before the outbreak of World

War I, and when the war ended both models were again offered by Vauxhall. By 1919 they were fully equipped with an electric starter and electric lights. These cars were amongst the fastest most comfortable machines of their period and yet were offered at very reasonable prices.

The first real attempt at offering a car which everybody could afford came in 1922 with the launch of the M-type. With its 2.3-litre, four-cylinder engine and reasonable price tag, the M-type did indeed prove popular.

In common with many British companies, the inflationary 1920s proved hard for Vauxhall and

despite fighting to produce good models its independence came to an end in 1927 when it was bought by America's General Motors. The first GM Vauxhall, the R-type, was a signal to move downmarket for more sales.

The 1950s Velox, Wyvern and Cresta provided the mainstay of Vauxhalls with their heavily American-influenced styling. A reputation for rusting plus a penchant for staid designs hurt Vauxhall during the early 1960s, but the advent of the stylish and innovative Viva HB and Victor FD models put the company right back on the map.

In the 1970s Vauxhall, never a

big seller like Ford, started to feel the pinch as sales declined. It took a bold decision by parent company General Motors to kill off the Luton-designed products in favour of re-badged Opel models. It was the right move because the launch of the Cavalier, almost single-handedly saved Vauxhall. Now the company is known as a producer of some of the best mainstream cars around such as the Tigra, Vectra, Omega and Astra.

Vauxhall

Now rebadged Opels, Vauxhall's status has never been better

Legendary Marque

VOLKSWAGEN

THE STORY OF Volkswagen is more than just that of a concept car that evolved into one of the world's largest vehicle manufacturers. It also reflects the contemporary history of Germany, as both are indelibly linked.

The Volkswagen started life in 1934 as an idea for a modest vehicle pitched at the masses. Its name translates into English as 'people's car'. That was exactly the dream of its originator, Dr Ferdinand Porsche, who had been working on a series of small and inexpensive car prototypes. He was regarded as Germany's finest car designer of the period. When Adolf Hitler

heard of Porsche's plans, he instructed the Doctor to produce a car that was simple yet advanced technologically; a car which could cruise at high speeds on the country's ever-expanding autobahn network. Despite the challenging specification, the vehicle had to cost just 1000 Reichmarks to buy (the equivalent of £90 at the time).

Until the advent of the Volkswagen, German cars had been an exclusive luxury item, so when Porsche submitted his proposal to the German Reich, it received a cool reception in many areas. In fact, the German car

industry rather hoped that the project would fail and consequently offered little support to Porsche.

As a result, the car was not ready for series production until 1938, by which time a prototype had been dubbed the 'Beetle' by The New York Times . The name may have been said in jest at the time but it became the car's – and the company's – fortune. Dr Porsche ensured that the prototype had been thoroughly sorted before committing it to production. This was an almost unheard of luxury for such a downmarket and inexpensive car at the time, but the Beetle's production longevity is testimony to the appropriateness of the original design.

By 1938 the car (and its dedicated factory) was ready for series production but the outbreak of war halted the project. After five years of conflict Germany was in ruins and the Allies didn't quite know what to do with the humble Volkswagen. The car was more than ready for production; the

German Army had used small numbers for military and propaganda purposes during the war years, but the factory had been badly damaged in bombing raids. Neither the British or American governments wanted to take the project on.

Instead, for the sake of German morale, the Volkswagen was allowed to be built by locals and refugees. There seemed little hope for the company's survival, despite the purchase of 20,000 Beetles for British Army use in their zone of occupation. Indeed, it was not until 1947 that private individuals were permitted to buy the car. It immediately struck a chord with the West German populous and Beetle sales were soon astounding other global manufacturers.

Volkswagen's rise was meteoric once the Allies handed the company back to West Germany. Soon, other variants based on Dr Porsche's rear-engined, air-cooled, separate chassis design were announced, including a convertible Beetle (which has now attained

cult status, along with the minibus), vans and a range of saloons and fastbacks. The Beetle also inspired some of the world's greatest sportscars, Porsche's 356 and 911. Both these classics were based on the same design concept.

The Beetle was Volkswagen's mainstay. By February 1972 it surpassed the production record of the Ford Model T when the 15,007,034th car pulled out of the Wolfsburg factory. Despite being dropped in Germany six years later, the Beetle still continued to be built in certain VW manufacturing bases across the globe. Indeed, it is still currently being produced in Mexico, where it has become a best-seller and duly pushed overall Beetle numbers passed the 21 million mark in 1994.

As West Germany thrived, so did Volkswagen, and in the 1960s the company began to buy-out other German car manufacturers who had been so reluctant to assist the company during its early years. Prestige makes Auto Union, Audi and NSU merged and then came under direct Volkswagen control in 1969 – a year after the 15 millionth Beetle had been produced. The move was a master-stroke as Volkswagen badly needed to expand its ageing car range, and fortunately both Audi and NSU had fully grasped front-wheel drive design techniques.

In fact Volkswagen's first 'conventional' car design was

Volkswagen

Left *A radical three-wheel scooter design shows that VW has come a long way since the Beetle and points the way for urban motoring for the next century*

Right *The stylish Corrado's outstanding handling quickly made it an enthusiast's delight, especially in VR6 guise*

195

a re-badged NSU saloon. Called the K70, it was not a sales success but it did provide Volkswagen with a blueprint for its next generation of cars – the Polo, Golf, Scirocco and Passat. Audi-badged vehicles, meanwhile, have cemented the Volkswagen group's market-share at the prestige end of the range, supplying high technology, quality vehicles, right across the globe.

The Golf is well on target to beat even the legendary Beetle, with sales recently topping the 11-million mark since its launch in 1974. The GTi version of the car started an entirely new fashion when launched in 1975. It was dubbed the 'hot hatch', and saw sportscar-like performance combined with the practicality and convenience of an estate.

In 1991 the Golf Mark I-based cabriolet became the best-selling convertible in automotive history – the car it assumed the mantle from was, of course, the Beetle!

Success through the 1980s saw the company expand into new markets, participating in joint ventures with other vehicle manufacturers such as Ford and Toyota. Volkswagen was rapidly and continually expanding.

In 1986 Volkswagen bought Spanish car-maker SEAT from Fiat, followed four years later by the Czech Skoda concern. Both these companies have since enjoyed significant inputs of both cash and technology to bring their ranges in line with modern rivals.

The unification of Germany saw Volkswagen potentially double its home consumer base overnight, although like the new nation, the company began to experience considerable financial difficulties which resulted in a major restructuring of the group and a redefining of its market strategies.

Volkswagen's Phoenix-like rise from the ashes of Germany in such a short period is nothing short of remarkable. It is entirely fitting that the car which started it all, the evergreen Beetle, still plays such a significant role in the company's plans for the future. VW has recently announced plans for an all-new Beetle for the next century. Quite possibly it will revolutionise motoring the way the original did.

Volkswagen

Previous page *The Golf Cabriolet took over from the Beetle as the biggest selling convertable*

Left *The Transporter light commercial has been another success for VW, enjoying cult status in the US*

Above *The Karman Ghia was a sporty derivative of the Beetle, available in Coupe or soft top. Very popular in the US, now a classic*

Right *The car which started it all: the Beetle's popularity was such that it became the foundation for one of the fastest-growing automotive giants*

Volkswagen

The Camper Van based on the Transporter commercial, has become ubiquitous around the world

VOLVO

SWEDEN'S VOLVO car company has always concentrated on cars which will last a lifetime, cars which could be passed onto their buyers' grandchildren. Based in Gothenburg, Volvos first started to flow out of the factory in 1927. Early Volvos were utterly conventional and it has to said, hardly the nicest lookers around.

However, that criticism cannot be levelled at the P1800 which achieved worldwide fame when TV's Roger Moore drove it in his role as *The Saint*. This two-seat sportscar never had the agility and performance of British or American rivals of the early 1960s period, but was pleasantly designed and proved to be long-lasting.

Interestingly, the P1800 was not just built in the Sweden, some 6,000 were produced for the UK in West Bromwich by Jensen. Assembly was transferred to Sweden in 1963 when the car became left-hand drive and gained an S badge. In 1969 a 123 bhp, 2.0-litre engine (the original engine was a four-cylinder, 1.8-litre unit) was put under the bonnet and in 1970 a fuel-injected version (the E) replaced the previous carburettor-powered car.

The 1800ES sporting estate was launched in 1971 with an up-rated 135 bhp version of the 2.0-litre engine and the last cars were produced in 1973.

The problem for the 1800, at least in its hey-day, was the image everyone had of Volvo as being makers of solid, dependable and yet essentially boring saloon and estate cars. Indeed, Volvo has nurtured such an image. This includes the Amazon cars of the late 1950s, a solid yet staid saloon, many of which amazingly still survive today.

In 1967 a new range of saloons and estates, the 144 and latterly the 200-series, was launched, and they – more than any other – established Volvo as a true quality car-maker. In 1974 Volvo bought the ailing DAF concern and entered the small-car market with its 300 Series using a mix of Volvo and DAF mechanicals.

By the 1980s Volvo were striving to shake up its rather dowdy

Wolseley *Started by Austin, Wolseley became the upmarket arm of BMC, producing cars like the Hornet, basically a repackaged Mini*

conservative image, by trying to persuade younger buyers that Volvos really were interesting.

Competing in touring car racing began the process and the launch of its excellent 850 series completed the job. Any motor manufacturer who can produce a 160 mph estate car which is available in bright canary yellow can no longer be considered boring!

Volvo's latest S and V40 car ranges – produced in conjunction with Mitsubishi – and a new alluring Coupe and Convertible based upon the mould-breaking 850 design of 1992, are forthright evidence that Volvo can be both sexy and safe!

Volvo

Quickly shaking off the image of a maker of rather safe and boring cars

---

WOLSELEY

IT ALL STARTED, rather bizarrely with the Wolseley Sheep Shearing Company. Herbert Austin had plans to build a range of cars but had a disagreement with the fellow shareholders and decided to quit. He took his ideas with him – and a few years later launched them with the now famous Austin badge. Wolseley, though, wasn't dead. Herbert Austin may have

gone but and the company he left behind went on to make some very interesting and technically advanced cars, renowned also for their high build quality.

Austin had helped to produce the Wolseley-Siddeley with its 3.3-litre engine before he left. He was mostly involved in the mechanical complexities of this vertical-engined car, while the actual design of this very popular little machine was carried out by one J.D. Siddeley, of Arstrong-Siddeley fame, hence the name of the car.

By 1930 the Hornet was introduced, a name which later kept appearing on various Wolseleys. This first bearer of the Hornet badge was aimed fairly and squarely at the ordinary motorist. It was very successful, thanks to the combination of an efficient six-cylinder 1.3-litre engine

and a light, yet spacious body. By 1935 the engine had grown to 1.4-litres. A year later Wolseley launched the Hornet Special which used a 1.6-litre unit producing 50 bhp which could reach 80 mph.

Despite the success of the Hornet with its evocative name, Wolseley once more reverted to numbers on their bonnet badges when they launched the Ten early in the 1940s. Once again the build quality was first class and Wolseley was considering moving the range up-market to cash in on the name's appeal. By the 1960s and 1970s, however, Wolseley did not look in such good shape, it was part of British Leyland's empire and fell foul of the marketing habit of using different car badges at will. Wolseley's image suffered and the marque was buried in the late 1970s. BMW now own the badge.

SPORTSCARS
The History

Ever since man invented the wheel, he has harboured a passion for speed and freedom. In the sportscar, he found both of these powerful forces entwined in an expression of beauty and style. Almost from the very dawn of the car's development it has offered these powerful inducements. The car has also given its owner a certain status and image, either real or imagined, that gives him or her a sense of identity and pride. A sportscar intensifies these values. In its form and function it evokes the romance of speed and the thrill of going fast. It provides an expression of individuality. In its very being it implies success, style, even virility.

It is largely the pursuit of these very human emotions and vanities that led to the birth and the popularity of the sportscar. Of course, there is far more to the sportscar than its use as a badge of success and everlasting youth. Beauty, engineering excellence, and the satisfaction of driving a responsive and powerful machine will often provide more than enough reason for owning one. To simply cast the eyes over a beautifully styled sportscar can give a buzz of pleasure. A Jaguar E-type or an Aston Martin DB7 is an image to savour.

Likewise, the racing of the heartbeat as a driver pilots a thoroughbred sportscar at speed across a mountain road is an experience that is impossible to put a price on. Some of the more advanced sportscars are able to deploy feats of control, grip and speed that can only be described as sensational. The engineering elegance behind these feats is not to be overlooked, and sometimes modern technical excellence has an innate beauty in itself. All of these things are powerful reasons why the sportscar has survived and thrived.

Logic rarely enters into the arena of sportscar ownership. Buying and owning one is an affair of the heart; a purely emotive decision. It's clear that for as long as the human species retains these primitive desires and emotions, the sportscar will always be with us.

To find the origins of the sportscar the enthusiast must delve back to the early years of the century, when the first motor races were being held in Europe. These were mainly on dirt roads and often covered hundreds of miles. To finish a race, let alone win one, was considered an achievement, but the very spectacle of these Spartan machines with their truck-like chassis and their big powerful engines stirred a demand for more and more to be built.

These were the very first sportscars, like the 60 bhp Mercedes of 1903 and the 1908 Austin 100 bhp Grand Prix Replica. Some of these racing-derived cars had massive engines of up to 20-litres capacity and were capable of going far faster than the tyres, brakes or handling could ever be expected to cope with.

America, too, caught the speed bug. A variety of stripped-down, large-engined cars in the style of the racers began to gain popularity. Among these were the 1910 Mercer Raceabout and Stutz Bearcat, both of which had engines of around six litres and 60 bhp. They were capable of propelling these primitive devices with virtually non-existent bodywork to speeds of 80 mph in the hands of a very brave driver.

Competition formed the structure around which sportscars were based. It led to cars being made faster, to handle better and to stop better, although almost all sporting cars were still big, heavy and cumbersome until after the First World War. Comfort did not really come into the equation until much later.

The Great War brought with it some major advances in technology that would eventually provide added sophistication and reliability to the sportscar. Wartime aircraft used piston engines and, in the pursuit of greater power and reliability, a vast amount of technology was learned that would soon be absorbed into automotive development. It led to a golden era of the sportscar in which they became lighter, smaller, more wieldy and, despite considerably smaller engines than those pre-war monsters, more powerful.

As the Roaring Twenties progressed some advanced engineering features were offered, such as four-valve, double overhead-cam, cylinder heads; forged aluminium road wheels; and supercharged engines. sportscar engineering had emerged from a hammer-wielding blacksmith's craft to the design sophistication of the science of precision engineering.

Among its most notable exponents was Ettore Bugatti. The artistry and engineering elegance in his Type 35B Bugatti is self evident. In the early 1920s, here

was a car able to deploy up to 130 bhp at 5,500 rpm from a supercharged engine of just 2.2-litres. This was enough to produce a top speed of 120 mph. This wasn't just a racing car, it was also a road-going sportscar. The Bugatti was different from all the others of its day in that its legendary performance was not merely a result of high power. The Bugatti's superior chassis design created excellent steering, handling and roadholding. It was a sportscar ahead of its time.

A decade later, we began to see sportscars gain in popularity as they became smaller, cheaper and more readily available. Marques such as MG and Riley came to prominence. As the decade wore on, there were clear signs that aerodynamics would take far greater prominence in the look of the sportscar of the future. Already some of the continental makes, such as Alfa Romeo, Bugatti and BMW, were taking great strides in this direction. The same was the case over the Atlantic, with Cord and Auburn producing some truly dramatic shapes.

Following World War II, a period of austerity together with a shortage of raw materials swept the world's car-makers into stagnation as far as sportscars were concerned. Mostly, pre-war designs were continued as before, with cycle wings and all.

However, as the 1940s led into the 1950s, a boom time arrived for the sportscar. Perhaps the car that typified this period most of all was the Jaguar XK120. Launched at London's 1948 Motor Show, it shone out like a bright star in a dark sky. The slender lines were the embodiment of grace and sophistication and its engine was an advanced twin-cam design that would eventually power later versions of the car to reach a giddy 150 mph.

The Jaguar XK120 was not a particularly cheap car, even though it was a bargain for its specification

and style. However, the sportscar was on its way back into popularity and, as the decade wore on, some excellent sportscars were produced by Triumph, MG and Austin-Healey. These were mostly relatively crude devices with many parts derived from more mundane saloons, but they were accessible, they were fun to drive, and they were a breath of fresh air compared with what had gone before.

In the meantime, continental Europe was beginning to show some tantalising glimpses of exotica in the form of Ferraris and Maseratis, while America was about to plunge into the era of the

Sportscar or supercar? The two are very closely related in their aims: to bring the sensation of speed to the car enthusiast

muscle car. It was an exciting time for any sportscar enthusiast.

Unfortunately by the mid-1960s, the era of the affordable sportscar seemed to be on the wane. People were buying Mini Coopers and Lotus Cortinas instead of traditional sportscars. There was very little progress on the technical front as far as sportscar design was concerned in England.

On the continent, however, Porsche was fast making a name for itself with the 911 coupe.

Matters were looking even more grim for the sportscar enthusiast as the 1970s began with constricting safety legislation. American muscle cars were shorn of their power and the underlying threat of a US ban on convertibles meant that any new sportscar designs were shelved or cancelled. Triumph's TR7 was one of the few new sportscars for the masses. It seemed that the concept of the sportscar was moving more and more upmarket and consequently becoming out of reach of all but the well-heeled.

The final blow for the traditional sportscar market seemed to be the arrival of the hot hatchback in the late seventies. This was the era of the GTI – the mass-market, pure sportscar, looked set for extinction. Only the auto-exotica or the specialists remained.

It was at this time that Japan came to the rescue – by re-inventing the sportscar. Toyota's MR2 showed that it was still possible to have affordable sportscar fun and when the Mazda MX-5 appeared it was clear that the sportscar's reprieve had come.

Also at the tail end of the 1980s, the upper sector of the sportscar spectrum began to ascend in ever increasing spirals towards the stratosphere. The age of the supercar had arrived.

Fixed by a desire to build the ultimate performance machine, regardless of cost, a handful of like-minded car-makers began the race for the fastest and most exotic car of all time. Lamborghini, Porsche and Ferrari started this rather futile quest for speed. For a while it seemed to pay off. Demand initially exceeded supply to the extent that people would actually pay over-the-odds to get their hands on the latest Ferrari F40 or Porsche 959, which meant in turn

that buying supercars became a money-making exercise in itself.

The fact that these high-tech, highly impractical machines cost many times the price of a perfectly good Porsche 911 or Honda NSX mattered not a jot; if it was possible to make money by re-selling the car because of its rarity value and long waiting lists, then it had to make sense. This kind of logic encouraged a growing throng of supercar-makers to plan ever more ambitious projectiles costing vast sums of money and offering 200-mph-plus performance!

The bubble burst in a big way when sales dried up. Jaguar's XJ220 was soon being offered at a considerably reduced price and McLaren's super F1 ended up reaching only a fraction of its planned production. Perhaps the mega-money supercar's demise was simply down to the fact that this type of car was not as desirable to own as it was to look at. Some were downright uncomfortable to drive, impractical to take on long touring jaunts and the only place they could show their true potential was on a race track. With the possible exception of the Formula One-based Ferrari F50, the day of the ultimate supercar seems over.

As we approach the Millennium, things have never looked brighter for the sportscar. This decade is surely the new golden age of sportscar motoring. For proof, we need look no further than the new sporting cars from MG, Fiat, Alfa Romeo, BMW, Mercedes, Porsche, Audi and Lotus. The quest for the ultimate supercar is disappearing with the realisation that cars with that level of performance have no place on today's roads. Instead, a new breed of talented, fun, and relatively cheap sportscar has arrived to re-assert the place of the sportscar for the next decade at least.

It's a refreshing thought that, despite threats of legislation and political incorrectness, the sportscar looks set to fight another day.

Caterham Seven

•••••••••••••••••••••

Anyone who has seen a Seven at speed is never likely to forget it. A flash of colour, a rush of sound, the glimmer of a smile on the driver's face… that's all it is possible to glimpse in that split-second. The sudden realisation that a car doesn't have to be dull transport takes a microsecond, but leaves a lasting impression.

In a world where the average car is a sophisticated cocoon of quietness and comfort, the Seven comes as a breath of fresh air. The anachronism that is the Seven has not only survived for close on 40 years, it thrives. Perhaps it's because this race car for the road is an effective antidote to modern-day stress or maybe it's simply

that the Seven is an appealing piece of engineering art in its own right. Whatever the reason, the fact that it does exist is genuine cause for celebration for every red-blooded sportscar enthusiast. The Seven provides an almost unmatched level of driving exhilaration, yet it remains so affordable.

Piloting a Seven places the sensations of driving onto a much more cerebral plane than is possible with a conventional car. Merely sitting in one quickens the pulse. Drivers must step over the side and wriggle down snugly between the aluminium propshaft tunnel on one side, the steel tubes of the spaceframe chassis on the other. It's low enough to place a hand flat on the ground surface simply by reaching over the side. In heavy traffic, the feeling is one of vulnerability, but out on a quiet back-road, it spells freedom.

Gripping the rim of the tiny leather-clad wheel, the gear lever is just half a hand's-span away. Through the screen the long bonnet and the curved swathe of the front wings is an unfamiliar though pleasing sight. Fire it up and the engine sounds rorty, impatient to rev, the vibrations course through the chassis in a manner that provides an insight into the directness and rawness of the car.

With familiarity, everything about it becomes almost an extension of the driver so that those initial thoughts of vulnerability are transformed into mastery and control. Driving by the seat of the pants is something that comes naturally in a Seven. The driver can sense every bump and pimple of the road's surface. The steering is alive with a constant stream of detailed information. It feels as if when the car runs over a sweet

wrapper the steering would communicate which brand it was.

The gearchange is direct and quick, the throttle precise and responsive. It needs to be, because the Seven demands to be driven quickly. To do so safely and with precision and control, all the responses must be true and immediate. The powerful brakes, strong engine, and a chassis that is faithful and well balanced through bends ensure that they are.

Driving a car such as this is not merely about outright speed. It's about control, precision, sensation and the satisfaction gained from driver and machine in harmony. These things haven't changed one iota since 1957 when Colin Chapman, the genius who was the founder of Lotus, first put his ultra-lightweight and already race-proven sportscar into production and named it the Seven.

Chapman's designs were always uncompromising in their emphasis on lightness and engineering elegance. The Seven was no different. Chapman knew that the key to good handling was a rigid chassis. Instead of the more usual practise at this time of a heavy, large-section chassis, he designed a frame built entirely of tiny tubes. These were all triangulated in such a way that any loads fed into them from the suspension, braking, engine and

driveline forces were opposed by a particularly rigid yet very light structure. To further enhance the car's ability to make directional changes with impressive agility, he placed the engine well back in the engine bay to allow equal placement of the car's weight on all four tyres.

Back in the early days, the Seven was endowed with far less grip and power than even the most basic of today's superminis. Skinny cross-ply tyres and the feeble Ford 1172cc side-valve engine, taken from the old Popular, conspired to limit potency. Yet it was still enormous fun. Anyway, most buyers of this self-assembly car soon set to the task of improving on the paltry 40 bhp by modifying the engine.

By the early 1960s, the engine choice had widened to include the highly tuneable Ford Anglia 1200cc and Cortina GT 1500cc engines, while the crude cycle wings were replaced by the now-familiar flowing design in glassfibre. The

nosecone and rear wings were also glassfibre, and it even had an optional heater and hood. This Series Three design is almost identical in appearance to that of the current Seven. Today, however, it's made not by Lotus but by Caterham Cars and is available fully built as well as in kit form.

The cockpit is little more than basic but its great fun once you are strapped in

The Caterham connection goes back almost to the beginning of the Seven's history. Caterham was the sole sales outlet for the Seven.

By the early 1970s, when Lotus was about to embark on the production of an exciting mid-engined sportscar named the Esprit, the Lotus directors agreed

that this low-budget kit car could only harm their aspirations. Lotus wanted to become a carmaker committed to producing sophisticated and expensive coupes. It seems ridiculous, even heresy, to think it now but at the time the Seven was little short of an embarrassment.

To Caterham, on the other hand, the car was its lifeblood. Caterham boss Graham Nearn approached Lotus and a deal was struck where the Lotus Seven would be produced by Caterham.

And so the Seven lives on, now immortalised not only by its reputation as a sporting car par-excellence, but also by its fame gleaned from appearing in the title sequences of the cult television series *The Prisoner*.

It would have been easy for Caterham to have continued the Seven in its original form but a commitment to continuous development for enhanced

performance, improved safety and the ongoing pursuit of sales in the international market has seen the car improve in many areas.

The rear suspension, for example, eschews the original solid axle in favour of a more sophisticated semi-independent De Dion design. The engine choice has been further extended with options of Rover, Ford or Vauxhall power, and the current Vauxhall twin cam 2.0-litre engine is good for up to 250 bhp – more than six times the power of the original 1172cc Seven. Chapman would surely approve: 146 mph top speed, 0-60 mph in 3.5 seconds and the standing quarter mile in 12 seconds! To take all this power, the chassis has been beefed up, of course, but Caterham boss Graham Nearn won't countenance any changes to the exterior appearance, and rightly so. It's sacrosanct, he says, and many agree.

Today, the Seven is a continuing

success story. It's sold in markets as diverse as Japan and Germany, although the US product liability laws makes it impossible for a small company such as Caterham to sell cars there. It remains a unique vehicle; a car that defies convention and which is a true joy to drive. This enduring appeal should see it through the coming decades to give similar unbridled pleasure to the next generation of Seven owners – but only if the increasing restraints set by safety and noise legislation don't kill it first. If that happens, we will have lost something truly precious; the combination of a Seven, a winding back-road and a warm summer's day is seventh heaven.

Mazda MX-5

• •

Perhaps the most remarkable thing about the Mazda MX-5 (or Miata as it is known in the US) is that it

exists at all. The simple and cheap sportscar was so successful in the 1960s but had faded by the end of that decade. Its heyday was over and it seemed that the affordable roadster had reached extinction just ten years later.

Yet when the new cheeky little Mazda was launched in 1989, it mirrored the basic design elements of those lovable but often flawed sportsters of almost 30 years earlier.

Instead of facing a dispassionately critical audience, this unashamed blast from the past became an immediate success. It struck a chord with those old enough to remember the MG Midgets, Austin-Healey Sprites, Triumph Spitfires and Lotus Elans of their youth, while a whole generation new to such a concept soon revelled in this more sensual automotive experience.

Were it not for two enthusiasts within Mazda's California design department, the MX-5 project would never have got off the ground. Bob Hall, a motoring journalist before joining Mazda, had grown up with MGs and Triumphs. He believed that the time was right to re-invent the classic, rear-drive, front-engined sportscar. He found an ally to his cause in Tom Matano, head of Mazda's US design team. Together they bullied and cajoled the senior management for two years until permission was granted to go ahead with the project.

Left: *Brilliantly simple Mazda MX5 relies upon smiles per mile rather than pure power*

Below: *This Lotus Elan of the 1990s appeals even more than that 60s classic due to its superior build quality and reliability*

Both men had a clear idea of what they wanted. The new car would eschew the complexity of a mid-engine layout or the hatchback-derived handling of front-wheel drive in favour of the honest simplicity of a classic sportscar layout. The target was to produce a modern-day version of the original Lotus Elan but with Japanese reliability and thorough attention to detail. It would possess a balance of abilities to make it fun. It would not be so fiery that it would be transformed into a grenade in the wrong hands. Above all, it would be small, light and uncomplicated.

Both men knew that to retain these values through the development stages would prove to be tremendously difficult. A major car-maker has many different departments aiming for different targets. It would be easy for the twin ideals of lightness and simplicity to fall by the wayside in the face of conflicting engineering, safety, and technological demands. Legend has it that to fend off the demands for added complication, Hall christened it the KISS car – meaning Keep It Simple Stupid. The ploy worked.

To bring a true understanding to the aims of the project, they brought a Triumph Spitfire and an original Lotus Elan. People working on the MX-5 were encouraged to drive these outdated but still immensely appealing machines to bring home to the designers and engineers the philosophy they wanted to recreate. They even dismantled them to help understand the simplicity and engineering elegance within.

No wonder, then, that the MX-5 is so similar to the Elan. The lines are clearly reminiscent of the sixties classic and the handling echoes the Elan's responsiveness.

Every so often, a car is conceived that is something out of the ordinary. In driving it, there's a perception that the whole is somehow greater than the sum of its parts. Such was the case with the Elan. It is true also of the MX-5.

On its introduction, the MX-5 drew accolade after accolade from the world's press. Perhaps they had forgotten just how appealing the virtues of a simple but talented small sportscar can be. Yet, in trying to understand why a car such as this is special, there are no easy answers.

Examining the bare bones of the MX-5, we see a traditional two-seat open car, with a twin-cam, four-cylinder engine of no great potency. It produced a mere 116 bhp when first introduced. The 115 mph top speed and 0-60 mph time of just under 9 seconds would barely warrant a second glance.

This was GTI-fodder. But the test track figures tell only one part of the story.

It looks clean, uncluttered and well proportioned. There's no overt sportiness, no racetrack innuendo. It's just plain pretty. The interior too, boasts no special gimmicks. Tradition rules here, with plain analogue clocks, simple seats and decor. It's a business-like cabin.

Under the skin, the suspension gives us a clue as to the true character of the MX-5. Independent double wishbone suspension at each corner is a promising start for a good-handling car. Likewise, the

A Japanese classic that was born in the USA, the Mazda MX5 is a landmark in the history of the affordable sports car and a sure-fire classic of the future

engine set back behind the axle line hints at the near equal front/rear weight distribution; a pre-requisite to balance and agility. The fact that the engine channels its power to the rear wheels also holds promise. It means that the front tyres, and more importantly the steering, will be unencumbered with the corrupting influences of harnessing and transferring the engine's torque. So it looks good on paper at least.

Behind the wheel, the MX-5 feels just right. There are no compromises in driver comfort, unlike so many specialist sportscars that suffer from offset pedals or offer nowhere to rest the left foot. The Mazda sounds right too. The engine has a certain crispness and responds with immediacy to any driver input. This crispness extends to the whole car. Turn the wheel,

and it feels free of the cotton-wool mushiness that afflicts so many passenger cars. When changing gear with the short-throw shift, the engineered precision with which the lever slides into place and the attendant change in engine note encourages further use.

Even so, the MX-5 may seem a disappointment on first acquaintance. It jiggles and bucks over the constant imperfections of city streets, while the lack of noise refinement is self-evident on the highway at speed. It's a little cramped too, and lacks many of the creature comforts taken for granted on today's cars. However, to judge the MX-5 by the standards of an everyday car is to miss the point.

To reach the true heights of the MX-5's abilities it is necessary to turn away from the confines of town or the boredom of the

highway and head for the hills. Here the delights of the car can be fully appreciated for those willing to search for its subtle charms. It's not fast in a straight line and neither does it possess huge reserves of grip. The key to its appeal lies not in what the MX-5 does but in the manner in which it does it.

On a twisty road, the car's honest and communicative responses place it onto an altogether higher plane. Once acclimatised to the MX-5's character and feel, it is easy for the average driver to appreciate this lightweight sportster's balance and agility. It doesn't need racing expertise to revel in the way the MX-5 dances through the twists of a mountain road. It flows through corners with little apparent effort and with inch-perfect precision. This fine little car involves the

driver intimately. This is the core of its appeal.

Nowadays, the novelty may have worn off and other car-makers have seized upon its success in attempts to emulate it. Part of the MX-5's charm, however, lies in the timeless appeal of the pleasures of driving a precision machine, one which will never date because it already has its character rooted in the past. By looking backwards to the sportscars of an earlier generation, the MX-5 helped the modern driver to discover a rich new seam of driving pleasure to explore. That it does so at a price that most can afford adds further significance to its distinguished standing as a landmark sportscar.

MGF

The name MG has always been synonymous with open sportscars. Those two letters conjure up a powerful image. For many, it's a nostalgic image too, a trip back to the days when even the most impecunious enthusiast could afford an MGB roadster or Midget. Or perhaps the name brings to mind the pretty T-series cars of the post-war era hurtling along traffic-free roads. Either way, it's almost impossible to think of MG without imagining the scene of a thoroughbred sportscar driven through sun-dappled English countryside by a dashing young blade, a pretty girl beside him with her hair flowing in the breeze.

Yet surprisingly, many MGs were old-fashioned in design and never particularly talented or fast, despite a host of factory-backed competition successes. The most successful MG of all was the MGB. It sold in droves and was a good car in its early years, even if it did continue with scant development for well beyond its sell-by date. Production halted finally in 1980.

The MG name is a powerful marketing tool but it has had its low points as well as its times of glory.

It survived the ignominy of some of the most appalling 'badge engineering' in motoring history when the MG logo was tacked onto a series of mediocre 1970s saloons and hatchbacks.

Then came the rumours of a new affordable MG for the 1990s. This time, it wouldn't be merely a dolled-up saloon or hatchback, but a proper sportscar in the true MG spirit. MG enthusiasts around the world clamoured for the new car.

By the time the MGF was launched in 1995, Rover had already stacked up more than 1,000 customer orders.

The bosses at Rover, and at parent company BMW, knew that the MGF would have to sell on more than nostalgia alone. Mazda had already dived in to capture the pent-up demand for open sportscars with the excellent MX-5. Meanwhile, Toyota's MR2 had acquired a great many admirers with its mini-Ferrari looks and fine performance. Nostalgia might sell

the first MGFs but it would take a solid range of abilities as well as alluring looks to make the MGF palatable to this new breed of more discriminating sportscar buyer. Also, with new sportsters from Fiat, BMW and Alfa Romeo ready to plunge into the same market, the MGF had to be good.

Those of us who have always harboured a soft spot for MG were mightily relieved when the MGF proved to be not just good... but sensational. Some feared that the new car might prove to be a throwback to an earlier period of motoring, as was the case with the underwhelming MG RV8 – a car that was little more than an old-style MGB V8 with added glitz – but the new F proved to be as convincing as it looked.

Styling chief Gerry McGovern created a shape that is thoroughly up to date. In common with so many designs of timeless appeal, the MG is sculpted in a rounded form, free of the constrictions of

Worth the wait! The return of the MG in 1995 with the MGF hasn't disappointed roadster enthusiasts

straight lines. Detail design is particularly impressive. The headlights and tail-light clusters flow into the surrounding bodywork; the bumpers harmonise with the overall design; the twin oval tailpipes exit neatly through the aggressively-shaped tail; the side air-intakes are smoothly integrated yet they create a styling feature in themselves. Even the fuel filler is automotive art, its outer retaining ring held in place by eight aircraft-type bolts. The six-spoke alloy wheels set the whole car off to perfection.

The mid-engined layout was more or less pre-determined. A relatively small development budget dictated the use of an engine and transaxle from an existing Rover product. With no rear-drive cars in the range, the power unit had to be installed either in the usual position at the front driving the front wheels or just behind the cockpit driving the rear wheels.

It would have been far simpler to have gone for a front-engine installation but there would have

The MGF may have delved into the Rover parts bin, but was a dedicated sports car design, in tune with modern times and mid-engined for ultimate road manners

always been too many compromises for a true sportscar. A mid-engined layout, with the front wheels freed from the influences of transmitting engine torque, would not only help achieve the steering sensitivity required, but the better weight distribution would also endow the car with greater potential for handling agility. Yet this decision meant a greater challenge for the engineers. Added complications arose from cooling an engine in a constricted space. The isolation of engine noise and vibration would also prove to be more difficult, as

would the packaging.

The natural choice of engine was the excellent Rover K-series – but this would be no ordinary K-series engine. The existing twin-cam unit, in use for many other models in the Rover range, had at that time a maximum capacity of 1.4-litres. For the MGF, the capacity would rise to 1.8-litres with a power output of 120 bhp.

Then Rover played its Joker card. The engineers had hit upon an old but undeveloped concept of managing the valve opening and closing periods, thereby allowing each cylinder to draw more air

and produce more power. By integrating this design with the latest electronic management, this Variable Valve Control, or VVC, allows an infinitely variable range of cam periods to give enhanced power at high revs but without sacrificing flexibility at lower engine speeds. It all adds up to an output of 145 bhp at a heady 7000 rpm – enough to propel the little MG to a top speed of 130 mph with a 0-60 mph time of around seven seconds. In anyone's language that's quick enough to be interesting.

It gets even more interesting

out on the open road. This MG begs to be driven hard and fast. The mid-engine layout, stiff body and classic double-wishbone suspension at front and rear provides responsive and agile handling. That it's super-quick through the turns is never in doubt, but the MG goes a step further in providing a surprising degree of adjustability and on-limit composure. This is a truly entertaining, but also safe, car to drive quickly.

The steering, electrically power-assisted, seems almost immune to the vagaries of imperfect road surfaces to produce a level of

Like all MG roadsters, the MGF is a joy to look at

accuracy that drivers learn to trust implicitly. Powerful brakes add to the driver's pleasure but the gearchange can occasionally baulk if the driver's actions are less than positive. The vivacious engine combined with a chassis of rare excellence places this fine sporting car among the greats.

For a car with such handling alacrity it's rare to also have a supple ride, yet the MG contrives to happily combine the two. This is possible thanks to special Hydragas damper units linked front and rear.

Obviously, a sportscar of such dynamic excellence and good breeding would be seriously lacking if it did not feature a driver environment to pamper the most discriminating pilot. This does not mean ostentation: there is a no-frills approach to the MGF's cabin. It is

enticing and well designed rather than luxurious or flashy. It makes you want to drive; it works and it's comfortable. Similarly, the hood provides a snug fit, useful for those MG customers living in northern climates. It is surprising how many exotic car designers seem oblivious to the needs of everyday practicality, but MG has managed to squeeze enough space within the clever design to accommodate some luggage behind the engine, even if that does mean that there's just a slim slot for engine access.

The MGF is clearly a sportscar of rare competence and ability. It's a genuine English sportscar, less expensive than most of the competition but with a manner and a talent that gives it enduring appeal. Some day, it too will join its MG brethren in achieving true classic status.

Alfa Spider & GTV

Smiles of approval mixed with sighs of relief greeted the Alfa Romeo design team when the Spider and its coupe cousin the GTV were released to the world's motoring press in 1994. These stunning new designs had already received a clamourous reception at shows throughout Europe, but there were serious doubts as to the ability of this brace of new sporting Alfas to be as 'bellissimo' to drive as they were to look at.

It was clear from the furrowed brows of the assembled car experts that each was concerned that that this might prove to be yet another disappointing Alfa to drive, despite the bold looks and its promising on-paper specification.

Alfa Romeo has a past history as illustrious as anyone's, but for the past two decades its products were characterised by inept chassis dynamics and mediocre overall abilities. Only the 164 saloon with its glorious V6 engine could lay claim to any greatness and even this was a car of patchy ability. It's front-drive chassis never appeared comfortable transmitting this much power. So the assembled journalists waiting to drive the latest sporting Alfas were prepared for, and perhaps even expecting, disappointment.

There could be no argument over the strikingly aggressive lines. This is automotive beauty at its best; a shape that assaults the senses with its dynamism and power. The low nose is punctuated by tiny twin circular headlamps flanking a classic Alfa grille that flows into a broad V stretching the full length of the bonnet. From here, a diagonal line rises across the flanks to emphasise the high chunky tail and splits the profile in a rakish statement of design flair. The observer can almost sense movement with the car at rest; seen

The Alfa Romeo: Glorious styling details simply delight car lovers

in motion it is difficult to suppress a smile of approval.

For the driver, that smile broadens into a wide grin. It takes little more than the first mile or so behind the wheel of this Latin beauty to appreciate that Alfa has

at last turned the tide. In the Spider, Alfa has produced a truly great sportscar; one that is worthy of the Alfa name. The GTV is more impressive still. The increased body stiffness of the fixed-head layout endows the car with a tautness

that the open Spider cannot match.

The GTV's steering has a delicious crispness about it that allows the car to be deftly flicked through the turns with a confidence and poise that places this among the very best of the class. The quicker drivers go, the more impressive are its abilities. Some sportscars possess just a thin veneer of talent; they become ragged and unpredictable when pushed to their limits. The beauty of the Alfa is that its balance, poise and grip remain intact right up to the point where the tyres give up this unequal struggle. Throughout all this, it remains unflustered, controllable on the throttle and with a flat stance that inspires confidence.

The big surprise for many is that Alfa has succeeded in producing such measured and adjustable handling from a front-engined, front drive chassis.

To attempt this with an engine that develops 150 bhp, as is the case with the 2.0-litre Twin Spark, can cause some problems. The combination of too much weight at the front of the car together with power delivered through the steered wheels presents two inherent difficulties for the engineers to overcome.

The first is that the weight distribution places too much mass over the front wheels, making it more difficult to turn into corners. The natural tendency is for the car to carry straight on, which is hardly conducive to the values expected of a sportscar. The second drawback is that torque applied through the steered wheels can often create tugging forces at the steering wheel, especially over bumps, on damp roads or when the car is on surfaces of mixed grip.

With these potential handicaps, it's all the more impressive that

Alfa's design team has managed to eradicate the symptoms. It's genuinely hard to tell from which end the car is driven. It's an achievement thus far equalled only by the front-drive Lotus Elan.

This talented chassis is matched by an engine of rare ability and charisma. However, it's not so much the performance that impresses as the manner in which it delivers its power. This engine won't win any ovations for either the horsepower available or the outright performance, despite an accomplished specification that embraces twin-spark ignition, four valves per cylinder and variable valve-timing. The top speed of 133 mph and the 0-60 mph time of 8.5 seconds are respectable rather than crushingly fast.

But the crisp responsiveness to

> **Left:** *The new Spider signified a welcome return of Alfa greatness*
> **Below:** *In GTV coupe form it was even better due to a stiffer bodyshell. Both are certain to be future classics*

the throttle, the gutsy pull from the mid-range and the throaty crackle from the exhausts as it spins smoothly towards 7000 rpm makes this an engine to remember.

It is surely one of the finest four-cylinder engines yet built. Its charms are magnified further by a gearchange that, unusually for a modern Alfa, is a genuine delight to use through the range.

Other, more powerful engines are available in some markets. Although the 2.0 V6 turbo and the 3.0 V6 both provide a more gutsy pace, the greater weight of these engines and the effect on weight distribution destroys much of the chassis balance and poise that makes the GTV and Spider so special to drive in their four-cylinder form.

One thing that all of these engines share in common is that they are beautiful to look at. Many modern car companies have forgotten that the enthusiast will delight in the sight of an impressive engine. Alfa hasn't forgotten .

There is almost always a penalty

to pay in a car of exquisite charms. Here, it's a combination of limited practicality and an interior build quality that fails to match up to the high standards of the brilliantly detailed coachwork. In addition, the ride from the stiff suspension never really feels relaxed away from the motorway.

Perhaps the most powerful impression that comes across with these Alfas is that they are true enthusiasts cars, designed for people who love cars.

Maybe the reason that the magic is so strong is that the men who design them also love cars. Walter da Silva, the man responsible for the charismatic styling, keeps a pair of classic Alfas, a 1962 Giulietta Spyder and a 1972 GT Junior 1300; Oreggioni Aldo, the designer of that wonderful engine, has a much treasured MGB at his home above Lake Como.

No wonder the new Alfa has one of the best shapes, one of the best chassis and one of the best 2.0 engines around. It's a great car and a future classic.

Morgan

Snuggled close beneath a ridge of hills they call the Malverns, there lies a sleepy factory that has been lost in time. Within the ramshackle collection of red brick buildings, the work of craftsmen goes on in precisely the same way that it has for generations. It's the work of making thoroughbred hand-crafted sportscars.

This is Morgan, a small family firm whose history stretches back almost as far as the car itself. Morgans have been built in this same factory for more than 70 years. Tradition lies at the very core of its foundations. Peer within the recesses of the brick buildings and wooden sheds and see body panels hand-formed in steel and aluminium. Pay close attention and it is possible to see these same panels being grafted to wooden body frames of steam-bent ash, built using the same methods as for furniture making.

A separate underslung ladder

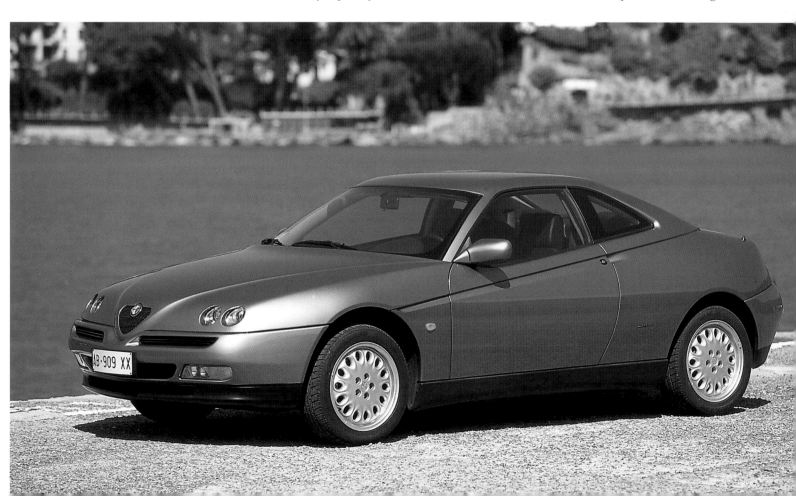

chassis, formed from a linked pair of Z-section longitudinal members, is the base for every Morgan. The inherent flexibility of such an untriangulated structure is easily accommodated by the forgiving nature of a timber frame. It's a method of car manufacture that has its roots deep in the mists of time. These same techniques once formed the art of making carriages – of the horse-drawn variety. It takes ten to twelve weeks to build each car and just ten cars roll out of the factory each week.

Even a Morgan's suspension is of a type used by this company for decades past. The sliding-pillar-type front suspension is of exactly the same design as the first three-wheeled Morgans of 1909, while the rigid back axle suspended by cart springs dates from before that. At least the body frames of current cars are now treated against fungal and beetle attack.

Apart from a more rakish slant to the tail and the change in 1955 from a flat radiator grille to the familiar bulbous shape, the current Morgan appears very much as the 4/4 did when it was introduced in 1936. Only with the engines does Morgan make any attempt to keep up with the times and that's only because these items are bought-in from other more conventional car-makers.

There is, of course, method in this madness. People buy Morgans precisely because they are brand-new classic cars, built in the traditional way. Charles Morgan, grandson of company founder HFS Morgan, will say that his customers simply won't entertain any changes. Such is the demand, that each customer must wait his turn for anything up to six years.

No other car company can boast this level of customer demand.

Over the years, the chassis and body have grown wider, the engines have become more powerful, with chassis strengthening and upgrading of the brakes to cope, but it remains effectively a pre-war car built in a vintage factory using time-honoured methods. It's this uniquely vintage feel of the Morgan that gives it a raw-edged appeal to the enthusiast driver.

Performance has always been uppermost in the Morgan's personality, a fact emphasised when Morgan squeezed Rover's 3.5-litre V8 engine into a slightly longer and wider version of the traditional Morgan shape in 1968. Although today's range lists four-cylinder engines from Ford and

The view from the cockpit shows vintage exposed headlamps and swept wings – a throw back from the 1930s! For all that the interior is comfortable and welcoming

The Morgan: Vintage values still hold

Rover among its choices for the Plus Four and 4/4 models, the real Morgan, the Plus Eight, continues with an updated version of that same all-alloy V8. This means 3.9 litres, 190 bhp and 0-60 mph in just six seconds. Put another way, it will keep pace with a Porsche 911 on a straight road for most of the way up to 100 mph.

The combination of gut-wrenching torque allied to a chassis and body that, by rights, should be housed within a museum, is, depending on a particular point of view, either a recipe for disaster or the perfect antidote to the mundanity of today's cocoon-like motor transport.

This level of performance within a flexible chassis that hops and skips over the bumps demands a healthy respect. It's well suited to smooth roads where the Morgan's suspension isn't taxed beyond its limits and the grip of the tyres can be fully exploited, but over rougher roads its limitations are clear. The flexible 'ladder-type' chassis and ash frame, together with inadequately damped short-travel suspension and a rear axle that is located by little more than a pair of leaf springs might appear a somewhat perverse combination in the age of stiff monocoques with precisely controlled all-independent suspension.

It's this sense of challenge that lies at the very core of the Morgan's appeal. The driver needs to work hard to get the best out of the Morgan. It needs to be taken by the scruff of the neck and driven hard. Drivers need quick reactions and a certain familiarity with the car's traits. It will buck constantly over mid-corner bumps, while the tail is easily provoked into a slide by a touch of over-exuberance with the throttle. Glorious fun, though!

There's never any doubt that this is a man's car... or a car for a woman who has been on a weightlifting course! The heavy steering, gearbox and brakes, the bone-jarring ride and the far from cossetting seat will confirm that, as does the meaty thump in the kidneys from a bootful of throttle. With the hood raised, a howling gale screams just inches from the

On the right sort of roads a Morgan can provide real thrills but its ancient chassis and suspension always demand respect

driver's ears to make swift progress an unpleasant experience. The buffeting is brutal when the sidescreens are tucked away in the only available luggage space behind the seats. Hood down and sidescreens up is the best way to drive a Morgan.

The driving position is just right for sports motoring, although the upright position of the wheel takes some acclimatisation. With the bonnet stretching out into the distance, a twisty road ahead, the front wings bobbing gently up and down over successive undulations, and that glorious woofly rumble of V8 beneath the bonnet, it's easy to see why people are so captivated by the Morgan's charms.

Add a smattering of rain and the

task of keeping it all on line on a bumpy back-road becomes a precarious balancing act. A restrained throttle is essential, but the Morgan's seat-of-the-pants feel serves as an invaluable asset to help maintain control. This intimate involvement of driver and machine against the odds is the very essence of why the Morgan remains such an enduring classic. It offers a tactile experience entirely absent from so many of today's hugely capable cars. Drive a Morgan smoothly and quickly and the driver is rewarded with a huge buzz of achievement and excitement. It really sets the pulse-rate racing.

It possesses an inherent beauty too. The rakish lines and the simplicity of its form, the long

Classic hand crafted bodywork and vintage style mark Morgans out as sheer class in a world of computer designed tin boxes!

louvered surfaces of the tapered bonnet, the traditional cockpit with its leather trim and the knowledge that this car has been hand-crafted from wood and aluminium: it all adds up to a feeling that the Morgan is unique.

Provided it can retain this excitement and challenge to the driver, the traditional values of the Morgan will always find a keen following. It means that, for a certain red-brick factory tucked away beneath the Malvern hills, progress can wait a while longer.

TVR Griffith

• • • • • • • • • • • • • • • • • • • •

It idles with the malevolent, low-pitched growl of a Rottweiler roused from its sleep. Blip the throttle and that evil snarl rises into a savage, ground-shaking crescendo that ricochets off the walls and assaults the eardrums. Pedestrians stand back as the tortured scream of rubber biting tarmac announces the full ferocity of five litres of prime British muscle being unleashed. Acrid tyre smoke fills everyone's nostrils and the car catapults toward the end of the strip like a Tornado jet on take-off.

That's what it's like to witness a TVR Griffith 500 on a standing start acceleration run. The astounding figures on the ticker-

tape read; 0-60 mph in 4.1 seconds, 0-100 mph in 10.2 seconds and a top speed of 167 mph.

All this is from a traditional British sportscar with a normally aspirated V8 that can trace its roots back 40 years. This is performance with which to crush Chrysler Vipers and destroy Porsche Turbos. Yet this car costs less than any rival that comes even remotely close to its crushing performance and sensational looks.

The unmistakable growl of a TVR Griffith is a familiar sound to those close to the traditional seaside town of Blackpool. It's a place famous for two things: its wild roller-coaster fairground rides... and TVR sportscars. Which of the two offers the greater entertainment value is a point of debate. For the better part of a century, the fairground has provided thrills for all the family. For nigh-on 40 years TVR has provided thrills of an entirely adult nature from the traditional hairy-chested sportscars that it builds within the shambling range of buildings that passes for its factory.

In common with so many of England's specialist sportscar makers, TVR has had its fair share of ups and downs, especially in its early years when it went through various owners. But for the past decade or so it has gone from strength to strength. The guiding force and the man whose ebullient

A Griffith in all its glory! With a massive 5 litres of muscle-bound might, this TVR offers shattering performance and demands the utmost respect; especially in the wet

and bluff character is central to every TVR is a man named Peter Wheeler; a chain-smoking, north-country businessman with a big personality and a penchant for fast and charismatic cars.

Ever since Wheeler acquired TVR the cars have become faster and better built, but in many ways the design concept is the same as it always has been at TVR. It's just that now the company is better organised, more professional and it has that little extra bit of magic that comes only from a car-maker whose boss has a genuine passion for cars. There can't be too many car company MDs who race their own products at weekends. Peter Wheeler does.

TVR's stock-in-trade right from its beginnings at the tail end of the 1950s has always been the sort of sportscars that enthusiasts love. The first of the MG and Coventry-

Climax-engined cars had a steel-tube backbone-type chassis and glassfibre bodywork, trademarks that endured right to the present day. Over the years the stubby coupe shape grew longer and wider, the spine chassis became better triangulated for improved stiffness and the suspension, independent from the start, changed from a crude trailing-arm system to a more effective double wishbone design.

As far back as the early 1960s, TVR was dabbling with V8 engines. The story goes that two US racers were fettling their cars at Jack Griffith's workshops. One had a V8 AC Cobra, the other an MG-engined TVR. Somewhere along the line, they decided to see if the Cobra's Ford 4.7-litre V8 would fit in the TVR's engine bay. It wouldn't quite but Jack Griffith saw the potential and set about

making it work. TVR's North American importers then brought the prototype car over to the Blackpool factory for further development and before long the car was on sale as the TVR Griffith 200, with the same engine as the mighty AC Cobra.

With such a big engine in a lightweight, short-wheelbase body, the Griffith proved to be stunningly fast in a straight line but somewhat temperamental in its everyday road behaviour.

It was not until 1991 that the name was seen again. This time, however, it was an all-British effort and the car was an open two-seater with a rounded aggressive shape. This new car was in stark contrast to the wedge profile with which TVRs had become associated throughout the 1980s but it was clear from its rapturous welcome at the 1991 British Motor Show

TVR Griffith: Only fun for two

that this charismatic form would be the key to TVR's future success. It looked sensational, with its far-from-subtle muscularity and bulging flanks. Power exuded from every pore. This was a TVR with real soul.

In true TVR tradition, the new Griffith was based on a tough tubular backbone chassis with the engine mounted well behind the front axle line and with double wishbones at each corner, all clothed in a glassfibre body. Rover V8 engines were no strangers to TVR and by this time Wheeler had acquired an engine plant, TVR Power, to develop the Rover engines into power units offering rather more than the stock motor. When the first cars eventually appeared from the Blackpool works, the engine had grown to 4.3 litres and could deploy a solid 280 horsepower through its five-speed manual gearbox.

This proved to be a car of rare charisma, thundering performance and a sense of style that any driver with red blood in his veins would die for. The performance was crushingly effective, the handling exuberant but unforgiving for the inexperienced. It was an enthusiast's car, and TVR couldn't build enough of them. But there was yet more to come. TVR somehow managed to gain a full five litres from the Rover's block and thus liberated a mind-blowing 340 bhp in a car weighing just 1075 kg. With a power-to-weight ratio of 316 bhp per tonne, it's still one of the most potent sportscars that money can buy.

In Griffith 500 guise, as the 5.0-litre car is known, the TVR is perhaps a little too potent for its own good. Given a little encouragement it hurls itself down the track in an explosion of brute strength and power. In contrast to the sanitised speed of a Ferrari or Porsche, the Griffith exudes raw, latent aggression. The bark of the engine is enough to make children run away and hide; those great nuggets of torque are sufficient to virtually rearrange most internal organs. Quite simply the power is sensational. Few cars, if any,

The he-man appearance of the Griffith takes no prisoners, nor does its 340 bhp power. It's not for the timid but in the right hands is awesome

actually feel this fast.

Any car with this much raw performance must be treated with respect, the Griffith with perhaps more than most. On a racetrack or on smooth roads the chassis is utterly predictable, the steering crisply communicative and the brakes work like tug boat anchors. Add a few bumps, the odd surface change and the occasional patch of damp, however, and it becomes a sight more demanding to stay in control. This car isn't for wimps and if the rear end does break away, it's difficult to catch. None of which takes away the pure unadulterated enjoyment of driving this car; it simply adds to the challenge and makes it all the more sweet when its foibles and faults have been mastered.

It is easy to see how the Griffith steals the soul. Not only does it look sensational, sound like a brigade of artillery, go like lightning and possess a thoroughbred heritage, but when an enthusiast slips behind the wheel and the leather cabin folds around like a favourite armchair, they wouldn't want to be anywhere else in the world.

Porsche 911

Any car that has become an acknowledged classic within its own lifetime has to possess an aura of magic about it. That's certainly true of Porsche's 911. This is the car that redefines the term 'continuous development'. In fact, it elevates it to an art form.

After three decades, the 911 remains one of the world's foremost sporting cars. It still captivates the enthusiast with its

blend of pace, ability and outright excitement. And yet, although the profile remains the same as the very first 911 to be unleashed onto an unsuspecting world back in 1963, only the badge remains the same. Every component has been refined, upgraded and honed to its ultimate development. Engine power has trebled. And at the Porsche research centre, the work still goes on.

That a concept such as the 911 should have proved to be such an enduring success almost defies belief. Pierce the depths of time far enough and it is possible to trace the 911's roots back to the humble VW Beetle, designed by Ferdinand Porsche back in the 1930s.

From this unpromising beginning,

Ferdinand's son Ferry Porsche, also a talented engineer, developed the Porsche 356 coupe, itself the fore-runner of the larger and more sophisticated 911.

And so it is that every 911 has its engine behind the rear axle line, just like the Beetle. No sportscar designer today would choose such a fundamentally flawed layout. Ideally, the major masses of a car should be as close as is feasibly possible to the centre of the car. To have the engine stuck out the back means that it acts as a pendulum when cornered hard. That is why

An early 911. Compare this shot to the one overleaf and note how little it has changed. But underneath the skin reveals a different story

early 911s were notorious for swapping ends unexpectedly, requiring a high degree of skill to master at speed. Some early 911s even had lead weights attached to the front bumpers in an effort to curb its tail-end waywardness. Over the years Porsche's engineers have overcome all the disadvantages of such a layout to achieve a car that compares with the very best for handling fluency and overall dynamic excellence. The 911 proves how engineering development can triumph over flawed design.

The rear-engined, rear-drive layout does of course have a degree of inherent merit. Traction under acceleration is outstanding, which allows the 911 to be powered away from corners much earlier than with a front-engined car. Also, the use of aluminium castings and air cooling for the engine lessens the adverse effects of a potentially heavy mass at the rear.

The latest 911s have come a long way from the first showing of the car in 1963 with its 2.0-litre flat-six engine and 901

BHR 728L
DICK LOVETT SPECIALIST CARS

nomenclature. Objections from Peugeot over the 901 name meant that by the time production began in 1964 the cars were labelled 911. From that date onwards the design has matured and developed in a continuously upward spiral.

Even the first 911 of 1964 with its compact and aerodynamic body was capable of 130 mph from its 130 bhp engine. Ten years later, the engine had grown to 2.7-litres and, in lightweight Carrera RS trim with 210 bhp at its disposal, the 911 could crack 150 mph.

A more significant development ten years into the 911's life was the introduction of the Type 930 – the 911 Turbo. This was the car to prove beyond doubt the ability of the turbocharger to work reliably and effectively in a road car. In profile, the Turbo looked like any other 911, but the pronounced bulge of its rear flanks together with the huge rear aerofoil gave it an overtly aggressive stance in keeping with the breathtaking performance. With 3.3-litres and 300 bhp for 1977, the 911 Turbo became a performance icon.

Amazingly, there was still more to come from the 911 concept. Its zenith of development was the amazing 959 of 1985. This pure supercar, its production limited to just 200, was conceived as Porsche's engineering showcase and its Group B rally contender. Porsche had always had a commitment to motor racing as a tool to develop ideas for its road cars and had dominated sportscar racing for many years. With no wish to re-enter Formula One, the next challenge was rallying.

Never complacent or content with anything less than the ultimate, Porsche's 959 encompassed all the latest technology. The body was still recognisably 911 and the engine remained a flat-six but these were heavily modified in this ambitious engineering showcase. From its advanced four-wheel drive and electronically controlled anti-lock braking system to the 450 bhp twin-turbo engine and kevlar-panelled body, this was cutting edge technology. The bottom line was a car capable of around 200 mph, with the 0-100 mph sprint in a spine-tingling 8.5 seconds.

Although the 959 missed out on the rally program because of rule changes that made the car ineligible, it has proved its all-terrain pace and durability by twice winning the arduous Paris-Dakar rally.

As proof that racing really does improve the breed, the latest Porsche 911 line-up encompasses much of the technology that went into the 959. The 911 Turbo, for example, with a potent 408 bhp in its 1995 form, shared a similar turbo layout to the 959, its twin rotors acting sequentially to improve response. Although the 959's four-wheel drive system has been simplified, the concept of 4WD is there just the same to help tame the effects of channelling all that power to the wheels.

Surprisingly though, it was not four-wheel drive that was to mark the turning point for the 911's transformation from a tricky-handling rogue to a sure-footed thoroughbred. That accolade must go to the engineers who masterminded the thorough redesign that brought about the Carrera 2 of 1988. A complete rethink of the rear suspension to incorporate an advanced multi-link design and a separate light-alloy subframe resulted in the twin

benefits of improved road-noise absorption and massively improved stability. Further improvements came with the introduction of the second-generation Carrera 4 with its subtle deployment of 4WD.

Another area where Porsche engineers have proved that they lead the world is in the development of the Tiptronic gearbox. This enables the car to be driven either as an auto or as a clutchless manual. There have been previous attempts at this but Porsche was the first to prove that it could be done while maintaining

the delicacy demanded by the most discriminating of drivers.

The Porsche 911 has become accepted as a design classic. The compact body makes effective use of space to make this a truly practical two-seat sportscar with occasional rear seating. Despite the lengthy development of the 911, it remains true to the original concept of a high-performance sportscar. Yes, it is more comfortable, it is quieter, it rides better, and it now handles as a true thoroughbred should, but the engineers have retained that rich seam of raw-edged sporting appeal that, for a generation, has so characterised the 911.

It still has steering that translates every subtlety of the road surface. It still has a ride firmness to remind car-spotters of its racing pedigree. It still has an engine that will make hairs stand on end. But it also possesses a confidence inducing stability to make this accessible to a far wider audience. It's no longer

the car that bites the unskilled or the unwary. It has a more rounded, better balanced character. Like a fine vintage champagne, the 911 has matured in its advancing age, yet it has maintained that youthful effervescence that has always given it so much appeal to the enthusiast.

Chevrolet Corvette

The Corvette has played a leading role in Chevrolet's sporting line-up for more years than anyone cares to remember. Spanning four decades, this archetypal American sportscar has acquired a reputation not just for speed and power, but for toughness and durability too. That mammoth V8 engine will smoke the tyres off the line time-after-time until the track driver either gets bored or wears out their tread. The tough old Chevy won't break. What the Corvette lacks in

sophistication it makes up for in solid engineering strengths. High mileage and high horsepower are its twin virtues.

This was not always the case. Back in 1953, the very first Corvette developed just 150 bhp from its 3.8-litre straight-six engine. Expediency meant that many of its components were based on the GM saloon cars of the time, so its road behaviour as well as its performance was clearly not all it should be. An auto transmission with only two forward gears didn't help. However, the overall design of a relatively lightweight glassfibre body – the first to be used in this scale of manufacture – together with a cross-braced chassis frame which placed the front-mounted engine well back for good weight distribution, meant that the Corvette had potential for further development.

Even so, it was not until 1956, when the Corvette gained a sleeker body and a more powerful

4.3-litre V8 engine, that the first hint of the Corvette's aspirations as a true muscle car began to emerge. It took the next complete redesign of 1963 – the classic Corvette Sting Ray – to prove beyond any doubt that this would be a car to reckon with. This had a new and audacious fast-back coupe body on a redesigned chassis that now featured independent rear suspension. It also had the punch to make the likes of Jaguar and Ferrari sit up and take notice. Initially, a 5.3-litre small-block V8 deploying up to 395 bhp nestled under the vast expanse of bonnet to provide a car with a genuine 150 mph top speed – but for those who wanted even more, a big-block 7.0-litre Chevy V8 could be specified. This produced up to 435 bhp. Serious power indeed.

Through the economically depressed 1970s, the Corvette's power and performance waned as GM, along with everyone else in the automotive business, struggled to keep pace with spiralling

> **Left:** *By the early 1980s the Corvette was becoming stale – until the sensational ZR1 hit the tarmac in 1983. This was followed by the LT1 – almost as good and cheaper*
> **Above** *The current Corvette relied upon Lotus to give it the power this cult American muscle car deserved*

emission and safety regulations. It was not until two body styles later that the Corvette was again a force to be reckoned with. This time its name was Corvette ZR-1.

The current-shape Corvette has been around since 1983 and even with its original output of 200 bhp from its pushrod 5.7-litre V8, this lighter and smaller car's clean and uncluttered shape was good for 140 mph and 0-60 mph in around seven seconds. By this time, some exclusive European marques were busy making in-roads into the Corvette's market and GM needed to fight back. The answer was a powerful new engine option capable of pushing this already impressive car to within spitting distance of 170 mph.

The catalyst to bring about this potent beast was Lotus Engineering, the British sportscar maker that, by the mid eighties, had established a worldwide reputation for engineering consultancy. GM needed more power for its top sports model and also for their racing activities at Indianapolis. Lotus said it could do the job in the limited time available. The original intention was for Lotus to engineer new four-valve cylinder heads for the existing iron L98 block but space restrictions beneath the Corvette's bonnet precluded this.

In the event, Lotus developed an all-new aluminium-block engine with twin overhead-camshafts for

each cylinder bank and four-valves per cylinder. This new 5.7-litre engine developed 380 bhp (411 bhp from 1993) but efforts to keep its fuel economy on the right side of 'gas-guzzler' status were proving elusive.

Lotus tried an ultra-high top gear ratio for the six-speed ZF transmission and an equally low idle speed for improved emissions. It still wasn't enough.

Finally Lotus hit upon the idea of using just one of the two inlet valves for low-throttle applications. Whenever there was a requirement for greater power each of the second inlet valves could be opened progressively and its separate injectors deployed by means of electronic control through the engine management computer. The result is a type of variable valve-timing that produces acceptable economy and good low-end flexibility but with no loss of top-end punch.

Having finally obtained the right engine, GM next set about improving the grip, handling and brakes. The car now wears fatter rubber, stiffer springs and better brakes than the stock Corvette. The end result is a hugely capable car with near-supercar performance and a traditional front-engine, rear-drive layout. In this respect it remains a refreshingly uncomplicated beast. There's no sign of the tricky

handling traits or inaccessible power of some of the more highly-strung mid-engined competitors we could mention. In contrast, the Corvette ZR-1 is remarkably easy to drive fast. Down the straights, it hauls in the horizon with alarming ferocity. Through turns, the fat tyres demonstrate prodigious grip. If the tail does begin to slide, and with so much power available it's relatively easy to unstick the back on tighter turns, the resultant slide can be brought to heel smoothly and progressively. These sort of tricks are strictly for the track, of course.

If there's a car whose engine is its heart and soul, this is it. It manages to combine the savage low-down brutality of a big V8 with the formidable top-end zing of a modern multi-valve screamer. With such awesome and accessible power, most of those six gears appear to be redundant.

The ZR-1 is still on the options sheet, though its significance is rapidly being overhauled by the less sophisticated but now almost as quick Corvette LT-1. Progress and development has meant that the good old iron small-block V8 now pushes out a beefy 305 bhp. Put another way, buyers still get 150 mph performance but for a lot less money.

In the latest LT-1 guise, the Corvette possesses an assured air of ability. It has surprisingly sharp

and communicative steering, demon grip and a degree of balanced handling that comes as a quite unexpected pleasure in a car this big. Perhaps its greatest asset is an engine that growls its pleasure with every depression of the right foot. A seemingly bottomless well of torque gives truly accessible power whenever its needed. That V8 sound is truly glorious.

These days the Corvette can't conceal its advancing years alongside newer muscle cars. It's no match for the lithe and light Porsche 911 or for the sophisticated charms of a Honda NSX. A Chrysler Viper would eat it for breakfast. But in terms of obtaining big power for not-so-big bucks, the Corvette remains a tempting alternative that offers one big kick of pure driving pleasure.

Honda NSX

Nobuhiko Kawamoto once had a dream: to create a sporting car to humble the world's most accomplished supercars. As if this were not a task challenging enough, Kawamoto's dream car would also be required to marry its dynamic prowess with the virtues necessary to cross a continent or a city in comfort and in grace.

It would prove a tough challenge even for Honda's President to convert this dream into a reality. And yet, some six and a half years later, the dream was achieved. The dream car's name: the Honda NSX.

The first step was to define the points of reference from which to start, so Honda's development team evaluated every sportscar from Honda's own CRX to the mighty Lamborghini Countach. Most performance cars were either light enough to be nimble but with insufficient comfort, or they were fast and powerful but too cumbersome. Also, many were too unrefined for long-distance travel or simply too difficult to master.

Among those singled out as the most dynamically efficient were the Porsche 911 and the Ferrari 328. Both were smaller and lighter than their supercar counterparts but ultimately more effective.

To achieve these qualities and more, the NSX would need high power but low weight. It would have to be aerodynamically efficient and it would need to have a large enough footprint to offer stability both in cornering and in a straight line. But it must also be compact enough to be wieldy. Everything about the NSX stemmed from these design criteria.

Uniquely, Honda chose aluminium for the structure. The heavier the body, the bigger the brakes, the stronger the transmission, and the more powerful the engine. Weight saved in the structure would be vital to the overall concept. So the NSX evolved with an aluminium monocoque, the first production car to do so. It cost five times as much as steel but the 40 per cent weight saving proved its worth. At 210Kg, the body is lighter than any rival, yet it's also immensely stiff, a vital pre-requisite for good handling. Following initial tests with the legendary Ayrton Senna, the prototype NSX received eight months of chassis development at the demanding Nurburgring circuit in Germany before emerging 50 per cent stiffer than any rival. This not only enhances handling but also allows for long-travel suspension to more effectively sponge away the bumps.

The pioneering use of aluminium alloys extends to many of the suspension components. The intricate alloy forgings and stamped extrusions weigh almost a third less than equivalent steel components. This vital reduction in unsprung weight allows more precise control over bumps and improves grip and stability. Yokohama produced literally thousands of test tyres to further enhance the levels of grip, bump absorption and low noise levels.

Of key importance to the superior agility of the NSX is the 42/58 per cent front/rear weight distribution, made possible by the design team opting for a compact engine and the fuel tank sited just behind the passenger compartment. With much of the weight concentrated at the centre of the car, directional changes can be quick and fluid.

With such a no-compromise approach to the chassis and suspension, no less ideals would be expected for the engine. Here, efficiency was the goal. V8s and V12s were ruled out because of bulk and turbos were rejected because of fears of lethargic throttle response and poor economy.

In the end, the optimum for smallest dimensions, lowest weight and best weight distribution proved to be an advanced quad-cam all-alloy V6 mounted transversely. It features electronically controlled valve-timing to enable a broad spread of power without sacrificing the high output at high revs. This is enhanced further by the use of dual length tuned inlet tracts, opening at 4,800 rpm and producing a positive ram effect into the cylinders.

Exotic materials figure in the relentless pursuit of high power and low weight. Titanium alloy con-rods cost ten times more than conventional steel items but they allow an extra 700 rpm, enough for this jewel of an engine to attain the target 8,000 rpm.

When introduced, the 3.0-litre engine had the highest power and torque per litre of any non-turbo production car engine. It can propel the lightweight NSX to 167 mph; not the fastest, but quite fast enough for real roads.

Of course, the aim in creating the NSX was to go further than merely developing a car with superlative dynamics. To demonstrate beyond doubt Honda's mastery of real-world talent, it also had to be user-friendly, free of compromise, and fastidious in detail design.

Perhaps the most surprising aspect of the NSX is just how easy it is to master. The glassy cabin is unusually clear to see out of, while the driving position defies the usual compromises of a mid-engined sportscar. The driver's feet are behind the axle line, so the pedals are in line with the body for greater comfort over long distances. It gives confidence and control. The NSX is also the right size to fit the road comfortably. Some high-performance cars are simply too big.

The secret of the NSX's appeal is that it does not sacrifice practical considerations in the pursuit of dynamic perfection. It remains unruffled in the city – not always within a supercar's repertoire – and it will traverse a continent at tranquil high-speed, yet it will attack the Nurburgring or an Alpine pass with finesse and commitment. It does all of these things brilliantly and that is why the NSX achieves its aims.

In combining high power and low weight, Honda can match its rivals for acceleration, yet be able to offer greater handling agility and responsiveness. Its chassis is outstanding and the long-travel suspension means that it sticks to the road on bumpy bends where others hop and skip in uncontrolled frenzy. It has impressive traction, mighty grip and powerful brakes.

The engine might sound whisper-quiet at idle but that changes into a full-blooded snarl as the fury of a competition engine is unleashed at high revs. The gearchange is possibly the very best amongst supercars. The light, short throw, flicks deftly between ratios and the

No supercar has ever matched the speed and civility of the Honda NSX. Arguably it is the most complete sportscar made

The NSX Targa arrived later on and provided fresh air thrills and gave the Honda a fresher, sexier appearance

lightweight clutch works with unflustered smoothness.

This is not a thinly disguised race car with all its attendant compromises. The critical might wish for a classier interior, a more overtly curvaceous exterior or perhaps a little more power, but in the end it's hard to dispute that this is a masterpiece. It's subtle yet powerful. It possesses awesome ability, breathtaking engineering, an exploitable yet surprisingly supple chassis. It's even practical, with room for a suitcase in the rear compartment, behind the engine.

The NSX is different to other supercars. It makes high performance accessible. It tackles potential problems with engineering solutions, not by expecting the driver's expertise to counter the car's shortcomings. In short, it is a sportscar that makes high-speed driving a satisfying, not daunting prospect.

Those who have been privileged to drive the NSX know that the truth is that it combines the glamour of a Ferrari with the engineering flair of a Porsche. Until the arrival of the Ferrari F355 it was a better car than either.

If we're looking at the ultimate driving machine, then clearly a Mclaren F1 is faster, lighter, and more exotic. Yet away from a racetrack and on real roads, the difference is surely academic. The fact that Honda achieves its aims at one tenth of the cost of the Mclaren is nothing short of a small miracle.

Chrysler Viper
● ● ● ● ● ● ● ● ● ● ● ● ● ● ● ● ● ● ● ●

If any car could lay claim to be the spiritual successor to the legendary AC Cobra, then the Chrysler Viper

has to be it. All the key values that made the Cobra such an icon of unashamed power and performance are clear for all to see in the Viper's squat and muscular lines. Perhaps the fact that a certain ace car-tuner and racer Caroll Shelby had a hand in the development of both of these tarmac-melting sportsters has more than a little significance here. Shelby knows how to build a heroic, fire-breathing, scare-the-hell-out-of-the-driver sort of car better than almost anyone else. That shows with crystal clarity in the Viper.

In the US, the Viper lays full claim to cult hero status. It caught the imagination right from the moment its curvaceous form was revealed at the Detroit Motor Show in 1990. From that time on, its rise to production status seemed inevitable. Two years later it hit the streets in awesome style. The combination of titanic thrust and a jaw-dropping shape strikes just the right chord of patriotism and pride. So much so that, for the hard-top Viper GTS version, the powers-that-be decreed that it would come only in the US racing colours of blue with white striping.

One look at the Viper affirms that it has its soul locked deep within the long traditions of the muscle car. Beneath the huge acreage that passes for the Viper's bonnet lies the mother of all V10s. It started life as an all-iron truck engine but after switching the iron castings for aluminium, Chrysler commissioned Lamborghini, at that time owned by Chrysler, to work a little of its engineering magic into its heart. Starting from a unit that measured a mammoth eight litres, Lamborghini's task of achieving 400 bhp-plus was never going to be particularly challenging.

The red cam covers might hint at Italian mechanical sophistication but in fact this engine is about as conservative as there is in a car of today. The massive castings

conceal a single camshaft driving pushrods and hydraulic lifters. Each combustion chamber has just two valves. The only nod to present-day technology is the electronic management system but even this is relatively simple, with the low compression ratio precluding the need for an anti-knock sensor to run on low grade fuels. With a specific output of a modest 49 bhp per litre – almost half that of a Honda NSX – the Viper's lump might seem tepid but with eight litres to play with, the end result is fiery hot.

An output of 400 bhp is serious power in anyone's language but in such an unstressed application as this, that power is spread over an unbelievably wide spectrum. So quite why the Viper needs a six-speed transmission is difficult to understand. Boot the throttle in any gear and it responds to crushing effect. Such is the flexibility that most drivers could drive all day without changing out of third gear and still cruise comfortably at 120 mph.

This vast engine is housed within an equally massive body that looks capable of swallowing Ferrari 355s and 911s and spitting them out whole. It's wide, low, and very, very mean. The broad flanks, bulging out from the body in pseudo racer style, cover wheels and tyres that look as though they belong on a Formula One car. The rears are an astonishing 13 inches wide, the fronts ten inches.

But there's more to the Viper than a truck engine with a mean face; this is more than a mere hot-rod. That engine is set well back in the sheet steel monocoque chassis to give a near equal weight distribution, the better to provide decent handling balance, while the

Over: *Subtle it isn't but few muscle cars have caught the imagination like the mighty hard-top Dodge Viper GTS by Chrysler, one of the most envied cars on the road*

suspension is a classic double wishbone set-up, just like a race car. Naturally, it channels its power to the rear wheels in time-honoured tradition. The body itself is of plastic composites, the logical choice for low-level production and one reason why the Viper possesses such an audacious form.

This level of specification could only be that of a true thoroughbred. There are few compromises here, even to the extent that those items not considered necessary for the pursuit of performance are discarded. There's no anti-lock for the brakes, no glass side windows, not even an outside door handle. If it rains, the only answer is to rig up the pathetic canvas cover and to fit the floppy sidescreens. Some would argue that this is going too far; no wonder the GTS derivative with its proper glass windows and weather-proof coupe shape is gaining all the customer orders right now. It also has an extra 50 bhp, not that it needs any more grunt.

To get behind the wheel of a Viper is an intimidating experience at first. The cabin itself is sparse and business-like with leather seats and a neatly leather-trimmed, three-spoke wheel. A battery of white-faced dials stare back from the dashboard and the bonnet stretches out for miles. That feeling of gargantuan size is hard to ignore in a car that's almost as wide as a Ferrari Testarossa. Not surprisingly, the Viper feels constricted by tight and twisty roads where the ample girth restricts driver confidence.

The Viper needs room to breathe before its true talents can be appreciated. Out on more open roads, the Viper begins to seduce the driver with its awesome power and grip. Accelerate in any gear and the beast gathers momentum until it's rocketing toward the horizon in a horsepower frenzy. That bottomless well of torque teaches drivers to treat it with respect, but the amazing flexibility also means that the Viper will trickle along at engine speeds that

would produce a stall in most high performance engines.

Given its head, this engine will topple giants in its headlong rush towards its formidable maximum speed of around 170 mph. To reach 100 mph from rest takes little more than ten seconds – which is only a couple of seconds longer than the time it takes to read this sentence.

Of course, this level of power needs treating with respect. An incautious boot of throttle from a low gear is enough to virtually vapourise the tyres. It's child's play to unstick the rear end in the wet but on dry tarmac the Viper appears surprisingly stable and grippy. It is not a heavy car despite its size and those giant tyres do their job effectively to produce a car that is devastatingly quick through gentle curves. Here, the neutral handling and impressive body control outweigh the negative aspects of steering which never feels as precise as that of a Porsche or Ferrari. With an often recalcitrant gearchange and no anti-lock for the dinner-plate-sized discs, this is not the easiest of cars to tame. Even so, it's fun trying.

If there's one area where the Viper fails to deliver, it's the sound of that V10. Think V10 and the wail of a Formula One engine comes to mind. Instead, it delivers a flat blare that never comes close to stirring the soul. It's not merely loud but unpleasant too, a factor that makes this a poor choice for a long drive. But then, the tiny load space within the boot and the pathetic weather equipment would preclude this car's use for anything more than a half-day blast, even if the driver and passenger could endure the noise. Which is a shame, because the Viper's pliant ride would suggest that, given a little more development in one or two key areas, this car would make a fine grand tourer as well as a short-distance sprinter. Perhaps there will be some improvements in this department with the fixed-head Viper GTS.

Aston Martin DB7

● ●

There are surely just two top contenders for the most beautiful British post-war sportscar – the Jaguar E-type and the Aston Martin DB7. Both are stunning in their own way; each possesses an understated elegance underpinned by sensational performance and an impeccable pedigree.

So it is a remarkable co-incidence that, were it not for a fortunate twist of fate, the Aston DB7 could so easily have worn the Jaguar emblem on its shapely snout in place of the winged Aston Martin badge.

Just ten years ago, the hard economic truth was known that, for the 80-year old company to survive, it would need to supplement the production of its hugely expensive, hand-built, V8-engined grand tourers with another product. The company needed a 'cheap' Aston that could be built in greater numbers to compete at the level of the Mercedes SL, BMW 850i and Porsche 911.

Aston Martin had built its reputation on its DB-series high-performance grand tourers under the control of tractor magnate

David Brown. The new car would follow a similar concept; exclusive but not to the extent that ownership was restricted only to the immensely rich.

Without a partner to provide suitable major components as well as financial backing for the new car, Aston Martin's future looked grim. Ford may not have been seen at the time as a knight in shining armour when it added the famous Newport Pagnell firm to its stable, but few would doubt now that its involvement was anything other than crucial to the company's current success.

However, the real opportunity for an all-new Aston did not arise until Ford placed Jaguar on its shopping list and subsequently acquired this famous marque. Jaguar had some fine engines; it had suitable suspension systems; and together with Ford's range, the possibilities for robbing the parts bins was almost limitless.

Of greater significance was the fact that Jaguar was already some way through development of a sportscar that was originally intended to be the spiritual successor to the E-type. Code-named XJ41, the prototype car had already been axed by Jaguar, but Ford revived the idea. A shape looking very similar to the XK41 was soon to be seen lurking atop an XJS floorpan as the XX prototype. This promising contender was judged too expensive to produce in this form to be of any use to Jaguar but, with an Aston Martin badge and built in relatively low numbers at a small purpose-built factory, it certainly had possibilities.

And so it came to be that the prototype Jaguar was honed and polished by race-car guru Tom Walkinshaw eventually to emerge as the Aston DB7. Powered by a supercharged 3.2-litre version of

> DB7 is the latest in the long line of Aston Martins and the most successful. Stunning looks and performance mark the DB7 as one of the best supercars currently made

the Jaguar XJR engine, clothed in an extraordinarily graceful body sculpted by Ian Callum, and built at the same Oxfordshire factory that was once home to the sensational Jaguar XJ220. The DB7 definitely has had something of a chequered genesis.

Yet it takes but a single glance to see beyond doubt that this is every inch an Aston. That much was clear right from the start of the car's tantalisingly slow rise from its announcement and first showing to its eventual launch late in 1994. Callum had struck precisely the right balance between Aston Martin tradition and nineties sophistication in his rendering of what a new Aston should look like. Likewise, the sculptured architecture of the interior clad in the finest hide and set off by the subtle sheen of burr walnut epitomised the very best of

English craftsmanship.

Everyone knew, before it had even turned a wheel, that this new Aston would be sensational. Even David Brown himself, who had owned the marque until 1971, gave his wholehearted approval both to the car itself and to his initials being given to the name, although sadly he was not to live to see the car into production. The orders started to roll in.

It was with more than a hint of anticipation that the world's press assembled at Aston Martin's Bloxham factory for their first taste of the DB7's charms. It proved to be a day of surprises. The factory itself is essentially an assembly shop where parts from Jaguar and other suppliers are hand-assembled to make just a handful or so of cars a day. The squeaky-clean, high-tech atmosphere is in stark contrast to the collection of

grubby sheds at Newport Pagnell in which the bigger V8 Virage is hammered out of sheet steel and aluminium by the hands of true craftsmen. This is more like a race-car workshop, as befits the most technologically advanced car that Aston has ever produced.

From every angle the DB7 exudes beauty. It has a presence and aristocratic dignity that few cars will ever match. Once inside, the eyes slip easily over the curves of the facia to rest on the view over the bonnet ahead. It is a moment of deep satisfaction.

So to drive the DB7 and to find even detail flaws in its character is tantamount to sacrilege. But they exist, just the same. The brakes lack feel, the gearchange is cumbersome, the switchgear is mostly Ford derived and seems unworthy of such a beautiful machine, and the driveline is less

smooth than it should be. Look beyond these relative trivialities, however, and most drivers will discover a car of towering ability.

It's clear from the first few miles that this Aston holds true to the 'grand tourer' traditions of the earlier DB6. It's no race-track warrior in the way of a Porsche 911 but neither is it as soft as a Jaguar XJS when the going gets tough. Instead, the DB7 holds that fine line of balanced ability that makes it such a capable machine in which to cover miles deceptively quickly. The XJS-derived chassis copes with the ravages of country roads with effortless ease. Its ability to soak up

bumps and resist body roll enables it to be driven very rapidly while maintaining composure.

The liberties that can be taken with this chassis are simply phenomenal, a point proved convincingly at the famous Goodwood race circuit. Pushed to its limits, the DB7 maintains a neutral balance right to the edge of its considerable reserves of grip. Only when driving hard on tight country lanes does this car's 1750 kg weight begin to tell. That the chassis is thoroughly up to the challenge posed by the likes of BMW and Mercedes is never in serious doubt.

Talent in one area of a car's performance so often reveals weaknesses elsewhere. Does the engine stand such close scrutiny? The answer is an emphatic 'yes'. With the aid of a giant Eaton blower pumping charge into the

cylinders, this six-cylinder 3.2-litre liberates an impressive 335 bhp. That's the same specific output as McLaren's F1 sportscar engine or, to put it another way, it equates to a top speed of around 160 mph and a sprinting ability that will enable it to reach 60 mph from rest in under six seconds.

More than this, it's an engine that offers accessibility to its power. Depress the throttle – almost any gear will do – and the DB7 picks up its skirts and goes. As it does so a distant scream from the blower punches through into the sumptuous cabin. Encouraging stuff indeed.

In 1995, Aston produced more than 700 DB7s to make it the most successful Aston Martin ever. It is not perfect but that does not imply that this isn't the classiest way to travel. Nothing on four wheels draws appreciation quite like it.

Ferrari F355

No treatise on sportscars would be complete without Ferrari. This small Italian car-maker has established a reputation for creating beautiful and fiery Latin wonders for the past 40 years, but with so many talented candidates to have passed through the Maranello factory gates, how on earth can just one be chosen?

It's a decision that is easier than a casual onlooker might expect. For driving on real roads in real-life conditions, the so-called supercar Ferraris are simply too much of a handful to be truly wieldy. Impressive, yes, but for the ultimate road-going Ferrari it is necessary to search a little further down the range to the nimble and potent F355.

This is a superstar even among

Ferraris. So much so, in fact, that not only does it outpace and out-handle other truly talented contenders, such as the Honda NSX and the Porsche 911, but it transcends class boundaries to make owners of Lamborghini Diablos and Ferrari TR 512s seriously question their choice of supercar. That the F355 manages to comprehensively outrank these others without pricing itself in the realms of the unattainable is worthy of celebration for sportscar lovers everywhere.

The mid-engined Ferraris have always been the best of the breed for those who have a passion for driving. It's a talent that reaches

With looks like this, it can only be a Ferrari but while the F355 is essentially a revision of the successful 348, to consider it an update sells this fantastic car short

right back as far as the classic 246 Dino, the very first of the road-going mid-engined Ferraris. Since then these small Ferraris – the 308, 328 and 348 – have numbered amongst the most beautiful sportscars in the world. Each represents a perfect form with engineering brilliance within. These are cars so special that they could be considered works of art.

For decades, Ferrari seemed to have the market pretty well sewn up. Porsche had its devotees too but no-one really disputed Ferrari's claim to be the best of its breed. Then the unthinkable happened. Honda decided to enter the game with the audacious NSX, an aluminium-bodied supercar which broke all the rules. Not only did the NSX prove beyond doubt that it was the best handling car bar none but it did so by such a wide margin that it left Porsche 911s and Ferrari 348's looking really rather sad and inadequate in comparison.

But there was worse. The Honda also showed that it was possible to achieve these levels of dynamic supremacy while retaining a remarkable standard of ride quality. If this wasn't humiliation enough, the Honda's engine also proved embarrassingly superior to the Ferrari in its specific output of almost 100 bhp per litre, yet it could be driven through town almost as easily as a shopping car. The NSX knocked the establishment supercars for six.

Something had to be done. Ferrari's response was both dramatic and swift, the result being a thorough redesign of the 348 to give us the F355. Yet to consider the F355 as merely an updated 348 is to sell it short. The leap in ability is little short of miraculous and amounts to major improvements in just about every single area. Ride, handling, performance, refinement and styling were all given comprehensive treatment. The

result is one of the finest driving machines ever to have emerged from Maranello.

The purity of the F355's Pininfarina lines is classic Ferrari at its best. The elegant proportions are set off perfectly by an interior that has a sense of occasion about it. Exquisite detailing forces the eyes to linger as they pass over the hand-stitched upholstery to the chrome-plated gate for the gearshift. The drilled pedals are pure Ferrari; so is the chrome ball that sits atop the gear lever.

Fire up the 3.5-litre V8 and the staccato crispness of the exhaust as the pedal blips the throttle gives the first clue that there's something different and rather special about this engine. The F355 designation provides the giveaway. Usually, the first two digits of a Ferrari's name give the capacity, while the final digit denotes the number of cylinders. Only in this case, that last number '5' means that this engine has five valves per cylinder. It's just one of a whole host of changes that sets this engine apart from the common herd.

Titanium conrods and 40 valves helps the V8 to achieve the highest specific output of any normally aspirated engine. It's higher than the Honda NSX, higher even than the McLaren F1. It adds up to 380 bhp of pure heaven. Listening to the sound as it reaches a crescendo of almost 9,000 rpm is like nothing else on earth.

Of course, it delivers far more than sound bytes. This engine has the thrust to zip the car and its occupants from rest to 100 mph in little more than ten seconds. Given enough space, it's good for around 180 mph. This is impressive enough but the manner with which it delivers its considerable punch is justification enough to make rivals look away in disgrace. The flexibility and response of this engine are devastatingly effective, made more so by a gearshift that, for once in a Ferrari, is a real pleasure to use.

Not so much of a pleasure is the offset pedals which the driver never quite feels accustomed to but this is about the only quibble with Ferrari's masterpiece. It's a flaw that is hard to find forgiveness for but it's certainly compensated for in the fine handling and ride. The old 348 was never particularly accomplished in either area, producing a constant jiggliness over any surface that wasn't supersmooth. But the manner in which

Previous page: *A prancing horse that is every inch a thoroughbred. The Ferrari has proved a formidable sportscar thanks to its sheer power and towering high speed manners*
Below: *While it's not the fastest or most expensive supercar made, the F355 surely ranks as the most complete and usable on the road*

the rear tyres could break free under extreme cornering was utterly unforgivable.

No such fears with the F355. The re-worked double-wishbone suspension and electronically-controlled dampers provide iron control on undulating surfaces while unobtrusively sponging up bumps and imperfections that would upset a less masterful chassis. Transformed as it is, the F355 emerges as a model of security but without forfeiting any of Ferrari's legendary finesse. The addition of power assistance for the steering gives welcome relief from the kickback that could often afflict earlier models, yet it doesn't rob the helm of that all-important feel. The driver will know exactly where those wheels are headed. The brakes are as powerful and effective as any car with this level of performance demands.

That this baby Ferrari reaches

such heights of accomplishment at a fraction the cost of anything that comes even remotely close is testament to its greatness. That it does so while providing a level of visual and aural stimulation to match any rival serves to underline the rounded portfolio of its abilities.

More attractive than a McLaren, more accelerative than a Ferrari TR512, and costing a fraction the price of either, this has to be the ultimate road-going sportscar – at least for now.

Jaguar XJ220

No-one who was there to see the unveiling of the Jaguar XJ220 prototype at the 1988 Motorshow is ever likely to forget the experience. Any new Jaguar is a major event but this one was a sensation. Long, low, and elegant in its silver coachwork, this

dramatic machine would be the fastest and the most expensive Jaguar ever built. It looked as much a record breaker as a road-going supercar. In fully developed form, it would prove to be both.

That show marked the turning point that changed the XJ220 from concept car to a viable road car project. This was the heyday of the supercar and the Ferrari F40 was drawing a queue a mile long. So perhaps it was no surprise that when a production run of 200 or so cars was hinted at, people were practically falling over themselves to hand over £50,000 deposits for this new Jaguar supercar. Suddenly the idea of producing the car seemed possible.

Until that point, the XJ220 was no more than a 'low-budget' development project dreamed up for Group B racing by Jaguar's head of Engineering, Jim Randle. Randle is a man of vision. In his

XJ220 he saw a car capable of taking on the likes of the Porsche 959. That meant four-wheel drive and 500 bhp for this mid-engined V12 but it also meant a limited production of at least 200 road cars. In the XJ220 he saw a car that would emerge as the ultimate road-going supercar and a mighty flagship for Jaguar.

Legend has it that Randle started work on the styling, chassis and drivetrain of this supercar with a handful of volunteers after Christmas 1984. It was all unofficial, with the work carried out after hours and at weekends, hence the project name, 'the Saturday Club'. Two years into the project, a limited budget was agreed to build a one-off car based on a styling proposal by Keith Helfet, and by spring 1988 a full-size model of the car was seen for the first time.

This mock-up was, in fact, the

Jaguar XJ220 is a true supercar which started off as merely a hobby

1988 show car and after its Motorshow debut, it was taken to JaguarSport's base in Kidlington for a viability study. By this time, JaguarSport's Group C racing efforts had ceased development of the big and heavy Jaguar V12 in favour of a TWR-developed twin-turbo V6 – basically the same engine as that of the super-quick Metro 6R4 rally car of the same era.

JaguarSport's latest proposal for the XJ220 had changed too. The revised design retained similar styling to the original but the engineering within had moved far away from Jim Randle's initial concept. The team now felt that the complexity, weight and cost of four-wheel drive couldn't be justified on a car that was to benefit from ground-effect aerodynamics. Also, the Jaguar V12 engine's massive size and weight was thought to be a huge handicap.

It was felt that the better alternative would be to share the V6 turbo engine and the rear-wheel drive of the race car, a move that would enable the production XJ220 to be smaller, lighter and less complex, with a wheelbase 200mm shorter. Jaguar management approved of the changes, so did Jaguar's new owner Ford, and the price was set at an ambitious £290,000 plus taxes, index linked to inflation. A production run of up to 350 cars was planned from the Bloxham factory, with the first deliveries to start in 1992.

History would prove that the commercial possibilities for such a car were over-ambitious. But although performance and power targets of 200 mph and 500 bhp were equally ambitious, these were actually exceeded by a convincing margin. This was despite the additional hurdle of having to meet new emissions regulations.

When the XJ220 was finally signed off, it produced 542 bhp from its 3.5-litre 24-valve V6, a figure that enabled it to achieve a speed of 212 mph while testing at Firestone's Fort Stockton test track in Texas. It proved conclusively that this was the fastest production car of all. Soon afterwards, racing driver John Nielson proved its handling and grip capabilities to be on an equally elevated plane in producing the fastest-ever lap of the tortuous Nurburgring circuit by any production car. The XJ220 went on to win Le Mans in 1993, thereby sealing its fame forever.

Performance figures for the XJ220 are a world apart from almost every other supercar. The XJ220 is capable of rocketing from rest to 60 mph in just 3.6 seconds and on to 100 mph in 7.9 seconds. The in-gear acceleration is simply phenomenal too, lopping whole seconds off the figures for anything comparable this side of a McLaren F1, a car which at the time was not yet available.

Comparisons with the McLaren are inevitable but the cars are very different in character. The McLaren was designed to be a road car from the outset, while the Jaguar comes across more as a sports-racing car developed for the road. The XJ220 might have a cockpit swathed in leather and properly trimmed but there's no boot worthy of the name and the chassis tub is built up from aluminium honeycomb, just as in a high-tech race car.

Any thoughts of driving to

Right: *The XJ220 never lacked race car performance or handling but as a road car its sheer width made it unsuitable for some roads*
Below: *Jaguar's supercar wrote itself into the record books by becoming one of the few road cars to win the Le Mans 24 hour race in modern times. This is partly due to a performance of 0-60 mph in 3.6 seconds and 0-100 mph in 7.9 seconds*

Monaco for the weekend are soon dispelled after a quick peek at the load space behind the engine, has confirmed that there's room for little more than a slim briefcase. Packaging is not amongst the XJ220's strengths.

Firing up the engine sends all the wrong messages too. At idle it sounds like rusty nails in a cement mixer and even when driving with the turbos pumping away for all their worth, the engine never sounds inspiring – just a flat drone, regulated louder or quieter by the throttle and revs.

That throttle produces an indecent level of pace given some encouragement but in dry conditions it's not of a form in which the driver is faced with an embarrassment of power. The long, progressive action of the throttle pedal sees to that, together with high gearing that means even first gear is good for more than 60 mph. Third gear brings 130 mph in reach, a speed at which the XJ220's superb

body control makes it hard to grasp just how fast this is.

It might be easy to drive on a racetrack but on real roads the ridiculous nature of such a car becomes clearly apparent. It's very, very wide, which is fine on the motorway but almost anywhere else places severe restrictions on driving. Suspension that is firm enough for 200 mph downforce transfers into a tooth-loosening joltiness at low speeds. The art of avoiding potholes has to be studiously learned right from the start. Then there's the clutch that demands precisely the right amount of throttle to prevent a stall and the unassisted steering that provides the driver with a thorough work-out when threading through town. Wet roads, however, are the biggest upset to the big cat. The combination of all that power through the rear wheels demands a degree of caution if disaster is to be averted.

Perhaps Randle was right after all. A V12 would sound terrific in this and four-wheel drive would provide that all-weather security. As an exercise in pushing forwards the parameters of the road-going performance car, Jaguar has made an emphatic point with the XJ220. It's an object of beauty too. Even so, it's hard not to dismiss this as an oversized, overpowered irrelevance to the sporting road driver for all its impressive presence, speed and dry-road handling and grip. Perhaps that's why so many potential buyers changed their minds and why the last cars are being sold at a knock-down price.

McLaren F1

McLaren's F1 is, without doubt, the ultimate road-going supercar. It has a V12 engine developing more than 600 bhp. It is smaller and lighter than any other. It is

the fastest production car ever, and the most expensive of all, by a considerable margin. If the pursuit of sporting excellence is the aim, money no object, then the McLaren F1 is the target.

That the F1 project happened at all is largely down to a chance conversation at an Italian airport amongst men of power, money, influence and foresight. Legend has it that the idea of McLaren building a road-going sportscar was first mooted at the bar of Milan's international airport.

The McLaren team were returning from the 1988 Italian Grand Prix but, with a delayed flight, it so happened that Gordon Murray, McLaren's chief designer, together with McLaren directors Ron Dennis, Creighton Brown and Mansour Ojjeh began chatting about which direction Mclaren should take in the next phase of the company's development.

To build the best sportscar in the

world was an idea that soon began to gather momentum amongst the four agile minds at that meeting.

Before many months had passed, Murray and Creighton Brown moved into a new building opposite the racing team headquarters in Woking, Surrey, and the two set to work on making the road car project work. Brown concentrated on setting the company up and getting things working, while Murray worked on design concepts while assembling a small hand-picked team of expert designers and engineers. For the styling, the designer of the latest Lotus Elan, Peter Stevens, filled the brief, one of several ex-Lotus personnel chosen to add weight to the team.

With the key personnel at last assembled under one roof, the day came in March 1990 when Murray laid down the design objectives in detail. Right from the outset, Murray knew what he wanted. The new car was to be a driver's car par excellence. It would be fast and agile, it would be capable of extended touring. It would be lightweight and compact. Also, the passenger layout would be almost unique in placing the driver centrally, slightly ahead of the two passenger seats, and the engine would be mid-mounted.

The choice of engine was crucial, and this was one item that would not be built or designed by McLaren. Murray's priorities of a large-capacity, normally aspirated and high-revving engine of compact design and capable of delivering more than 100 bhp per litre could be met by just a handful of manufacturers. Honda, Ferrari and BMW were all in the running as suppliers here, but Ferrari could hardly be considered because of the

conflict of interest.

Honda seemed to make the most sense, especially with the Grand Prix team connection. However, although there was plenty of talk initially about V10 or V12 engines from the Japanese manufacturer, the project never really got off the ground.

A chance meeting between Murray and BMW Motorsport engine wizard Paul Rosche at the 1990 Hockenheim Grand Prix acted as the catalyst that led to BMW producing the V12 engines for the F1. Targets were a safe rev limit of 7500 rpm, a power output of 550 bhp with good flexibility, a capacity of at least 5.0-litres, and an overall length of no more than 600mm.

BMW's existing V12 proved to be too big, too heavy, and too slow-revving for this specialised application, so Rosche announced that they would build a brand new engine in order to achieve these lofty goals. The new engine proved to be a minor miracle, its eventual 6064cc capacity capable of developing a reliable 627 bhp at 7,400 rpm and over 479 lb ft of torque over a broad rev range.

With the engine finalised, the overall packaging of the car could be decided. This was based around the three-seat cabin, the length of the engine, and the compact transverse six-speed gearbox. Everything else within the car would be a logical progression from these vital criteria.

Throughout the entire design stage, weight was a critical factor. Murray was obsessional about it, maintaining that every effort be made to achieve the 1000 kg target. This target was literally hundreds of kilograms lighter than supercars from Bugatti, Lamborghini and Jaguar, although Ferrari's F40 and Honda's NSX come close. Even so, light weight as well as compact dimensions would be crucial to maintaining a significant performance lead. To this end, technology would be stretched to its absolute limits.

The cat is out of the bag! The XJ220 has proved to be an excellent racing car and has scored numerous memorable victories

It dictated that the monocoque body itself would be formed of carbon-composites and that the components that make up the double-wishbone suspension are of forged aluminium alloys. Aluminium or magnesium alloys also form the base materials for brake callipers and dampers, to name but a few of the items that this fastidious obsession with lightness demands. No component was thought too insignificant to be unworthy of exquisite detailing and weight saving. The throttle pedal, crafted from titanium, is one example; seat runners are machined from solid alloy; and a starter motor half the size and weight of a conventional unit is employed.

Equipment, too, is pared down in the interests of weight saving. There are no anti-lock brakes or traction control, no power steering, not even a brake servo.

Even though the engine is a symphony in full flow, McLaren has at least deigned to allow some music on the move. But even this is half the weight of a normal CD system. Likewise, the air conditioning unit is ultra-compact and light.

These last two concessions to creature comfort, along with sound-proofing of the cockpit and a beautifully made titanium toolkit, must take some of the blame for the eventual dry weight of 1,100 kg, yet this is still the lightest supercar of all. An amazing achievement.

As with any new car, the F1 has had its share of development testing to ensure that it holds together in any number of harsh environments. It was during testing at Italy's Nardo test track that the car reached its headline-grabbing top speed of 231 mph at the hands of ex-Formula One driver Jonathan Palmer. It told the world emphatically that McLaren had achieved at least one of its goals.

Other tests proved it capable of sprinting from rest to 60 mph in just over three seconds; to 100 mph in little more than six seconds, and to 200 mph in less than 30 seconds. These are figures that firmly underline McLaren's authority as the quickest of all supercars by a huge margin. Even Jaguar's XJ220 couldn't match this. But as everyone who loves fast cars will know, how fast it travels is only a small part of the story.

Few people have had the opportunity of driving a McLaren F1 in anger, but those who have all agree on one thing – that this provides the ultimate in dynamic performance of any production car yet built. There are others that are quieter and more compliant. There are others that are more user-friendly – just getting to the central driver's seat is an exercise in agility – and there are others that offer more creature comforts and less driver effort. But nothing this side of a true racing car is quite like the F1 for unparalleled stability, grip, and acceleration response.

In some ways, to judge the McLaren F1 by the way it drives is to miss the point. The McLaren costs ten times a Honda NSX or Porsche 911, for perhaps a ten per cent benefit of real-world performance. The figures just don't add up. No, this is an exercise in pushing forwards the frontiers of automotive development further than they have ever gone before. In achieving that goal it is impossible to place a value on McLaren's F1 – a road car which dominated the Le Mans 24-Hour race at first attempt. Quite simply it's the greatest supercar of them all.

Right and Over: *It costs around half a million pounds to buy but McLaren's F1 supercar can rightly claim to be the lightest, fastest, most expensive and, of course, greatest supercar of them all*

INDEX

ACKNOWLEDGEMENTS

The publishers would like to thank the following sources for their kind permission to reproduce the pictures in this book:

Advertising Archive: 198, **Alfa Romeo (GB)**: 27, **Allsport**/ Karlt Desmoulins 248/9, **Aston Martin Lagonda Ltd.**:73 b, **Autocar Motoring Archive**: 16, 16/7, 20, 23, 25, 26, 28/9, 29, 31, 33, 34, 37, 38, 39, 41, 42, 43, 44, 47, 49, 56, 59, 60/1, 63, 64/5, 66 br, 67 c, 68 b, 69 tr, 70 tl, 71 l, 74 b, 76 bl, 78 tl, 84/5, 86/7, 90, 91t, 93 t, 94, 95 bl, 98 tl, 101 br, 103, 108, 109 r, 113 tr, 115 tr, 116, 119, 122, 123, 125, 132, 134, 135, 136, 137, 142, 143, 153 c, 155, 157, 159 t, 161, 162, 166/7, 169 tr, 171, 172/3, 173 br, tc, bl, 179, 182, 183, 186/7, 189, 192, 194, 195, 209 b, 213, 214, 225, 238, 239, 240, 247, **BMIHT/Rover Group**: 51, 53, 75 tr, 121, 148/9, 149t, 215, 152/3, 153 br, **Bristol Cars Ltd.**: 81 t, **Neill Bruce Motoring Photolibrary**: 16/7, 32 c, t, 46, 58, 72 tl, 80 b, 82/3, 118, 120, 131, 140, 156, 184, 203 /Peter Roberts Collection: 102 t, **Caterham Cars Ltd.**: 208, 209 t , 210/1, **Chrysler Jeep Imports UK**: 92 bl, 130, 236/7, **Classic Z register/Datsun**: 97 b, **Daihatsu (UK) Ltd.**: 96 t, **De Tomaso/Emilia Concessionaires Ltd.**: 98/9, **Ferrari UK**: 106/7, 244/5, **Fiat Auto UK**: 112, **Ford Motor Co. Ltd.**: 113 b, 138 bl, 147, **Honda UK**: Nexus Advertising Marketing Ltd.124, 234/5, **Hulton-Getty**: 4 cl, bc, 8, 10, 13 tr, 30, **Hyundai car (UK) Ltd**: 126, **International Motors Ltd.**: David Finch 128, 181 t, 185, **Jaguar Cars Ltd.**: 45, 64 cla, 129, **Lotus Cars Ltd.**: 138/9, **Marcos Sales Ltd.**: 141, **McLaren Cars Ltd.**: 144/1, 250/1, **Mercedes-Benz (UK) Ltd.**: 22, 146, **Mitsubishi Motors/ Colt Car Co. Ltd.**: 154, **Morgan Motor Co. Ltd.**: 221 b, **National Motor Museum, Beaulieu**: 4 c, 9 b, 13 b, 14, 18, 19, 21, 24/5, 35, 50, 52, 54, 55, 57, 62/3, 79 b, 88/9, 100 t, 104/5, 110/1, 114/5, 158/9, 164 tr, 164/5, 176 tr, 188, 202, 206/7, 217, 220, 222, 230, 232, 233, 245 t, 252/3, **Peugeot Motor Co.**: 163, **Porsche**: 228, 229, **Quadrant Picture Library**: 1, 4/5, 12/3, 15, 36, 48, 64/5, 87 br, t, 116/7, 127, 133, 150/1, 193, 196/7, 198/9, 204/5 c, 212, 216, 218 t, b, 219, 221 t, 226/7, 231 /Autocar 9, 11, 200/1, /Auto Express 40/1, 204/5 tl, br, 246 /Phil Talbot 241, **Renault UK Ltd.**: 168/9, Roll-Royce Motor Cars: 65 bl, 77 tl, 174/5, **Saab GB Ltd.**: 176/7, Seat UK: 178, **Skoda UK**: 180/1, **Susuki UK**: Nexus Advertising Marketing Ltd.186, **Sutton Motorsport Images**: Brooks 242/3, **TVR Engineering Ltd.**: 2/3, 190/1, 223, 224 t, bl, **Volkswagen UK Ltd.**: 199.

Every effort has been made to acknowledge correctly and contact the source and/or copyright holder of each picture, and Carlton Books Limited apologises for any unintentional errors or omissions which will be corrected in future editions of this book.